# *FROM*

# WORKING

# *TO*

# WISDOM

George,
Thank you for
your wisdom and
example.

Best,
Brendan

# FROM

# WORKING

# TO

# WISDOM

THE ADVENTURES AND DREAMS OF OLDER AMERICANS

## BRENDAN HARE

ISBN: 0996003401
ISBN: 978-0-9960034-0-7
Library of Congress Control Number: 2014910597
LCCN Imprint Name: Joppa Flats Publishing
Arlington, Massachusetts 02476

*Every reader finds himself.*

—Marcel Proust

# CONTENTS

## III. CREATIVITY

## IV. ENJOYMENT

## V. SPORTS

## VI. FAMILY

## VII. COMMUNITY

## VIII. SERVICE

## IX. CHANGE

## X. ATTITUDE

## XI. THE LONG VIEW

# INTRODUCTION

This book began two years ago, during a period of anxiety. After four decades of work, I found myself about to retire, unable to imagine the next phase of my life. I was faced with many questions: *Would my days be meaningful? How should I spend my time? How did others approach this experience? Would the challenges of growing old prove too great?*

The roots of this anxiety, I later realized, reached all the way back to my childhood. I've always been practical and somewhat impatient, and never inclined to spend much time pondering the larger mysteries. Philosophy, in the ancient sense—the study of how to live, the search for transcendent truths, the love of wisdom for its own sake—always seemed like an indulgence. The unexamined life, I decided early on, was the only one worth living.

For decades, I retained essentially the same outlook and motivations I had as a boy. In college and graduate school, I chose a practical field of study, economics. Later, I chose a practical profession, the law. And after falling in love and having children, I lived as practically as I could, focusing all my efforts on providing my family with a comfortable, well-ordered life.

Then one day, to my amazement, I was about to turn sixty-five. Instead of celebrating my birthday, I tried to ignore it. If I could somehow forget about time, I thought, it might somehow forget about me. So I put my head down and worked harder than ever, as if, simply by working, I could force all the world's clocks to grind to a permanent halt.

Months passed. I stuck to the plan. It was everyone else who refused to cooperate. First, my peers let me down. Each morning, I searched the train for someone my own age or older, usually with little luck. At my favorite lunch spots, I endured awkward meals with colleagues of long-standing. We talked about old times, old cases, old victories, and then, instead of discussing new business, they informed me that they were hanging it up. Strangers were also little help. I remember how affronted I felt when a young clerk at the local hardware store offered to help carry my purchases. He was only being nice, I knew, but something in his tone irked me: the natural condescension of youth.

After I turned sixty-six, I began to wind down my law firm. While I continued to work on a number of projects, I wasn't nearly as busy as I had been in previous years. People began to refer to me as "retired" or "semiretired." It became impossible to ignore. I was in unknown territory. The well-marked paths had all vanished. One weekday afternoon—an afternoon that, only weeks before, I would have spent at the office—I found myself at the local bookstore, grabbing any title that looked halfway helpful: books about retirement and about aging; literature concerned with older characters; even surveys of philosophical and religious traditions. At home I spent hours searching the newly bought pages for some measure of guidance, wisdom, or comfort.

The books about retirement and aging proved least helpful. In general, they fell into two categories. The first might be called the "how-to-retire" books. These were full of clichés, platitudes, and one-size-fits-all tips, as if there were instructions for growing old. The second category might be called the "I-have-a-theory-about-aging" books. These were written by academics, were full of statistical data, and, as far as I could tell, existed principally to demonstrate the author's mastery of the subject and the correctness of his or her conclusions. None managed to ease my anxiety. None taught me anything vital that I could apply to my own life.

"Ripeness is all," said King Lear. I couldn't argue with Shakespeare, of course. Nor with Keats, who wrote that the autumn of a man's life has a music all its own. Nor with Camus, who called this autumn another spring, in which all the leaves become flowers. These were beautiful, exalted thoughts. Reading them, I felt ennobled, though not entirely reassured. For me, poetic and fictional creations, no matter how masterful, lacked the force and sting of real life. Next, I turned to a subject I'd always avoided, philosophy. First, I looked to the Greeks. "Happiness," according to Aristotle, "is the meaning and purpose of life." Fine, I thought, but I need details. After Athens, I headed to the East, which, given my temperament, may have been a mistake. "For certain is death to the born," the *Bhagavad Gita* informed me, "and certain is birth for the dead; therefore over the inevitable, do not grieve." I wasn't grieving. I was just looking for some tangible sense of what the next years might hold. "When your work is done, retire," said the *Daodejing*. "Focus on the empty space." This was inscrutable. I needed to know that the coming years would be more than mere empty space.

After several weeks of study, I decided to give up. I would, I thought, have to figure out this next phase of life on my own. I began adding my new collection to the shelves. As I did, I came across a book I'd bought when I was preparing to graduate from law school: *Working*, by Studs Terkel.

The subtitle of *Working* is long but direct: *People Talk About What They Do All Day and How They Feel About What They Do*. This neatly summarizes what the book is about. Terkel interviewed people and asked them to discuss their jobs and lives, then used the edited transcripts of those discussions as the basis of his book. Decades ago, as I prepared to enter the workforce, *Working* supplied me with a much-needed sense of perspective and a rich store of insight. It occurred to me that I could attempt a similar project, one that would address the concerns that I and others felt as we prepared to retire.

Now I had a project. More than that, I had Terkel as my guide. The strength of his approach, I knew, was his great interest in people. He spoke with a diverse group: geographically, ethnically, and economically. He didn't ask them to recite "how-to" lessons, abstractions, or clichés. Instead, he invited them to tell stories, to share their thoughts, and, at times, to confess their fears, misgivings, and dreams. Throughout, Terkel tried to convey a sense that the people he met were speaking directly to the reader. In this way, he produced a series of oral histories that transcended the details of individual lives and offered insights into the universal experience of searching for "daily meaning as well as daily bread."

Following Terkel's example, my project was transformed. Although it began with personal concerns, it's not a memoir. It's also not a book-length essay. It doesn't present a unified theory on the experience of aging in contemporary society, nor a series of abstract lessons on how best to approach one's golden years. Instead, like *Working*, it's a collection of life stories, all told in a compressed, conversational style and in the first person. Throughout these pages, I've tried to make myself invisible. My goal has been to present each interviewee's story directly, to convey a sense that each is addressing the reader personally, in a spirit of absolute frankness and sincerity.

My methodology has been straightforward. Starting in the summer of 2011 and continuing through the summer of 2013, I set out to find a diverse group of older Americans. Some I knew or knew of. Others I approached cold, with nothing more than a letter or a phone call. Like Terkel, I wanted to find a true cross-section, one that was geographically, ethnically, and economically varied. I was not interested in speaking with only the very accomplished or the very wealthy. (During the interviews, I declined to speak about money, investments, or income, thinking that these subjects would distract from my central purpose.) Many months later, after I'd completed all the interviews, a friend I'd asked to review an early manuscript remarked that it was "impossible to find any losers" among those profiled. I agree. To some extent, the absence of any "losers" may be due to a self-selecting bias. Those who were unhappy with their lives were unlikely to agree to be interviewed. However, only three of the many I approached declined to participate. More than any self-selecting bias, I think that the absence of any "losers" in these pages suggests the richness of every person's life, each of which, according to the old chestnut, can supply the basis for at least one good novel. I also believe that the absence of any "losers" in this book points to the positive results of reflection and storytelling, of forcing oneself to shape experience into a coherent, sustained narrative.

As I drove or flew to the first meetings, I had a general sense of the initial subjects of discussion, and sometimes a few questions, but seldom anything more. In each case, I used these prepared ideas only to start conversations, never to direct them. I wanted natural, free-flowing talk, with room enough for genuinely surprising and revealing moments. Usually, these discussions were conducted over lunch, dinner, or coffee. Sometimes, they lasted ninety minutes. Sometimes, they lasted much longer, and included subsequent meetings and follow-up phone calls.

I captured all the interview sessions on tape and then transcribed the conversations in full. This created a record of several hundred thousand words. Like much natural discussion, these transcriptions were often disjointed and discursive. In editing, my goal was twofold. First, I wanted the text to be accurate, and to remain true to the language used by each interviewee. Second, I wanted the text to be intelligible and engaging for the reader. As such, I tried to find the most interesting sections of each transcribed conversation, to eliminate any unnecessary words, and to organize the material to create a sense of cohesion and progression. After I'd finished my edits, I sent each interview subject a draft to ensure that the language was accurate and that all facts were true as of the time of the interview. My final step was to organize the completed profiles. I did so by grouping each interview based on a prominent theme discussed therein (e.g., Adventure, Community, etc.). I believe that such a categorization was necessary, although I acknowledge that it was also somewhat arbitrary. Each profile addresses a variety of topics. The scope of each cannot be limited to the section in which it is grouped.

I'm credited as the book's author, but this is true only in a nominal sense. Its real authors are the remarkable people I was fortunate enough to meet and interview over the past two years. I found them fascinating, charming, generous, vibrant, and inspiring. The opportunity to know them and to learn from them has been the chief pleasure of this experience. In many cases, they became friends and role models. During the two years I spent working on this book, some of the interviewees grew ill or passed away. I knew this was a possibility when I began, but I was not prepared for how deeply it would affect me. I owe each of the interviewees a debt of gratitude and always will. They helped me, not only to make this book, but also to grow, to change, and to feel prepared to enter the next phase of my life.

When I began, I thought I was assembling a book about retirement. Soon, I realized that, although this book was that, it was also much more. It was even more than a book about the experience of growing older. Fundamentally, this book is concerned with choice. Again and again, the people profiled in these pages remind us that if we expect to find any measure of happiness, meaning, or fulfillment, doing so is up to us, and a good life will find us or elude us based on the decisions we make every day. The people in this book are elderly, but they speak to everyone, even to the very young. They ask: Why wait to examine your life? Why wait to change? Why not live, really live, as much and as best as you possibly can right now? They tell us that it's never too late and it's never too early.

# I. WORK

# *"Why? It's Fun!"*

## JOSEPH KELLY
### Born 1925

Joe was born and raised in Providence, Rhode Island. His father was a carpenter. His mother, one of thirteen children, emigrated from Ireland. She worked and, one by one, brought many of her siblings over to America.

Joe has been a practicing trial lawyer since 1951. He loves to try lawsuits. He's tried some several hundred jury trials in his sixty-three years of practice. He's one of the longest-practicing trial lawyers in Rhode Island and recently tried a four-week medical malpractice jury trial. He has been honored by the Rhode Island Bar for his contributions to the community and for serving as a role model to other lawyers, exemplifying the ideals of ethics, civility, professionalism, and legal skills. Joe is a fellow of the American College of Trial Lawyers and a member of the Rhode Island Board of Bar Examiners.

He exercises an hour daily and attends Mass four times a week. His wife of fifty-six years suffers from Alzheimer's and lives in a nearby assisted-living facility and Joe visits her several times a week. His daughter is a lawyer and practices with him. Joe has three grandchildren and two sisters, and many nieces and nephews, all of whom he sees regularly. Our interview is at a restaurant near his office. When he enters, Joe is escorted to "his" table overlooking the Providence River, where patrons and

**lawyers stop to chat him up, and introduce him to clients as "the famous Mr. Kelly."**

I have always loved to have fun. Even in grade school I'd infuriate the nuns with one antic or another. I remember one nun got so exasperated that she pushed me into a three-foot-deep trash barrel. My butt went deep to the bottom and my arms and legs hung over the side. When she couldn't loose me from the barrel, the local fire department was called. Everyone still laughs about that.

I didn't want anything to do with college. My mother filed an application to Providence College without my knowing. When I got in, she said, "Well, what are you going to do now?" And so, I went. After World War II, I returned to Providence for a while, and then went up to Northeastern University Law School.

The first law firm I worked at had a connection to the legal officer at the Quonset Naval Base and would send us a ton of work for sailors—drunk driving, divorces, everything. On a Saturday morning there'd be fifteen to twenty sailors in our offices, all with their problems. I had a lot of independence about how to handle cases. My God, from 1951 to 1957, all I had was trial cases. In fact, when I was a lawyer for only a few months, I went to court on a Friday, to get an extension on a criminal manslaughter case, and the judge told me to show up on Monday to try the case. I tried that case for three weeks...I didn't know what I was doing.

There was a time when lawyers could get a lot of trials. I went down to one county for a call of the calendar. That's when the court goes through the list of what's up for trial for that month. I had a number of cases on the list. So I started case number one, just had it submitted to the jury when I get called to start my next case, and so on in sequence until I tried my fourth case in sequence back-to-back.

Those dice on my desk are just for luck, but they do remind me that sometimes jury trials are like shooting craps. You never know. You see, we're gamblers. The most you can do is work hard. I use to say about any case, you can pick the side you want as long as I get first crack at the witnesses, because if I get first crack you ain't going to win that case, especially if I get the chance to talk to them first.

When I wasn't trying a case, I'd be at the courthouse watching the old-timers try their cases and getting all their tricks, and their various theatrical techniques. [*Slipping easily into character, Joe begins to rehearse the performance from the 1950s of an old lawyer arguing to a jury that contracting parties' reasonable expectations ought to control over fine print boilerplate. Joe mimics the lawyer. He picks up the contract and makes an effort to read it and can't, even squinting. He pulls it closer to his eyes and still can't make it out. He puts on his glasses; same result. Then finally he pulls a magnifying glass out and puts it and his nose close to the document. After a dramatic pause, he looks up and declares with great sarcasm, "By God, they're right!"*] That was the total argument. The jury laughed. Of course, it won the day.

I thought about retirement. When I was sixty-five I said maybe I should retire at sixty-five, but before I knew it I was sixty-eight, then I said seventy, then I said seventy-five. When I first thought about it, it never really settled in that I would retire. Cases got longer, so if you got a case at sixty-five and you signed on it, you were in it for a long time. I was on a big case here. It started in 1999 and closed in 2010, eleven years. You own those cases, or they own you. Never thought about retirement again.

Forty years after my partner and I started our firm and grew it to ten to twelve lawyers, my partner wanted to retire. At the time, we had a lot of work from major insurers. We had all the work we could do. We decided to cut our shares and give the firm to the remaining lawyers. It didn't bother me. Money never bothered me. And yet I made a lot of it.

Some cases I'd take on a contingency basis—a large trade secrets case and a medical malpractice claim—got great results. [*Joe points to a framed, hand-drawn diagram on his wall.*] This was the trade secret case. It involved a medical device that would suction out your lungs.

Retirement doesn't really cross my mind. Now three years ago, I noticed my wife was failing with Alzheimer's and I realized it's not going to do me any good to stay home because I can't take care of her. So I hired a nurse to come in every day. This went on for two years. I'd come to the office, go home, and spend the evening with her. The nurse said the arrangement had to be changed. So, we moved her to an assisted-living facility with an Alzheimer's unit nearby so I can see her. As long as my wife is in the facility, I want to be near her, so I won't be traveling or leaving the area.

My wife was a smart girl—she worked for a small law firm, did everything, took care of the books and all of this stuff—but she never liked doctors. So I got the best neurologist in Alzheimer's and dementia, but every time they get together, they get into an argument. So the last visit, the doctor tells her that he's going to ask her a question later on in the meeting and the answer to the question will be "tree, trunk, and green." So he goes on for fifteen minutes and picks up a questionnaire and says, "Question?" She says, "Tree, trunk, and green." And he says, "No, no, not now, that's later." But she says, "I know what you're trying to do. Trying to make me look like the village idiot!"

I suppose I'll stop if I'm going to get in over my head. That'll make me stop. Hasn't happened. What I've done is have somebody come in with me in my cases as a backup. Every once in a while I'm looking for a word and I can't find the word fast. But that's it.

Right now I'm working on a brain injury case for a bus driver who fell on black ice and really hit his head. I want to try it. They talk about football players and hockey players who get whacked. He's got the same sort of thing that these players have. You know, the brain goes bang, bang, bang. [*Joe makes a motion of a brain swinging inside a skull.*] This is the perfect time to try a case like that. If these big players with helmets falling on grass can get hurt...

Well, if I stopped doing this I'd like to dictate all my cases, because so much of it was fun, not just business. People don't realize what a great thing trial practice is. It's fun! A chance to make things right.

I've hired guys, smart as whips, and I'd send them up to try a case and they'd fold. They come back in a sweat. If you don't like the practice, you got to get out. I like this. I really do. The stress is just the price of the fun. I always think I couldn't just do the same thing over and over. Sometimes you just come away laughing. When the day comes, I would still like to golf. The distance is gone, but I still like to get on the course. I'd like to make another trip to Ireland. Those people would stop at the drop of a hat for a good time.

Regrets? My mother worked hard, died early. I've always been generous to my sisters and my wife's family, but I never got the chance to do something for my mother. One of her biggest joys was me coming into the law. Every time she'd go to church bingo, she'd come back with a list of things for me to do. She'd take out the list and say, "Joe, you need to write a letter for Mrs. McCarthy—*a threatening letter.*"

# *"An Identity Revision Process"*

## CAROL KIMBALL SIGELMAN
### Born 1947

*Carol and her late husband, Lee, in Portugal.*

Carol is a **PhD** professor of psychology at George Washington University, where she has worked for over twenty years after holding similar faculty positions at Texas Tech, Eastern Kentucky, and the University of Arizona. She has studied and written extensively on child development and the issues people face as they move through life stages, including a college text on life-span development. Recently, she has faced two major upheavals: the death of her husband of forty years, and a return to classroom teaching and research after thirteen years as an associate vice president in charge of research, graduate studies, and other aspects of academic affairs. She has no children; all her relatives

**are in the Minneapolis area. Most of her friends and social contacts are in the university community.**

I wanted to talk about this topic because I teach adult development, and having turned sixty-five I am acutely aware of aging and retirement.

I'm not worried about these topics. In fact, I actually avoid thinking about them. I have had a lot of changes recently and have a lot of support from the university community. After my husband died, I wanted to get back, to have a purpose, to have my social connections. So the last thing on my mind is retirement. I am focused on resuming my career as a professor. That takes some work if you haven't taught for thirteen years.

Getting back into research is hard, too. I'm looking for a new idea, a new project. It makes for an unusual situation. It's almost as if at this age I'm trying to build a new career, or at least revive an old career, at a time when other people are thinking about retiring. But I have every reason to maintain my connection to the university. It is the source of my social life and my sense of purpose and challenge, and everything else good. I'm happy at work. I've always been a workaholic—spending a lot of time on work, whatever it is. I enjoy it.

Since my husband died, I see this uncertainty in my future. I've been very focused on the present. Getting by, taking care of my house, taking care of finances. Things I didn't have to mess with before because he handled these things. So now I have to think ahead. Before my husband got sick, I just assumed, "Oh well, we'll figure something out. We'll be together. Probably he'll have more say about what we do than I will, but I'm open to a lot of different things." I had a sense of what my future looked like and now I don't. The future is something I should be thinking about. Yet, on the other hand, I don't want to. Most of me is saying, "Let's see what happens."

I haven't made major life choices for forty years, and even some of my decisions before that were more accidental than deliberate. I married at twenty-three. I got into my particular graduate program because a professor handed me a flyer and suggested I might be interested. Even my career choice was fairly accidental. I didn't intend to be a university administrator. I was picked to be one. See what I'm saying? I have the sense that I've never planned anything and I think, *Oh, I'm supposed to plan now?*

Age sixty-five is a milestone. Though I know better, there's a tendency to think, *Oh, now I'm in the category of old people.* That's partly due to bereavement, which dominates your thoughts and makes you feel that your mind doesn't work right. I have been more aware of memory lapses, just difficulty concentrating. But it's hard to separate the effects of bereavement and aging in what's going on. My difficulty getting back into research has made me wonder, *Well, maybe I don't have any good ideas anymore, or maybe I'm going to have trouble doing the kind of work I could do in the past.*

In thinking about the future, I haven't thought about it as a list of accomplishments I want to achieve, or a list of things I want to do. I don't have a vision of what I want to do after working. I'm not the kind of person who sets a goal and then drives to achieve it. I try to do what I am doing well. I look at the future and I think it would be unusual for me to set big goals and pursue them. Part of me feels like I may need to do that, particularly if a partner doesn't come along. I'll have to create a future myself.

I think I'd like a relationship again, if the right relationship came along. I think I would find fulfillment in a new relationship. I have thought about moving to someplace warmer, but I don't see myself doing that alone. I would have to be with a friend or maybe a partner to consider it.

I'm a workaholic, but I'm discovering that I can enjoy being lazy, too. Returning to teaching means I have summers off. I mix work and play better in the summer, and I love the freedom of deciding what to do when. I figure retirement may feel like that. Just mix it up better.

Even though I just witnessed a death in my bedroom, where we provided hospice care to my husband, I feel invulnerable and believe that I'm going to live to an old age. I'm very healthy. I have a few of the aging kinds of things, osteoporosis and high cholesterol, but basically I'm very healthy. So I'm not thinking about death. But I have thought on a more personal level about some of the concepts I teach. That's not unusual. People in their later years want to step back and think more broadly about life.

There are a number of tricks older people use to feel good—the academic term for one is selective optimization with compensation. And that's something I should work on more. Rather than writing a textbook on the entire life span, maybe I should write a more narrowly focused book—something that doesn't require as much breadth of knowledge and reading, something that allows me to specialize in what I know best.

I've been interested in the question of how to maintain your optimism when you're able to do less and less. The picture is very good until you get up to really old age, eighty-five or older, with multiple health issues. Up until then, older people seem to focus on enjoying life more than younger people do. At the same time, there's an increase in spirituality. It has been shown that when you see time running short, you emphasize emotional fulfillment with loved ones over other goals like acquiring more information and meeting new people.

It's also been shown that on a day-to-day basis older people have more positive emotional experiences than younger people. Older people may also have more emotional control. They don't get all bent out of shape over things that would cause younger people to go ballistic. It's about getting in touch with, not blunting, their feelings. Older adults have a full range of emotions, but better emotional control. That may tie in with spirituality and figuring out the larger meaning of your life. There's the concept of a "life review" that's been around for a long time. It gets you thinking about the life you led and helps you make sense of it.

Also, we change how we judge ourselves as we get older. Right now, I'm beating myself up thinking that I should meet the same standards as younger people. Maybe at some point I'll shift and start comparing myself to other aging colleagues and decide I'm not doing so badly after all.

All things considered, the research is very positive about old age. On the other hand, when you are around someone who is having multiple problems, you know there is a point when it's hard to maintain your optimism and people start to think, *I'd just as soon die now.* I just think that point comes very late, and doesn't apply to all of us, either, because some just keep ticking until the very end.

I'm still in an unsettled transition period, with conflicting feelings about myself, my life, and what the rest of my life is going to look like. I don't have a plan, but I didn't earlier in life, so that's not surprising. Perhaps, I'm waiting for something to happen, and maybe it will. It's like an identity crisis. My identity was tied up with my husband, with my administrative job. I've been forced into an identity revision process. It can be interesting and invigorating, and it can lead in new, good directions.

# *"A Final Spurt of Satisfaction"*

## JACK WINNINGHOFF
### Born 1924

**Jack is a former WWII pilot, engineer, entrepreneur, designer, and boat builder. He loves to work with aluminum and wood. He's currently planning to regroup and relaunch his business.**

My paternal grandfather was a blacksmith in Philipsburg, Montana, a town of one thousand in the Bitterroot Valley. At one time the town had the richest silver mine in the world, and at the height of the boom had a population of ten thousand. Granddad was a blacksmith, making his living shoeing horses and fixing wagons, but he was also a metal artist. I still have a small anvil and hammer set he made on my shop desk. Some of his ability got into me. My maternal grandfather ran away from a Vermont farm to Alaska at age twelve. He ended up as president of the Philipsburg bank and served as a Montana state bank examiner. The family lore is that my mom and dad met at ages three and four, playing in the sawdust of one of the town's saloons. My grandmother gave my dad a ten-dollar gold piece, and with that and a lot of hard work in the mines, he financed his way through the University of Montana. He then got a scholarship to MIT. In 1914 he got one of three doctorates granted by the school. He studied physical chemistry.

I grew up in northern New Jersey and after high school went to MIT. It was 1942, and after one semester it was clear that we would get called up, so I signed up for the Army Air Corps. I wanted to be a pilot, but I had some slight failures on the eye test. Most notably, my depth perception was poor. Everything else was fine. They sent me to an eye doctor for a consult. He told me that the depth perception test was bullshit and would not endanger my crew—you never use it. So he coached me on how to deal with the test. I went back and retook the test. Everything was dead nuts! One of the highest scores ever. The training was some of the best damn education I ever got. Boy, did they know how to do it. After training I went to Tinian in the Marianas. It was the busiest air base during the war. I flew B-29s over Japan.

After the war I returned to MIT, went straight through and finished up in September 1948. Then I went to work for Alcoa as a sales engineer. At the time, I had some ego, you know, MIT and a pilot, but I learned. I know I'm smarter, or at least have a better memory, than some people, but I've worked with a lot of guys who are smarter.

I got called up for Korea in 1950. At the time, I was engaged. We had to move the wedding up about a month. I was married to my first wife for thirteen years. I had three kids with her. They live in North Carolina and Seattle. I remarried. My second wife passed away a year and a half ago. I was married for forty-six years and have a son who lives in the area. I have five grandchildren, all smart and motivated kids.

After Korea, I resumed my work on government projects with big science-focused companies. Much of it was in electro-optics. I worked on the camera for the U2 and SR-71 spy planes and on the Hubble telescope. The work was fascinating, but you know big companies. I think I wanted to start my own company even during my early days with Alcoa, when management quashed a proposal I made. The disapproval made no sense, and it rankled me.

Anyways, in about 1974, we came to Gloucester to look for a summer home and decided to stay. During this period I met some UMass professors who had a patent on the explosive forming of aluminum sailboat hulls. They had a backyard pool and were using dynamite to create pressure waves that would form the aluminum sheets into shape. The process would not produce repeatable, consistent results. It wasn't working.

I was very comfortable with the material from my days at MIT and Alcoa. I knew it was a great material for boats—light, strong, economic. Won't rust, rot, or crack. Someone recommended forging the hull hydrostatically, rather than with explosives. I got some help from one of the professors and an old friend who had made some money. We tried a sailboat hull and it worked, but it wouldn't scale and wasn't economic. I then wanted to do a lobster boat using more conventional methods, but my partners weren't interested.

So I was off on my own. I wanted my own shop, and there it was. Age fifty. A small business presents all kinds of challenges. Will you make the product? Will you make the payroll? It means risking your economic future. It can be satisfying, but it is challenging. Also, you have to be tenacious and adaptive, staying in business for over thirty-five years. Luck is also a big part of it, but when I started I thought the merits of aluminum commercial fishing boats were so clear—economically and technically and proven in the Northwest and Alaska—that I would have no problem selling them. But the Northeast fishermen run on small margins and were reluctant to risk any change. They'll never let progress interfere with tradition!

Anyways, I set up in a converted horse barn. There's a tidal river nearby where we launch when we're ready to go. I use two fifty-six-foot bays for actual construction. I've converted the hayloft into my office and put two apartments in. I'm really satisfied with the one I'm in. Plenty of height, space, and light. It's great for entertaining, cooking, and shooting pool. And, I have a great commute, just downstairs.

Over the years, I have built around two hundred boats, some my own design. Early on I ran into a guy who needed a small boat for getting around in the tidal rivers, the shallows, and sometimes in open water. So I designed and built a model. Flat bottom, with chines for directional stability and strength—a good-planing hull. He fell in love with the design, but the guy who was going to use it didn't. I took a chance, went ahead and built it. I sold it to a local marine dealer and it became pretty successful. It's called a Rowley Skiff. Since, we've built fishing boats, fire/workboats, research boats, tour boats, including a sixty-eight-footer that works the Charles River. I've been at it so long I got full membership in the Society for Naval Architects and Marine Engineers. Last year, I custom-built a thirty-foot oyster barge for a guy who was susceptible to skin cancer—it had a bigger-than-usual pilothouse.

I've got a boat in the yard now—a twenty-eight-foot workboat for a New Hampshire electric cooperative. It'll be used to take on and off heavy loads, like a generator pulled on a trailer by an ATV. The boat has a landing-craft-type bow door.

I like design and producing things that have an artistic element to them. I've made a gazebo top for a lighthouse on Nantucket, and some docks and ramp bridges that have attractive parabolic shapes—one that I worked on with a local architect has that shape, combined teak tread, overhead fascia for lighting, and a light-blue coated-aluminum door. It bridges the house on stilts over the harbor and spans yards and yards of sea grass. The overall effect is very Zen.

I had my hip replaced and I'm through rehab. Otherwise, I'm good. I have a girlfriend. She's seventy-three, very attractive, and keeps me going. I knew her casually years ago. But fast forward the years and our paths crossed when I was looking for advice on a book I intended to write. She had been in the publishing business. We had dinner and it's been going on since.

My self-esteem is unjustifiably high. I like what I'm doing. It's satisfying in that rare case where we have a happy customer and make money. The worst thing is an unhappy customer. I've had a long run with some headaches, but overall I have a pretty short shit list. I don't know who number three is, but I know numbers one and two. Number two stiffed me for a bunch of money. Number one, I can't say enough bad things about that son of a bitch.

I don't see retirement. I would need a situation where I don't need to worry about making money. You only need enough to stay safe, warm, and buy a dinner and a drink every once in a while. Money doesn't have the same power over your life that it once had. I'm not far from that, but the work—boat building, the shop—is my whole thing.

I'm in the process of recapitalizing and starting over. Focusing on a small number of high-quality small boats—easier to predict the hours and cost. I'll take every damn thing I learned about people, about doing stuff, and try to apply it. You know, have a final spurt of satisfaction.

# "What's the Barrier Now?"

## GAIL DEEGAN
Born 1946 – Retired 2001

Gail was born near Albany, New York. Her father was the local postmaster and her mother was a nurse. She began working as an elementary schoolteacher, and in midcareer switched to finance, putting her in the vanguard of women breaking into the male-dominated world of business. Over a thirty-year career, she moved into the upper echelon of the Massachusetts business community.

Gail served as a senior executive and chief financial officer at Houghton Mifflin publishers, and at predecessors of Verizon and National Grid. She has served on numerous corporate boards, including: iRobot, EMC, TJX, Hartford Life, Houghton Mifflin, and EG&G. She has been an executive in residence at Simmons College and Babson College, and on the advisory boards and councils of several nonprofits, including: Simmons, Babson, Girl Scouts Patriot Trail Council, Woods Hole Oceanographic Institute, United Way of Massachusetts Bay, and the Greater Boston Chamber of Commerce. She has sought to advance other women and continues to look for ways to reach a wider audience with a message encouraging young women to enter the business world and seek top positions.

Gail graduated from The College of Saint Rose, The Ohio State University, and Simmons School of Management. She has

**received honorary degrees as well as numerous awards and honors. She is married and has two adult sons.**

When I went to college, the available career paths for women were limited to teaching, nursing, or social work. That message was clear. At the same time, I was exposed to women who worked outside the home and ran institutions. They delivered, subtly and by their example, different messages that shaped my life.

My mother was a nurse. She was accomplished and made things happen. Also, the nuns, the Sisters of St. Joseph of Carondolet, who ran the local hospital and the schools and college I attended, delivered the message that women could be successful leaders if they had high expectations for those they were leading and enabled them to be successful. Just as significant—never display a big ego because, in the scheme of things, you're not that important. Those messages became part of me, though I was unaware of it at the time.

After college and graduate school, I taught elementary school. I had a life plan of raising a family and working part-time, but that wasn't working out. A couple of breakups and rumors of teacher layoffs made me question my chosen path—maybe what I thought was going to happen just wasn't going to happen. About this time, a friend introduced me to a new MBA program at Simmons founded by two women Harvard Business School professors. The program taught both technical skills and the social dynamics of being a woman in business management. It made the point that you should always assess your business environment. What is the problem? What are the resources? How is the problem affecting others? Then, ask where and how can I help? Analyze the environment.

At the time, there were few women in middle management. Now, thirty-five years later, the problem is that few women are CEOs, COOs, CFOs, or are on corporate boards. What's the barrier now?

After graduation from Simmons, I got a job as a financial analyst at Eastern Gas and Fuel, a male-dominated company. It had varied businesses: utility, coal mining, and barging operations. I worked closely with the CEO and the CFO. Both were incredible people, but couldn't have had more different personalities. I think the CEO appreciated the challenges women faced, but I can't say he was all that comfortable around me. There were several times when I was not included in the boys going out. Of course, I felt badly, but I knew it wasn't personal. They just were not comfortable with me.

The MBA degree helped with the technical skills, but the training in the behavioral aspects was as important. I understood that I was going from elementary teaching, where women were the majority and independent actors, to a male-dominated culture where team play was critical. I found support elsewhere; Simmons classmates and other women in business would get together regularly.

Despite the gender differences, I got along well. I was named treasurer, the first woman officer in the company. Still, some of the old awkwardness persisted. At times, you just had to laugh. When I got the position, I decided to go by my maiden name. Up until then I had used a hyphenated combination of my maiden name and my husband's surname. When the CEO learned of this, his first question was whether I was getting divorced, and his second was whether I had my husband's permission!

Raising kids and working was challenging. I remember reading 10Ks and proxy statements while nursing. It was the time of year and a part of the job. We got through it because my husband is a clinical psychologist and had a flexible schedule and because we had great child care. Also, my employers were supportive. When an issue with child care arose, my boss packed my office up and told me to work from home for as long as it took. I still think of that as an example of how one person's support can make a huge impact.

I never had an issue with my kids being cared for and loved by another, but that doesn't mean that I didn't miss going to some events, or worry about how quickly I could get home. Of course, there were some poignant memories. When I got my first big promotion, I was sitting on the stairs with my sons. I felt like a big deal in my new suit. I said, "Boys, this is a really big day for Mommy." In reply, they asked, "You don't have to work anymore?" They didn't mind, but their ideal probably was different.

Pew Research recently came out with a survey showing that women are the breadwinners in 40 percent of households. There's definitely a cultural change under way. Going forward, it'll be difficult to achieve a work/life balance. Companies are global, operating 24/7, and technology is ubiquitous. It can be done, but will be especially difficult if the culture of the company puts a premium on face time.

I coach young women in business, and I see them shy away from top positions because of the stress the current officeholder operates under. Women don't want that lifestyle. I tell them that when they're in charge, they'll decide how things are done.

After thirteen years, I was recruited by New England Telephone to be CFO. It was the biggest operating public company in New England. I liked the people and the responsibilities were challenging. Basically, if an issue involved money, it involved me. Of the fifty corporate officers in New England and in our New York affiliate, three were women. I was the only woman in upper management in New England.

I felt extremely welcomed. The company had an established women's network, and as luck would have it, a childhood friend was the COO of the New York affiliate. So I saw what it was like to be included, and what it was like for people to go out of their way to introduce you to other people.

Discrimination is subtle. Over my career, the companies and people I worked for were quality people and would never tolerate harassment. I was never harassed, but I was treated differently, occasionally left out. Sometimes, people held back information, maybe due to bias, or maybe resentment that I was acting as the CEO's right hand and they had to deal with me. I remember delivering a proposal to the CEO of another company with a deadline for response. He asked in an imperious tone, "On whose behalf are you speaking?" Obviously a woman couldn't have such authority. By the time I got to New England Telephone I had the clout, and no one was asking such questions.

From my days at Eastern Gas, I knew the CEOs of Houghton Mifflin publishing, and of EG&G, a company that ran nuclear power plants. They were instrumental in putting me on their boards. Houghton Mifflin was a perfect fit. It already had two women on its board, and elementary education was its biggest product. On the other hand, EG&G was a male, male, male company. It had decided to put not one but two women on its board, so they wouldn't feel alone. I thought, *How sweet*. Subsequently, I served on the boards of TJX Companies, EMC, and iRobot. I never proactively networked for these positions. I got recruited because it's risky when you put an unknown on your board. I had experience and was known in the community. I presented a minimal risk.

I was recruited to be CFO of Houghton Mifflin. It was the perfect job. The company was one of few independent, publicly owned publishers, but it was tough to stay public. The required investment in technology kept increasing and the cycle of book adoption kept lengthening. The investment community did not like our business model.

At the same time, big companies were acquiring independent publishers. I wondered how long it would be before we were acquired. It wasn't long. Vivendi, the French company, had always been interested in acquiring one of our core assets, *Curious George*, and in 2001 acquired Houghton Mifflin. That acquisition ended my tenure with the company and marked the beginning of my retirement.

I was fifty-five. I hadn't planned on retiring so early. But, circumstances happen. I didn't know what I was going to do. I didn't know a lot of people who had retired. Now I was home and my kids were off to college. I thought we'd travel, but 9/11 put a real chill on those plans. I knew people who died on one of the flights that took off from Boston. It felt like the world was falling apart. It affected my psyche. The question of what I wanted to do felt so much less important.

My board activities kept me busy and engaged, especially one with the Girl Scouts. I loved the mission—reshaping its message to keep it competitive. It fit with my skills in strategic planning. Also, in conjunction with the organization, a friend and I created Camp CEO to teach girls about business. Surveys showed that most girls had only the vaguest ideas of the activities people perform in business. They thought business meant money and computers, and weren't inclined to pursue it as a career. The same surveys showed that boys didn't have any deeper understanding, but were inclined to pursue the field. We set up a curriculum that addressed marketing, communications, operations, business planning, etc. Most importantly, we had successful women come tell their stories and work with the girls. We had a terrific response.

I also coached young women as an executive in residence at Simmons and Babson. From this experience, I know that stories are tremendously helpful to young women. It's how they learn what's possible. I am looking for a way to reach a wider audience with these messages.

I don't miss the corporate life. In fact, I wonder how I did it for all those years, but you do what you have to do. I am sure enthusiasm and youth made it easier. Now, I see more complexity in issues, from health care to the financial system, and wonder how it's going to work out. My husband says things have to get ripe rotten before they'll get straightened out.

My mother lived until she was ninety-one, and I'll be sixty-seven this summer. So I have become more health conscious. I've also rethought what I want to do. I've always defined myself by accomplishing goals, making things happen, seeing concrete results. Now, it's not as easy to make things happen. I am more of an advisor than a doer. I have to step back and tell myself that I am still getting things done, just not as fast as I'd like. As a type A, I have to redefine my goals and how I measure success. I know I have become more reflective. There was a time when I found meaning and satisfaction in contributing to an organization's success.

Now, I'm beginning to understand that it's not about doing; it's about being. I don't see things as all-or-nothing. I have a portfolio of activities that contribute to my well-being and satisfaction: family, community, health, spirituality. I try to do something in each area every day. Completely contrary to the spirit of the effort, I've even created a spreadsheet to track it. Typical finance person! Old habits are hard to break.

I am not seeking balance for its own sake. I just want to find the joy and satisfaction that exists in daily life, helping with my niece's children or visiting with my kids. Those things are pleasurable for me. Just slowing down and being more conscious of what I'm doing, and the joy that's there. Recognizing meaning and fulfillment when it's there in front of you.

# "A Long Detour"

## WILLIAM E. WICKENS
### Born 1939 – Retired 2001

**Bill Wickens looks like central casting's version of a senior US senator, perfectly tailored, with an unlit cigar in hand to punctuate his speech. Ten years ago, he left a highly successful career in the law to pursue business ventures.**

I was born an entrepreneur, but raised a lawyer. There was a long line of entrepreneurs in my family. Some of my ancestors were among the first Dutch settlers who purchased Manhattan. There was also my great-grandfather who emigrated from England while a teenager and settled in Lorain, Ohio, which was then a small fishing village at the mouth of the Black River on Lake Erie. A cabinetmaker by trade, he built the first lighthouse for the village, and established successful funeral and furniture businesses. In the 1890s, he convinced the citizenry to approve a $100,000 bond issue to make the Black River navigable for commercial purposes, then the biggest bond issue in Ohio history. People called it a wildcat scheme that would never bring industry to Lorain. But it did, and Lorain boomed. The largest pipe steel mill in the world located in Lorain, as did Ford and American Shipbuilding. It turned Lorain into a significant Great Lake port and industrial center.

My father put himself through night law school, served as a local prosecutor, and then founded his own firm. He had the dream that I would join him in the practice, and I did, right after law school.

Through high school and college, I was drawn to school plays and debating. I always preferred the unpopular position; I could see potential where others couldn't, or maybe I just assessed it differently. Anyways, that approach seemed to work—I won a number of statewide and national debate contests. I went to Michigan Law, and at graduation I turned down offers from New York firms to practice with my father.

When I returned to Lorain, I did a couple of things. I renewed a lot of old friendships, many of whom were of Eastern European descent—Hungarian, Czechs, Ukrainian, and Slovaks. A few years later I worked to elect Bob Taft Jr. to the Senate. He was a Republican and his campaign faced a huge obstacle. Northern Ohio cities—Cleveland, Youngstown, Akron, Lorain, all of which had large Eastern European populations—were overwhelmingly Democrat. I knew I had good relationships in these communities and proposed a strategy for turning them to Taft's camp. It was basic. We'd go to the Croatian Club, tell them in Croatian what Taft was going to do about Communism in Eastern Europe, then the accordion would play and the people would dance. Then we'd do the same at the Hungarian Club, the Lithuanian Club, and so on. Taft won the election due to a huge swing in the Eastern European ethnic vote in northern Ohio. After that, Senator Taft asked me to come to Washington. A couple of years later, he recommended me to serve as counsel in the Watergate investigation. I was staff counsel at thirty-three or thirty-four to Senator Weicker.

When the story of the Watergate burglary first unfolded, Senator Weicker wanted me to go to Mexico to trace checks that were being run through Mexican banks. Everyone thought that was the way to go, but I could see that the story was there in DC. I told the senator that running off to Mexico was a waste of time. I explained that President Nixon and Attorney General Mitchell conceded that they had met right after the break-in and yet, unbelievably, claimed they never talked about it! Talk about the dog that didn't bark! It was clear somebody was paying somebody hush money.

Well, while Senator Weicker was considering my views, I encountered an older lady from Lorain who expressed concern that Fred LaRue, a Republican operative, was going to get hurt. (It was later revealed that LaRue had been the bagman who paid $300,000 to the Watergate conspirators.) She was concerned because LaRue was a decent guy who had done many good things with affordable housing in the Mississippi Delta.

I got in touch with LaRue and promised him a better deal than his lawyer could ever get, which I had absolutely no authority to do. Senator Weicker was miffed that I had made the commitment, but LaRue came through with a signed statement to the effect that he had been told to pay those burglars until their lips were sealed, and he did so because the president wanted it done.

With that statement in hand, Senator Weicker then announced that we had the goods on Bob Haldeman, President Nixon's chief of staff, aka, his "son of a bitch." The very next night our locked file cabinets were broken into. We planted some bait and they went for it. This action confirmed that we were on the right track. It was a big moment.

After Watergate, I left government and then joined a large DC firm. It was a great outfit and the founders were superb lawyers. Just about when I arrived, huge disputes were erupting between the government and major oil companies. So I started doing litigation work for Shell, Getty, Taylor Energy, and lots of others, like Honeywell. My experiences during the energy crisis really left a mark. They expanded my vision and network of contacts. They created a lasting interest in energy-related business ventures. Even today, I am pursuing ventures in the field.

One of my early forays into business was on a small scale, but personally satisfying, and probably whetted my appetite for independent business ventures. During the years I was practicing law in DC, I started an apple farm out in Rappahannock County. I don't know how I got interested; I'd never grown anything before. A lot of people were growing all kinds of apples by the truckload for processors for juice, applesauce, etc. Yet, at the same time, I saw all these farm stands that were natural outlets for a wide variety of apples and fruits. So I grew seventy-nine varieties of fruit; sixty types of apples, then peaches, plums, nectarines. I had all kinds: a strawberry apple, a mother apple, a limbertwig apple. I sold them to these stands at a premium. Did that and commuted to DC for eleven years, but the commute finally got to me. I sold the farm and moved closer to the city.

The legal profession was changing. Huge emphasis on billings, rather than value to the client. This wasn't the way my father practiced and it wasn't consistent with basic Midwest values. I saw an opportunity to bring some of those old-time values to the law. I started a litigation boutique that focused on high-value commercial cases throughout the nation. Our mission was to provide top-quality, aggressive representation to our clients, many of whom had become close friends. No unnecessary discovery, a willingness to adjust our charges, no pyramiding of associates—a flat organization that could go toe-to-toe with any firm. Well, this model was a hit! We got all kinds of "bet-your-company" cases from the Fortune 50.

Yet as I entered my sixties, I looked back and saw that the most satisfying things in my life had been discovering opportunities others didn't see, and taking whatever risk was necessary to exploit them. I decided to pursue that path, contingency cases and business ventures that had huge potential payoffs. Part of me said that the law had been one long detour—I should have always been an entrepreneur. I thought briefly that maybe at my age all the opportunities were gone. But that's nonsense. Opportunity is always all around you. You just have to have the staying power to bring the horses into the barn.

I never thought about retirement—I thought about opportunities with big potential. For five-plus years, I focused all my energy on one case—a good case, but it didn't work out. Now I'm more interested in purely business risk, not litigation risk, but business opportunities take a lot of time depending on the cycle. I was on the phone all night trying to raise money for a project in the clean energy field, getting close, but haven't put the deal together yet. My attitude is that this venture will take off. If it doesn't, something else will. I've always bounced back—I've always been optimistic.

When I was a child about eight or nine, I was diagnosed with polio. My parents took me to a hospital in Cleveland. Right outside my room was an iron lung. The nurse said it was there because the chances were I'd need it. My mother and father were very religious, and they prayed and prayed. Two weeks and their prayers were answered. I was out of the hospital with no loss of function. If that wasn't an act of God...My optimism is hope—faith, really. I believe there is a God who looks out for fools and others, including me. I believe if you say it's all going to fail, life's not worth living. Where does that get you?

# II. ADVENTURE

# "As Mortality Gets Closer, You Get Serious"

## JON TURK
### Born 1945

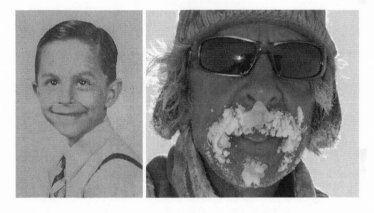

In 2011, Jon Turk, sixty-six, and Erik Boomer, twenty-six, completed the first circumnavigation of Ellesmere Island, the northernmost island in the Canadian Arctic Archipelago, just west of Greenland. The journey covered 1,500 miles in 104 days. They completed it by cross-country skiing, dragging two hundred pounds of supply-stuffed kayaks through jagged ice packs and kayaking through nearly frozen slushy waters, including a narrow channel that acted as nature's giant ice grinder. Along the way, they braved encounters with wolves, polar bears, and walruses.

At the end of the journey, Jon's body shut down; his kidneys failed. Near death, he was airlifted to an Ottawa hospital where he recovered. National Geographic named the Ellesmere expedition one of its Ten Adventures of the Year 2012.

Jon has a forty-year history of great expeditions, including an unsupported mountain bike crossing of the western Gobi and a three-thousand-mile kayak passage from Japan to Alaska that ranks as one of the all-time greatest kayak expeditions.

In addition to his adventures, Jon has a PhD in chemistry. He has written twenty-five college-level science textbooks, including the first on environmental science, as well as three nonfiction narratives about some of his adventures: *Cold Oceans: Adventures in Kayak, Rowboat, and Dogsled; In the Wake of the Jomon: Stone Age Mariners and a Voyage Across the Pacific;* and *The Raven's Gift: A Scientist, A Shaman and Their Remarkable Journey Through the Siberian Wilderness.* These recount his kayak expeditions around Cape Horn, rowing the Northeast Passage, running a dogsled up the east coast of Baffin Island, his kayak passage from Japan to Alaska, and his journey in the Siberian tundra. His time in Siberia led to a faith healing of a long-standing pelvic fracture that had been diagnosed as requiring surgery. The healing was performed by Molynaut, a shaman of the native Koryak people of Siberia. This led to a spiritual awakening and understanding that his travels have been more than a series of physical accomplishments.

Jon lives in the Montana forest, but spends his winters skiing in British Columbia. Jon's wife of twenty-five years died in an avalanche in March 2005. He remarried in September 2006, and he and his second wife are "learning each other's ways, wants, and personalities." Jon has three children and six grandchildren.

As we talked, Jon was preparing for a mountain bike expedition across the Tibetan plateau, near the birthplace of the Dalai Lama.

For whatever reason, I've always been naturally passionate about being in the outdoors. As a young boy, that's what I did all the time. Whenever I had an opportunity, whenever I wasn't in school, I was in the woods. I grew up near a reservation, maybe six square miles, a little Connecticut wood lot near a lake. That's where I would spend my time. That was the deck I was given to play.

Just about everybody has some innate component or activity that they're passionate about as children. Society tends to squelch that and say the activity is not efficient. It won't work in reality. You must learn to conform. I'm not recommending that everyone become an outdoors adventurer, but rather I'm saying that everyone should look deep inside themselves to find out what was it in their childhood that brought them the most joy. What did they gravitate towards?

I went through a standard education: Phillips Andover, Brown, and then the University of Colorado for my PhD in chemistry. Then, something occurred that made me stop. Near the end of my PhD program, I was out running my dog and he started digging in a field. I went over, put my nose down in the earth and breathed deeply.

Right then, I asked: "What was it about childhood that gave me so much joy? Is what I'm doing now giving me that much joy?" I suddenly had an "Aha!" moment, when I realized that I had to go back to that, whatever the cost.

My first outdoor adventure was when I was seventeen and my brother was twelve. We went down the Allagash River in Northern Maine in an old leaky canoe with a bent bow that wouldn't run straight in the rapids. As the older brother, I had the idea that we wouldn't buy any food. The trip was a couple of weeks or more. I think we brought some cornmeal, a .22 rifle, and a fishing pole. We'd live off the land in Daniel Boone fashion. The Fish and Game wardens were flying overhead in a floatplane when they saw us hunting ducks. They landed the plane and said, "Hey, guys, what's going on?" They took our fishing pole and our .22 and left us. We said, "But we don't have any food." They said, "That's your problem."

We made all the mistakes you could conceivably make, and we didn't die. We went down the river and came out hungry and mildly chagrined. So when you do something like this you come to one of two conclusions. This was a really dumb idea and I'm going back to the comforts of home. Or, it was a really good idea with a dumb execution, and try to improve the execution and keep the concept. My preparation has improved greatly since I was seventeen, but I still tend to be a little casual about things, which can sometimes open doors and cause problems.

The physical conditioning, especially at my age, you can't let it go, ever. For the last thirty years I worked out in the gym three to five days a week for up to an hour. If I stop working out for a month, it takes a long time to get back. Your body is very attuned to the exact activity you're doing. So no matter how much biking I've done, when I start skiing, I don't have my skiing legs. The only way to get strong skiing is to ski.

Frustrations? That's the great thing about expeditions. In life, most of the little bad things that happen to you are not life threatening. You have the luxury of doing something stupid like being frustrated. It's a luxury; it's a waste of time; it's a waste of energy. On an expedition, when something bad happens, it's the first step to dying. So you don't have the luxury to go off on a tangent. You don't have the luxury to let your ego say, "I wanted the world to be this way and now the world is this way."

That's a luxury, a stupid waste of time. It's something we all do. But when you're looking at the potential of dying, then it becomes immediately obvious, so obvious that it clubs you on the head. You can't let your ego go on a rant. You have to take care of the problem. Automatically, you get a great calmness. The wilderness is the greatest teacher. It teaches you to see frustration for what it is—worthless—and throw it out the window and get on to the task at hand with renewed concentration and attention to detail because now you're in trouble. As mortality gets closer, you get serious.

I often use the phrase "the ineffable joy of vulnerability." I find joy because vulnerability strips away all the bullshit. Buddhists would say there are a lot of ways to enlightenment. So when you face vulnerability and you face uncertainty, it clears away all the cobwebs. And when this vulnerability is something huge that you can't control, you get hit over the head with a very heavy stick. Look, you can't control your sled breaking or a blizzard coming in. "Now you're vulnerable, dude." That is a path to clarity because you can't afford to play this charade that I'm master of the universe; you have to accept reality. That's a joyful thing that happens—you get this great calmness.

The Dalai Lama says that the wilderness will teach you the path to enlightenment. I've done these things all these years without seeing it in this way. But after my experiences and doing hard adventures, I stopped for five years to be in the presence of Molynaut, a shaman of the native Koryak people of Siberia. I wandered around the tundra, being cold, but it wasn't really big or really difficult, and I took those five years. I came to understand these adventures as journeys to seek equanimity, and not just hard-core physical quests.

Then I decided to do this Ellesmere trip, which was the hardest trip I've ever done. It's gotten so much acclaim. I launched it when I was sixty-six years old. It was very important to me. It was a shamanic vision quest, the idea that I can do something at this age that for any people, at any time, at any age, would be a very hard trip to pull off. I had to test that. That was the point of the Ellesmere trip.

Looking back at it, to push yourself to the doorway of death, quite literally. Not from an accident, or polar bear attack, but just from day-to-day, to push your body where it absolutely goes into metabolic shutdown. I never want to go there again, but I'm really glad I went there. You push through a lot of doors, and hopefully...we're all getting older, and as we go into the final doorway that experiment will help me through that final transition.

When I was being airlifted, I was drugged on morphine in a major way. Through a morphine haze, I remember radio chatter as we were flying to Ottawa. "How much time does he have? Are we going to get there in time?" It was a detached feeling; the morphine was part of it. I wasn't bummed out, amazed, or frustrated that this was happening. I was kind of interested, in an abstract way. Detachment. *This is interesting. I could die here.* There wasn't a value judgment about it, whether it was good or bad.

Sometimes when you don't complete a journey it's because your preparation is bad. If it's because of an abysmally bad job of planning, then I'll feel a sense of failure. I made a mistake. I screwed up, not a good feeling, failure. Or, if I cut an expedition short because I didn't push hard enough, then yeah, I'll have a sense of failure. And there have been a few of those in my life where I could have succeeded had I waited a little longer or pushed through another door.

But if the environment gave me an overwhelming stop, or if huge meteorological events combined against me, then there's no sense of failure whatsoever. Not long ago I was doing this kayak trip through the Vanuatu Chain in the South Pacific. I had some long crossings that I needed to do. One was fifty-eight miles and another was 125 miles. The trade winds were abnormally strong that year and currents were stronger than normal. The fifty-eight-mile crossing was all I could do. I was getting pushed out to sea in the Pacific and in danger of missing my landfall. Just washing out to sea and dying. The next leg was twice as long. I looked at that leg and said there's no way I can go twice as long, twice as hard, so I'm not going to do it. There was no sense of failure. There was a sense that it was a good trip, a good idea; it didn't work out this year. I'm coming home safe.

I've been aware of aging since I hit sixty. I realized things were changing pretty fast: my day-to-day stamina, joint problems, knees, elbows. My ability to push really hard and my desire to push really hard started to slow down. I don't know why. I pushed hard on this Ellesmere trip. If I go out mountain biking, if I can do a twenty-five-mile loop, if I can get partway through, very often I'm content to come home a little early and sit on the couch and drink a cup of tea.

I still push pretty hard. It depends on whom you're comparing yourself with. Self-esteem is your own self-evaluation of what you're doing. Look, my knees are starting to show definite signs of wear. It's quantifiable; an MRI shows they're wearing out. So I go skiing and my knees start to hurt and I think, *My knees have only so many miles left, then they're not going to work anymore.* Maybe I'll go home and take a rest so I can go skiing tomorrow. I mean, I still ski more vertical in a year than many twenty-year-olds, but there're also people who ski a lot more.

Does this bum me out? Does this lower my self-esteem? Not at all! This transition we're going through, this transition into old age. Well, here we are, vulnerable and uncertain. It's quite wonderful to just accept your body the way it is and watch this process of getting old.

Aging has had no effect on my curiosity or optimism; my curiosity is still there. When I came out of the hospital and I was almost dead, I said, "Oh, maybe I'm going to quit being an expedition person." But that wasn't quitting life. That was making a transition. I live in the woods in western Montana and I thought that I would just spend more time gardening and being close to home. Well, that didn't last. As I got better, I realized that I have a few more expeditions to do.

Aging didn't affect my joy, wonder, or excitement at the world. No, no, no. It's just ratcheted down a bit. I just have to match my choice of activity, my itinerary, with the reality that I'm sixty-six years old. I don't want to sound groovier than I really am, but the conversation with myself on this was just fine. I live in a really beautiful place in the woods. I have a wonderful wife who is totally content to be out here in the woods. My alternative to expeditions is to live here in this relationship with this wonderful woman, to grow a bigger garden, to live in this wondrous natural environment. If I walk out my front door and start walking due west, it's 120 miles to the next road. I live in this big wilderness.

Getting old is not pretty, and it's not fun and it's not cute. It's nasty, but it's inevitable. Either we accept it and go graciously with it, or we don't and go out as very grumpy, very unpleasant people, unpleasant for ourselves and for the people around us.

I often say that we're driven by happiness, intensity, and ego, and these are undermined by selfishness and ego. Well, we all try not to be selfish. As I've gotten older, I realize that we're driven by ego and how important we are. But, we lose our importance as we get old. You lose your job, your wife, your children move out. Your place in the office hierarchy, your physical ascendancy, all that gets wiped away. I've watched a lot of people get old.

I'm committed to at least try to age with some element of grace. That means throw the selfishness and ego out the door and try to be creative about aging. Maybe you lose your ability to formulate sentences in a coherent way. Then you can no longer be a writer. That's been my creativity, but there's still other ways to be creative. Creativity is important, but I would put connectivity and awareness as more important because creativity is producing something. Connectivity and awareness are joy in being where you are. As we get older, we're likely to lose our ability to be creative, but we will never lose our ability to be connected and aware.

My goals have changed. I've promised myself not to push as hard as I did on this Ellesmere trip. So I have no goals on a point A to point B destination. My next expedition will be to mountain bike with an old friend on the Tibetan Plateau, where the Dalai Lama was born. We'll be traveling in about a month.

The prospect of decline in health is scary. It's not pretty. Anyone who says otherwise just doesn't have his eyes open. I think that the only sensible approach to old age is to develop patterns, ways of seeking equanimity, develop patterns in your mind of being at peace with yourself. Learning to sit by a creek and learning to appreciate sitting by a creek does that. I think that the patterns we develop in our younger age carry over to our older age. So if we follow a pattern of seeking our maximum economic opportunity, then maybe when we get old, we won't know how to sit by a creek and watch the water flow by. That's the most important skill I'll need when I'm old and can no longer work.

I can roll my wheelchair or ride my three-wheel bike or get pushed in a wheelchair and sit by a creek and be peaceful with that. That's the best preparation for being old.

I love to write. I go to my office early in the morning. It's thirty to forty yards down the hill. It's a tight space and heats up quickly. I intentionally don't use a chain saw to cut the wood, but do it with a little band saw. I start a little fire and then I write. It's a totally enjoyable process. I love it. I love the process. Musicians love to make music. Painters love to paint. It's who you are. And when I start being stupid and writing gibberish, I notice it right away. "Whoa, this is junk!" I notice it right away and shut the computer off.

Then, I go outside and do chores, go for a hike, ride my bike or ski. That downtime is a very important part of the process because I reflect on why the last two paragraphs were so horrible, egregiously bad, and it goes through my subconscious about how to start again. Sometimes in the evening I'll scratch some notes on a piece of paper, and I'll get going again in the morning. Beating your head against writer's block is really just counterproductive. If it doesn't come from deep inside and it comes just because your butt is Velcroed to your chair, it's not going to be worth reading.

We have these ideas and if we convey them well enough, we can convey a message to a lot of people—to be connected, aware, and passionate in whatever you're doing, that's the only route to being truly yourself. You have to be at peace with the whole thing.

The biggest trap that we face as Americans is the trap of consumerism. I was driving home from Missoula and there's this huge billboard that shows a woman with all these gift-wrapped boxes sticking out of shopping bags, and the billboard touts euphoria as shopping at a mall. The most blatantly consumeristic advertising I've ever seen.

You're going to be happy if you buy stuff. My message is: "Don't buy that stuff. Find another route to euphoria." I can't tell you what that route is because you're different than I am. But once you fall into that consumeristic trap, man, you are looped! They've got you, and they're going to run the show for you, and that doesn't have to be.

# "So What to All the Nonsense!"

## MARY B. HURLEY
### Born 1943 – Retired 2008

**Mary retired from the position of director of adult education for a local town and opened a small business that provides quality leisure activities to those just entering retirement. The business uses biking, walking, and cross-country skiing tours to explore local history, art, and nature. Mary is married. Her husband is still working. Mary has three children and six grandchildren. One daughter and two grandchildren are temporarily living with Mary. Her son-in-law is a diplomat posted in Kurdistan.**

I was born and raised outside Chicago. My dad was an artist and an alcoholic. He died in a homeless shelter. My mom was quiet, gentle, and religious. She named all her daughters Mary, in tribute to the Blessed Virgin Mary. My siblings were very intelligent and gifted. My sisters won college scholarships, one was recognized as a gifted artist at a very early age, and my brother had a photographic memory. I had a severe learning disability, severe dyslexia, and I didn't learn to read until age twenty. But I also had an extraordinarily high energy level. My mother didn't know what to make of me. She called me her energy bunny! She always treated me as special and gave me unconditional love, which I credit with sustaining me through difficult periods.

My sister died prematurely from breast cancer, which she had tried to cure through prayer alone. My brother, who was having difficulties with drugs, died at twenty-three in a solo canoeing accident.

I got through high school, despite my learning disabilities, by relying on my personality, and my ability to read social situations and talk around rules and requirements. Finally, at forty, I went back and finished college. After graduating I got the job of director of adult education for a local town, even though I had no experience, just personality. Sometimes I think I can talk a dog into giving me his bone.

What I'm doing in retirement goes back to childhood. When I was a little girl, I was a mad biker. I loved to bike. It was an escape from my family. I used to take my Schwinn...I cannot tell you how many miles I rode. I was riding because I was in pain. This is the sad part of the story, but I needed to get away from the house. There was alcohol abuse.

Even now, I do not pay attention to distances or elevation gains or that sort of statistic. I'm not a numbers person at all. Some of the type-A bikers can't understand that. I think more of wherever we go I'll be back at the scheduled time. I have an innate sense of where I am in time and space, even on new routes. It's the exact opposite of how I felt as a kid. I was really just out there somewhere.

When I was approaching retirement, I wanted to expand the biking and walking tours to more days and a wider audience. This small business has permitted me to do that. Whenever I'm about to start out on a tour, I feel like I'm going to be a little kid for two and a half hours.

Over and over and over, people tell me it's the happiest time of the week for them. For me, I'm at the happiest time in my life. I'm doing exactly what I want to do every day. I'm a very fortunate woman. I have chosen something where I can put together art, history, outdoors, independence, teaching, all together in a package. So what to all the nonsense! Who hasn't had a terrible past? If you had a great past, good for you. I have had so much stuff in my life, I'm happy to be out biking. I feel as if I've put my life in order. I'm doing everything that's important to me. All the stuff I love to do.

I get to explore local art, architecture, and history. I have a walking tour called "Art and Sole," where we go to out-of-the-way museums. A recent one was an exploration of the local Shaker villages in the towns of Harvard and Shirley. The Shirley visit was to a restoration of a small village. It was on the grounds of a maximum-security prison and all the restoration work—painting, carpentry—was done by the prisoners. It was eye-opening on a couple of levels. As part of that theme, I took a tour to the Holy Hill and Graveyard of the Shaker community in Harvard. The Shaker women lived into their nineties. They didn't have kids. People forget or just never knew about the Shaker connection to this area.

Another example: we were out on a tour and we passed the lawn of a private home where there stood this remarkable fifteen-foot granite statue with different images on the front and back. I stopped the tour, and with about twenty people behind me knocked on the door and asked about it. I learned that it was the work of a local, internationally acclaimed sculptor. I followed up and, as a result, my tour groups have met her and learned about her work. She quarries the granite right there on the property and renders the sculpture right there.

I think that's what I enjoy—getting the people in my tours to stop and look at things they would never stop and look at themselves...open their eyes to things they go by every day, but never see. Curiosity is a huge part of me. I see those things and am not hung up about going to ask someone or exploring a little, even if it means breaking a few rules.

I don't know why I'm like that. I think people take themselves too seriously, maybe because I can't. I want them to lighten up. I mean, how much trouble can you get into? I've never seen the rules. So when I'm told I can't do something, I see it as a challenge to bend the rule or push it. I get the tours to stretch the rules, not be so bound up, and be spontaneous. I think they like that, and the fact that I don't have a worry gene, and I'm not at all judgmental.

I do wonder what I'll do when I can't ride at the pace necessary to run the tours. At one time I raced bikes and would ride at a nineteen-mph pace. These tours are more moderate, but I still think maybe another five years and then I'll have to increase the walking tours. I wouldn't want to hear some type-A say, "Oh my God, she's so old." But right now my basic goal is to continue the business.

Through the years my husband and I have traveled extensively. My daughter lived in Australia. We visited and used it as a base to get to New Zealand, Fiji, Hawaii, and the South Pacific. When she was in Rome, we did the same thing there and we traveled through Europe. I love to travel. I'm not traveled-out. I don't think I'll ever be traveled out. It changes me. It really doesn't matter where I go because it stimulates new thoughts, new ideas. Recently we visited Croatia, including Dubrovnik and the Islands. I went with torn ligaments in my thumb and a broken collarbone, which I got in a fall from my bike a day or two before our departure.

I also think there might be another chapter in my life. Maybe a move to another area to be near my daughter and grandkids if her husband were to be stationed in New York, DC, or Rome. We have to have the capacity to think and do new things. If you keep doing things the same way, you're going to get the same results. I really believe that. I like to change things up.

I find spirituality in the outdoors. Just being on a trail in the woods or in a conservation area. I know these trails. I love the trails. Sometimes I feel that in a former life I could have been an Indian scout. My spirituality is in the woods and the movement of the air by my ears like when I was ten years old.

# "A Way to Replace Some of the Excitement"

## GENERAL WALTER E. BOOMER, USMC (RET.)
### Born 1938 – Retired 1994, 2004

*General Boomer with wife, Sandi, and fishing on the Zambezi River, Africa.*

General Walter Boomer was born and raised in a small rural town, set by the Roanoke River on the North Carolina Piedmont. As a child, he developed strong family ties, a love of the outdoors, and a reservoir of energy, focus, and ambition that would influence every stage of his adult life. After excelling in high school and college, he joined the US Marine Corps, where he served with great distinction for thirty-four years. He saw combat duty in two tours in Vietnam. During

Operation Desert Storm, he served as the commanding general of the US Marine Forces Central Command and the Marine Expeditionary Force. In his last duty assignment, he served as the twenty-fourth assistant commandant of the Marine Corps. General Boomer is highly decorated and has been awarded, among other honors, the Legion of Merit, the US Navy Distinguished Service Medal, two Silver Stars for valor, two Bronze Stars for valor, and a Marine Corps Commendation for valor. He is one of only sixty-five four-star generals in the 237-year history of the Marine Corps.

In 1994, General Boomer retired from the Marine Corps to pursue a career in business. Despite his relative lack of business experience, within a few years he became CEO of a publicly traded international company. In 2004, General Boomer retired once more. Since then, he has enjoyed hunting big game all over the world, and spending time with his wife, three children, and three grandchildren. During these years, he has also served on several corporate boards, and as chairman of the Marine Corps Heritage Foundation, which is responsible for constructing the National Museum of the Marine Corps.

On a recent fishing trip, some colleagues and I discussed aging, retirement, and what it means to be content. Until then, I hadn't thought much about these topics. The folks I was speaking with were all pretty driven—driven to succeed, driven to do things as well as anyone. We all agreed that kind of drive doesn't go away just because you retire. And if any of us ever thought that, just by retiring, we were going to find some kind of peaceful contentment—well, we haven't.

I'm not certain I've ever felt contented. I'm not certain that I even know how to define "contented," or to tell you how the idea pertains to my life. I always keep thinking, I need to get this done, or I should do this, or I need to go and talk to somebody about that. For me, retirement hasn't been about slowing down, as I might have expected. It hasn't been about catching up on reading. For me, life after retirement has been a lot like life before retirement—action-oriented.

I don't spend time thinking about past accomplishments, even the ones that some might call significant. To the extent I do, I just think, *That was a job pretty well done.* I'm almost always thinking about what's coming up next. That's true of most people I know who've accomplished things. They don't dwell on the past. They look to the future. And they're not always thinking about themselves. They're more interested in other people and in the world around them.

My mother was a driven person, and she was the driving force in my life, without question. She was my best friend. Unfortunately, she passed away at fifty. That was a tremendous, tremendous loss.

She'd often repeat something to me—an old phrase, but I've never forgotten it. She'd say: "Son, hitch your wagon to a star." As far back as I can remember, she'd tell me that. She'd say: "Son, don't just be satisfied with where you are." She'd always be telling me that I was going to make something of myself. We came from a very small town, a very rural town, but there was never any question about whether I was going to college. I was going—she made that clear from the start.

She was a genuinely good person, liked and respected throughout the community. She was deeply religious, but she wasn't a fanatic. She was practical. She was critical, absolutely critical in making me who I am. In high school, if I brought home anything less than an A, she wouldn't go into hysterics. She'd say: "Son, you got a B. You're capable of an A. Now, I don't understand why you didn't get an A." Soon, I was making all As. Then, she decided that I was making them too easily. In her mind, my As weren't real As. So I went off to private school. That was a positive thing for me, and I got a great education.

After high school and college, I was interested in the military. At the time, I planned to spend two or three years in and then get an advanced degree. I thought I'd join a big lumber company in the Southeast. But the Marine Corps resonated with me. I decided to join, and I stayed in for thirty-four years.

Retirement from the Marine Corps was not a big issue. You can only stay in for a fixed time. I got lucky and was promoted to general. If I hadn't, I would've had to retire after thirty years like everyone else. When you're in, you know that. Hopefully, you also prepare for it. Not everyone does. In my case, I got promoted to brigadier general—I always describe it as lightning striking—and that enabled me to stay in for a while longer.

It was my intention to leave the Marine Corps after I came back from Operation Desert Storm, where I'd had the great good fortune to command more marines in the field than anyone has since World War II—and more than anyone has since. I thought, well, it's not going to get any better than that. And so I intended to leave. And then a friend of mine, the commandant of the Marine Corps, called and asked me to go to Washington and to serve as his assistant commandant. Of course, I agreed. But, later on, when the time came, I chose not to throw my hat in the ring to possibly become the next commandant. I wanted another career—a career that wasn't in the defense industry.

I had this crazy dream of becoming CEO of a public company. In the Marine Corps, I'd met a lot of people in business. I thought it was something that I could do. Hard to say why I thought that. At the time, I was about fifty-five and didn't have any business experience—I just thought that I could do it. Now, back then, I didn't know enough to realize how crazy my plan was. I just knew that if I didn't leave the military, it would soon be too late and I wouldn't ever get a chance. So I left. And it worked out fine. Quite frankly, some people have a problem shutting that door. I've always tried to tell them, there's life after the Marine Corps.

I went from being a general—and that was how I was addressed, as General—to being part of a business enterprise, where everyone, from the chairman on down, is addressed by his first name. At the company, I was just Walt. It wasn't an issue for me. I enjoyed the change, and I enjoyed business a great deal. But it was a challenge. I spent those first years working as hard as I ever did at anything.

I ended up running two companies, both of which were composed mainly of engineers. Now, I'm not an engineer. I wouldn't have made a very good one. I know my limitations. On the other hand—aside from maybe being an engineer—I never thought there was anything I couldn't do. I don't mean to sound arrogant. That's just always been my attitude. So, when I had an opportunity to join a company full of engineers, I wasn't put off. I knew that I'd bring something else. I provided the adult supervision, so to speak. And that's what the board was really looking for.

I served as CEO until I reached sixty-five, the mandatory retirement age. At the time, I'm not sure that I had a goal. It came around very quickly. For me, work had always meant twelve-to fourteen-hour days, working on the weekends. I was looking forward to not doing that anymore. But, when it happened, it was a real adjustment.

What helped me was that I had an interim letdown period. I was on three corporate boards, all of which required travel, all of which met five times a year. So that kept me relatively busy. It eased my transition. It wouldn't have been healthy—psychologically or physiologically—for me to just go home and sit down.

The other thing that really helped was that my wife and I really like to travel. We've done that a lot in our retirement. Also, I grew up in a small town, and hunting and fishing were two of the biggest things going. So after my business career, I was able to pursue another dream of mine: to hunt big game. My wife enjoys it as well. We've gone all over the world—to South America, the Yukon, Africa, you name it. Hunting isn't everybody's game, I know. But it happens to be mine.

Since 1997, I've probably participated in twenty big-game hunting trips. I have one coming up, in Cameroon, and then I'm going back to Africa again in July. It's a magical place. I've been all over: Botswana, Tanzania, Zambia, Zimbabwe.

I think maybe big game hunting has been a way for me to replace some of the excitement that I found in the Marine Corps. I don't know— I suppose that my appetite for risk hasn't changed much, and there's significant risk in hunting big game. Every professional hunter I know ultimately gets hurt. That's not what I'm seeking. And I've never had an animal I was hunting pose any imminent danger to me, at least from my perspective. On my last hunt, we had an encounter with a group of female elephants, which are extremely dangerous. They don't ask any questions—they just charge. Luckily, the wind was right so we weren't charged right away, and we managed to get out in time. Those kinds of things happen. It's part of the game.

Now, as my big-game hunting winds down, I'm sort of wondering what's going to replace it. At this point, I'm not sure. I'd like to spend more time with our grandchildren. Thankfully, we've settled in a beautiful place. We love it, and our grandchildren love to come visit. Plus, we have good hunting right here—three thousand acres devoted to it. And the community where we live attracts other people who love the outdoors—bird-watchers, artists, photographers—fascinating, impressive people. It's not a golf community. I tell you, if I had to live in a community where all people could talk about all day is some shot they made out on the ninth hole—well, put me out of my misery. That's not the case here.

I think that the greatest challenge for me is continuing to find things that add meaning to my life and to the lives of my loved ones. That's what's preoccupying me lately. Of course, my wife and I often reflect on how lucky we've been. And we're always thinking about how we can best give back. A couple of friends here are mentoring children. I worry more about this country's education system than any other thing. I've been trying to think about how I could help. I don't know if I have the temperament for it.

One thing that's been very meaningful has been my work with the Marine Corps Heritage Foundation, where I'm serving as chairman. We're building the National Museum of the Marine Corps. It isn't complete yet, but we've already had two and a half million visitors. We still have a lot to do. We have to raise all the money needed to finish constructing the museum. It's been more work than I anticipated, but it's also been a labor of love, a way for me to give back something to the Marine Corps. On a personal level, that's gratifying. And it's what I like to do most, what I do best—bringing a team together to achieve a mission. That's right up my alley. If there's one thing I know, it's how to lead a group on a mission.

Like I said, I'm always looking at what's next—what's the next phase of my life? I'm not afraid of old age, but I don't like it. And I especially don't like the thought of not being able to do all that I want to do physically. I understand that it happens. It happens to all of us. I realize I'm not always going to be able to go off to Cameroon and walk all day long in the hundred-degree heat.

So what's next? It's a bit of a dilemma, I suppose. Sometimes, I feel like my transition into retirement is still going on—like I'm still settling into it. At times, I think that I should challenge myself more. Other times, I think that maybe my biggest challenge is just trying to find my own sense of contentment. As I said earlier, it may be that I'll never be content—whatever it is that being "contented" means. I suppose, in my mind, it means being totally relaxed. And I don't know if I'll ever be that. I don't know if I ever want to be that. I don't think I'm capable of it.

# *"The Magnificent Blue Waters"*

## PHIL DASCHER
### Born 1937 – Retired 1979, 1996

**Phil founded and managed three successful businesses in the garment industry. At forty-two, he sold his interest in the first, then retired to sail the East Coast and the Caribbean with his wife. Three years later, he returned to Manhattan and started his second and third businesses, which he ran until retiring permanently at fifty-nine. Phil and his wife live in Manhattan, although they are contemplating a move to Florida. He has three adult children and two grandchildren.**

In the '60s, the garment district, from Thirty-Fifth to Forty-First and from Seventh to Ninth, was flourishing. Everywhere you went—the deli, the elevator—you ran into your competitors. By the '70s, things had started to decline. Manufacturing was moving to low-cost centers. I ran operations overseas, and lived in Taiwan, Hong Kong, and Greece.

In '72, a group of us set up some apparel companies. They grew. After about seven years, I sold my shares. Then I had to decide what to do. When I was in Greece, I'd spent a lot of time in Athens. I became fascinated by the sailboats and the magnificent blue waters. Seeing that every day gave me a longing to sail. So after I sold my shares, I decided to also sell my co-op and buy a forty-eight-foot ketch. It took me three months to learn how to sail the thing. After I'd learned, my girlfriend, Amy—she's now my wife—and I set out on a three-year adventure.

We started in New York. The plan was to track down the coast to Cape May, to the Delaware River, and then to the Intracoastal Waterway. En route, there were storms. Forty-foot waves. Winds at seventy knots. The first time you're in the trough of a wave and it's two-thirds of the way up your sixty-foot mast—well, it gets your attention.

But the getting there, the end of the journey, the first time you make it, wow. However much time it took, whatever you went through—all that becomes irrelevant. Point is, you've made it, and everything you see is new: dolphins, fish jumping out of the water, another boat on the horizon, a sunset, a sunrise. Everything.

Before I set sail, I was excited. More than excited. Cruising like that had been a lifelong fantasy. But once it became a reality, it lost some of its flavor. Even fantasies can turn into routines.

I'm really glad I did it. It was a great adventure. But I felt like I'd taken myself out of life. After two years, Amy moved back to New York. So for twelve months, I was out there alone. Sailing alone isn't much fun. When you see something beautiful, you've got no one to tell. Anyhow, maybe three years was the limit. After that, I was happy to sell the boat and get back to Manhattan.

In New York, I started thinking about getting back into business. I didn't want to start at zero. Zero to one is really tough. But one to ten is relatively easy. I'd been a player. I knew everyone. And now I had a great story to tell. They all wanted to hear about my big adventure at sea.

At first, it all went great. But the garment industry runs in cycles. Nothing stays forever. At some point, the writing was on the wall. The revenues had peaked and were in decline. So after eleven years, I made a move. Took me a year to plan it, but by '96, I was at zero inventory, with an expired lease.

So at fifty-nine, I was a second-time retiree. As far as I'm concerned, retirement isn't what it's made out to be. It's boring. When people ask me about it, I say it's like joining the living dead. I don't feel unfulfilled, really. But I don't necessarily feel fulfilled, either. I don't feel anything. For sixteen years, I've largely been bored. When you're used to social contact, challenges, even mundane things like inventory risk, and then when all that's gone—well, it can get boring. You can wake up every day with a clear head and plenty of energy and nowhere to go.

After a while, your social contacts from the business world fade. Before, I'd call and schmooze. There's no need for that now. They were my business friends, not my friend friends.

My youngest daughter just graduated from college and has been staying with us while she gets set up in the working world. Next year, she'll likely move out. My wife and I have started talking about buying a place in Florida. Live six months and a day down there, eliminate city and state taxes. And then, when it comes time to go off to the happy hunting grounds, there'll be no estate tax. Also, you know, change is great.

My family life is meaningful. My daughters are great, and their families are great, too. I'm close with my kids and grandkids. I love helping them and hearing they're OK. All these things are where I find a sense of purpose.

My youngest daughter is a superstar. I have a relationship with her I could never have built without all this extra time. It's been a joy to watch her grow. And now she's a grown-up. She'll be on her own soon and we'll have to find our own life.

I'm seventy-four. You read about people that age in the obits.

I've lived with risk my entire life. At this stage, I'm sort of anti-risk. I don't want to be foolish about anything. Life is risk. I know that. There are no guarantees, I know that, too. But there's a time and a place for risk—and for everything else. What was, was.

# *"A Fantastic, a Brilliant, an Instantaneous Decision"*

## ERV SCHOWENGERDT
### Born 1928 – Retired 1989

Erv graduated from the University of Missouri with a degree in mechanical engineering and from MIT with a degree in business. He worked for more than twenty-five years at MIT in the design, manufacture, and quality control of miniaturized guidance instrumentation. Erv is twice divorced and is in a long-term relationship. His daughter, who is completing her doctoral thesis in social psychology at Cambridge University, currently lives with him.

**Erv arrived in a black sports car (his "James Bond" car) dressed in tennis shorts, a blue knit shirt, and jogging shoes. He brought with him a bottle of chilled wine to enjoy with lunch.**

Retirement was an instantaneous thing. I didn't plan on it or anything like that. It was in 1989. What I mean by instantaneous, they came around and offered fifty or sixty guys early retirement benefits. So out of the clear blue I got this letter in the mail saying, "We'll pay you a year's salary if you want"—or whatever it was—"you gotta decide in three weeks or so if you want to retire."

I had zero interest in retiring. I knew nothing about retiring. Never thought about it. Never cared about it. I was having a good time. Working with some interesting people. Some neat guys and women. So...I decided to do it! I didn't actually flip the coin, but it was that kind of decision. Out of the clear blue I was given a chance to retire with a big package that goes with it. And I decided, "OK, I'll do it." I didn't apply any brainpower to it. I wasn't thinking about what I was going to do afterwards, or if I would have enough income. I've always lived frugally. None of that stuff ever entered my mind. It wasn't an involved process. I was queasy at that point, and I wasn't sure if it was the right thing to do. I was going through a divorce at the time. Three years later I realized it was a fantastic, a brilliant, an instantaneous decision. They started having further cutbacks and the lab really downsized.

The only thing that changed was that I was not going in and working with high-powered microscopes. I'm still doing the stuff I was doing then. At that time, I was trying to restore my home and I'm still working on it. I've always done a lot of skiing, all over the world. Mountain climbing; I've climbed all the White Mountains. Canoeing, white-water canoeing, lot of the New England rivers. When I got arthritis in my hip that screwed me up. I quit climbing mountains for that reason. Oh, I get to the gym and play around there. I don't like that. I just don't enjoy that kind of thing. I'd rather be sailing or canoeing or mountain climbing. Like I used to canoe down the shore and then pull a canoe up and spend the night there, sleeping in the canoe.

Yet, things changed. I had the freedom to do even more of the things I wanted.

For example, a couple of schoolteachers in town and I mounted our own expedition down to Mexico and climbed El Popo, an eighteen-thousand-foot active volcano. It blew a few years ago and you can't get near it now. But I climbed all over that in my seventies.

Also, early on, I went into Africa with a friend and we bummed around Africa for a month or so and climbed Kilimanjaro. We flew into Nairobi and joined the expedition we were going with, and then afterwards we came back to Nairobi and did local transportation. We spent several days wandering around Nairobi, felt very safe. None of these problems that they are having now. Walked around, walked around at night. Talked to the locals. Then we hopped a train, the "Lunatic Express," and went to Mombasa on the ocean. We spent several days bumming around on the beach. Then we headed up to an island called Lamu. It's an area full of British ex-pats, full of people who have given up; guys in their twenties roaming around the world, that kind of group. An interesting old settlement on this island.

In between all of this, I did a lot of sailing, from St. Petersburg in Russia through the Baltic, the North Sea, the fjords of Norway, down the Seine and across the Mediterranean, and along the East Coast. A guy from MIT bought a boat and we sailed it from Corpus Christi, Texas, up to Sea Island, Georgia. Right now, a buddy of mine has a boat in dry dock. So I go down and help him with that. We'll get that in the water soon.

I've always been interested in redoing houses and that sort of thing. I got a whole lot of tools that my grandfather gave me when I was a little boy, and I played with them all my life. Just carpentry. Nothing really fancy. I'm not building furniture. I've put in some bookcases that are different, my own design that's a different way of doing something. While I was working, I took some courses on architecture. That really sparked me. It gave me a lot more confidence in what I was doing. I took courses on design and a couple of courses on visual design. It opened up my visual interpretation of stuff. What's good design, what's not? What proportions are right and all that sort of thing. So I played with that in my restoration projects. I've done a lot. I rebuilt my house, an old middle-1800s thing. I can't do that anymore. No desire of doing that. Now, I hire somebody to do it. I'm surprised that I lost my desire to do that stuff, to say the least. Luckily, I got all this other stuff done before that hit me.

I don't pay attention to age because I don't want to think about it, and I resist connecting age to these activities. If you tell me I'm ninety years old, then I also have to start hobbling around. Age doesn't matter at all. I just don't remind myself.

I missed the guys at work, but MIT puts on a party every year for people who had more than twenty-five years of service. Unbelievable. We get together as a large group for a big banquet in the wintertime. So I see people that I normally don't socialize with. The guys I used to work with, some of them I still have contact, still socially stay involved. A lot of them are dead.

Retirement felt like a continuation; it didn't feel like I was entering a new phase. But I did start a couple of new things: I got interested in trips that focus on archeology and on trying to do some good. I have been on archeology digs all over the world—Fiji, Argentina, Spain, Majorca, Belize—and on some humanitarian missions. After a huge hurricane devastated the island of Montserrat, I joined a group that went and built a hospital roof. The next will be a trip to South Africa, to research and rescue penguins.

There is absolutely no difference in my appetite for doing things. I feel very lucky because I'm basically in good health. Very lucky, very fortunate. I'm as fulfilled now as when I was working.

I don't spend a lot of time thinking about spirituality or meaning. I quit going to church in the formal way. I'm a good person, I think. I contribute to organizations that provide for the homeless and that sort of thing. I just don't go to church regularly, and I don't spend a lot of time thinking about our purpose here. I think our species is like all the species on earth—whether you are mealworm, fruit fly, or a dinosaur, whatever species—it's all an incredible technical thing that's happened over the last billion years. And it's still evolving.

From now forward, the biggest challenge for me will be staying healthy. Getting this hip fixed if possible. Yeah, I'd like to go back to skiing. But I will continue to do what I'm doing now. You know, polishing up my house, and I'm almost done with it. That's gonna be sad when I get done with that. I'll be done with it. Then I'll have to start redoing things. It needs painting now.

I am enjoying life and I don't dwell on things, or past events or people. I don't have any regrets about retirement or life in general. If you fail at something, you learn to do it a different way next time. Failure is teaching you something. If you failed someplace, you learned. I don't go off and do something and expect to fail. When I climbed Mount Kilimanjaro, it didn't enter my mind that, you know, what's gonna happen if I don't do it. If I didn't make the summit, then it would just be a fact that I wasn't able to do it, because I couldn't breathe, or lost energy, I had no strength left. That luckily didn't happen, but it wouldn't have impacted my self-esteem.

You got to have something that you're really interested in doing and pursuing. You got to keep doing something. You stop working one job, but that's not the end. You pick up and do something. You pick up another job. That is a loose word to use, but...Obviously, when people retire they start traveling and take the wife and go on a cruise ship. Well, if that's your style, that's OK. My style, I'd rather be down there at the helm of my own boat. Independent. For me, going off on an adventure is exciting. New culture, new environment, all those things are exciting. At least they are for me. I would urge people to go and do something. Do something different.

My aging has been: I just quit one day and continued doing things and got involved in things that I never thought about getting involved in. Things that weren't in my mind beforehand. They just occurred. I'm just full of things I'd be interested in doing.

# *"Adapt...Be Spontaneous"*

## BOB HAYDEN
Born 1942 – Retired 2008

Bob was born and raised in the Dorchester section of Boston. His father was a Boston policeman and his mother was a home-maker. After college he joined the Boston Police where, over the next twenty-eight years, he served as a patrolman, motorcycle policeman, and deputy superintendent. He later became chief of police in Lawrence, Massachusetts, an old mill city where crime, drugs, and gang activity were epidemic. After reinvigorating the Lawrence police force and greatly improving the city's crime sta-tistics, he served in high-level positions in the state's Department of Public Safety. Bob has been married forty-seven years, and has four children and seven grandchildren. Bob has an unusual

**hobby. About once a year, he hops on his bike and takes a four-hundred- to five-hundred-mile trip with no maps and little more than the clothes on his back.**

My high school offered no real learning, but it was such great fun that I'd never miss a day. It didn't prepare me for college life, and after six years, the college recognized that. It told me that I would be leaving in three months, with or without a degree, depending on how I fared on the last required course. I took the test, but felt that I had not done very well. So I called the professor's wife and convinced her that I needed to graduate for the sake of my soon-to-be bride. She, in turn, prevailed on the professor. Did he resent me!

After graduation I was with the Boston Police Department, rising to the rank of deputy superintendent. I applied to be commissioner. I didn't get the job. A rival did. About this time the chief of police job in Lawrence opened up. I wanted it, but I had to find some way to distinguish myself and get noticed. So I put on civvies, walked around for three days talking to all kinds of different people. Then I went knocking on the mayor's door and told her that I was the man for the job. After a three-hour impromptu interview, she agreed.

Crime and gang activity were epidemic, and the police were demoralized and feeling impotent. On my first day, I went out jogging in sweats and a hoodie just to see what I could see. As I passed a liquor store, a large gentleman asked if I wanted some "blow." I asked if "blow" was drugs, and if he had it on him. When he said yes to both, I threw a headlock on him and wrestled him into the liquor store. Once backup arrived and the arrest made, I was an instant hit with the street cops. They loved me.

After that, I put in programs that heightened police visibility and esteem. Through donations, we acquired a custom-built drug wagon emblazoned with a badge and the logo in English and Spanish, "Say No to Drugs, or Say Hello to Us!" I made a point of parading that wagon and fifteen motorcycles throughout the city as a prelude to a crackdown on drugs, crime, and gang activity. These programs did the trick. In a three-year period, arrests increased tenfold, and community spirit and civic involvement improved markedly.

I was looking forward to retirement. I had worked from the time I was a kid. I thought I'd write a book. I had had bit parts in movies; I thought maybe I could do a little work as an extra. I always liked some sort of Point A to Point B adventure. About ten years ago, I got selected as one of six out of sixteen thousand to be on an NBC reality show, an early competitor of *The Amazing Race*. The premise was to have three teams of two put down somewhere, some unidentified spot in the world, to compete to see who could get to the Statute of Liberty first. We were put down on a mountain in Bolivia with ten dollars and a cameraman. It took us three days to find out where we were. It took us twenty-five days to get home, through Brazil, down the Amazon...a great adventure.

After that and before retirement, when it looked like my father was going to die, I felt I needed to get my head clear and get strong. I took my bike to San Francisco and rode solo to the Mexican border with no advance planning, not even a map. I like that kind of ride. It's physical and you have to adapt to the unexpected...be spontaneous.

So when retirement was on the horizon, I thought, *I can run every day, bike, join a gym*. There was never any question about leaving the area. My goals were: don't drive my wife crazy, try to help people, and be there for my grandkids. We've gone all over the world, so travel was not a priority. It's worked out like I thought. I've been exercising every day, enjoying my grandkids, going to the beach, doing stuff around the house.

And I've had time to take some of those long rides. It turns out I get the urge every year or so. The first was Boston to Montreal. I did it on a mountain bike with two fat tires and no toe clips. I had no plan. I didn't have a map. I've always thought them overrated. Just a general idea of where I'm headed and then I'll ask along the way. On the Montreal trip, my wife, exasperated at such foolishness, got a map from a gas station the day before I left and highlighted a route. I got the map, tried to follow it, and got lost ten miles from home in Cambridge!

This last September I decided to ride solo from Malin Head, the northernmost point in Ireland, to Mizen Head, the southernmost point. It's 450 miles. I started the ride in October, which is a miserable month, especially in the north and west of Ireland, with so much weather coming off the Atlantic—cold, wet, wind, hail, dark—generally miserable. I had known this and thought about doing it in August or September, but I wanted to stay at the beach with the grandkids.

I got to Dublin, assembled my bike and took a bus north. I made my way to a B&B; that was my starting point. My destination was 450 miles away. The next morning, I got two things from the owner, a good breakfast and great directions: "At the end of the driveway, take a right and go straight."

It was cold and wet. No big deal. I eliminated all negative thoughts. The first day my bike broke and I walked it to a repair shop. The repairman knew Dorchester! In fact, he spent his honeymoon there! A first for me and probably for Dorchester. A honeymoon among the three-deckers.

The second day I got caught in a hailstorm and was thrown off my bike twice. The second time I went over into a ditch, landed on my left shoulder with the bike on top. My shoulder hurt. I was soaking. I got up. Pushed the bike three miles uphill in the wind and the driving hail. I found a house and a new best friend, a seventy-year-old, who gave me shelter, tea, some warmth, and a good talk about kids and grandkids. Over the six days I was on the road I had some challenges, but mostly many pleasant encounters. I shared Fig Newtons, tea, and cop-talk with a Garda who stopped me from riding on a high-speed interstate highway.

I basically wore the clothes on my back. At night I'd hand wash them and dry them over lampshades. My bike was a hybrid with twenty-one gears. My handlebar is an upright setup, like Peter Fonda

in *Easy Rider*. I have back trouble if I get into a bending-forward position. At the end I was greeted by friends and relations and the beauty
of Mizen Head—like the Big Sur coast. I loved the trip; met wonderful,
wonderful people, and I accomplished what I set out to do.

I think the biggest challenge is not allowing myself to become
old, not let old age sneak in on me, because I think we embrace
old age too quickly. I'm fighting the stereotype of old people, you
know, eating their prunes and hanging on the shopping carts at the
supermarket.

I'm the same person I was when I was nine and punched a kid
for throwing rocks at some poor neighborhood dog. I asked the kid to
stop, but he was a bit of a sadist. That was the first time I thought that
I had a purpose. Later on, I'd step in to stop bullying of weaker kids
or kids with disabilities. I didn't really think about it...I'd just react
to it. The instinct is still there and I can't stop it. It's just instinct. A
couple years back me and a retired marine subdued a couple of guys on
a flight from Minnesota. These guys refused to sit and were shouting,
"Your lives are going to change today forever." The passengers were
terrified and relieved when we stopped them. My wife, on the other
hand, never looked up from the book she was reading. She later explained to the people that she knew how the situation would end, but
didn't know how the book would end.

Over the years I've learned everything is not legal or illegal, but
everything is right or wrong. Sometimes the right thing won't be in
the general laws, but it's the right thing. I never had any trouble knowing what the right thing is...it's instinctual. Every decision I've ever
made, whether it's been a snap one or not, has been the right one. It's
moral certitude and the confidence to embrace it. It's just part of me;
it's always been there...I don't know how that happened. I don't think
it's going to change.

Later in life my father taught me a lesson about attitude that really
means a lot now. He was in his mid-eighties and I was taking him to a

boxing match. I was helping him down the stairs from his apartment and said, "Dad, I'll put in a railing." He said, "Why?" I said, "To stop you from falling." He replied, "I fall all the time." I said, "Where do you land?" He says, "On the grass, on the asphalt, on the concrete." I was getting ticked, him falling and not telling me. So I said, "Well, what do you do when you fall?" He says, "I get up."

# III. CREATIVITY

# *"Gigging...at Eighty-Five"*

## JOSEPH HANLEY
### Born 1952 – Retired 2008, 2010

**Joe worked as a laborer and in factories for over thirty-six years until he left to pursue his lifelong ambition of making a living playing music. He has been married thirty-three years and has a married daughter living in California.**

I was raised in the Mission Hill projects in the Roxbury section of Boston. I was one of six kids. My dad was a liquor salesman and cabdriver. He died at forty-two, when I was seven. My mother was forty-one and left alone to raise us. At the time street violence and racial tension in Boston were on the rise. So, when I was around twelve, she moved the family to a working-class beach community. It was barely populated in the off-season, desolate, maybe two hundred families on the nine-mile island.

Until the move I had the run of the city. I could always find something crazy to do...go to a construction site and climb into and all over the large equipment. There were lots of kids to play ball with and always something going on. The move to the beach was traumatic. My three older brothers refused to leave the city, and two of them, at fifteen and sixteen, dropped out of school, got jobs as dishwashers, and later joined the service. When I arrived at the beach, it was a culture shock; so few people, no open stores.

My oldest brother bought me a guitar shortly after the move. I started teaching myself the guitar and hanging out with people trying to play music. So music started to become part of my life. As I got older it became quite prominent in my life. It sounds kind of corny, but music was the thing that brought me the most pleasure, even just going to concerts or listening to music for hours on end. It just rang in my whole system. I needed music.

My mother was supporting the family on social security. We were probably on the verge of poverty, although we didn't know it. We had a house, one of the few that was winterized. We had meals, but nothing extra. College was not an option.

After high school, I began work as a grave-digger and landscaper. Then I got a job as a floor boy/laborer in a local factory that manufactured electrical components. I stayed in manufacturing for the next thirty-six years.

But I was always involved with music. In the early eighties, I tried to get into the music business, going to open mic nights and looking for people to form a group or a duo or something, and played at local clubs. It was awesome, after you get over the initial fear of performing in public. The feedback was positive and encouraging. So I started doing solo performances in the area in the late eighties, still working full time. I would do one gig a weekend, but I picked up the guitar every night, if only briefly. I met other people and developed a couple of different groups, including a five-man band that's been active for twenty years.

This setup was perfect. I was very lucky. I had a great working career, was fulfilling my responsibilities, and had the music on the side. I looked at the music as a counterbalance to the stress and hours of daily work life, but I often thought, when my daughter is out of school and we pay off the mortgage, maybe I could do it full time.

Then in 2008, I tried it. I had played at clubs and parties, and it was clicking. I was getting all this positive feedback. The decision was helped by the way business was going. The business world required you to do more with less, to work a lot of hours. I was proud of my work, but I was working a lot of hours, and had to ask: "Do I want to do that for the rest of my life?" So at age fifty-six, I said, "I'm going to go for it, make a jump." I thought I could get enough gigs to make it happen. I wasn't nervous or scared, I was hopeful. I had enough confidence that I was going to make it happen, plus I could always go back to manufacturing if I needed to.

But my first effort didn't work as well as I thought. There were weird hours and there was an absolute shift from having a social life at work. Jumping into the music was a radical shift from that. I had a hard time adjusting to spending the days on my own and then working nights, getting home late and then sleeping late. One big adjustment: isolation. Plus the musical format I was in, a duo, wasn't so satisfying. The full five-man band is an amazing experience. It's quite satisfying to have five guys clicking just unconsciously and doing it so well. The duo was more work and not as fulfilling, and I was struggling with the change in lifestyle, bodily rhythms, the isolation, the different schedule from my wife. Even though we were successful in getting work, after six months I concluded that it was not sustainable.

So I went back to manufacturing and doing music part-time. But I found it to be nothing like my past experience. I didn't warm up to the new job or the people. It wasn't the old environment. There was a strict hands-on micromanagement, fifty-five stressful hours a week. After three-four months I became concerned for my health. Even when I was home from work I was still at work. My wife noticed that when I was distracted or preoccupied, I'd whistle unrecognizable tunes. I didn't even know I was doing it. I always prided myself on hard work, getting it done, being a go-to guy. But in this job there was nothing nourishing about it and the longer I was there, I got less and less out of it.

I thought: *What are my options? What do I know? Manufacturing and music.* I thought, *I'll try the music again. It's what I love and what I'm good at.* So I started slowly building gigs to three to four per week. Now we've got bookings six months out.

This time it's more satisfying. I'm better prepared to do it and absolutely certain that the time had come health-wise. I know what to expect. Now, the schedule and routine feels quite normal. First year it's been hustle, hustle, hustle. Get the gigs. Now that's working and it's rolling pretty good.

I'm now more emotionally and spiritually nourished. Now I feel like a young fifty-eight. The change has been positive. My wife says that it's nice to have me back. My long-term dream is to continue playing in the duo, which is our bread and butter, and to put together a band where I'd have more creative control—playing jazzy, original music, something unique, and doing solo work.

I use the time during the day to practice music and explore and research different belief systems. I never bought into the idea of heaven and hell—never believed it, didn't know, didn't have any direction. So I've spent pretty much of my adult life looking into other belief systems. That study and music have been big parts of my life. This period of change has given me an opportunity to reflect, more time to read. The change is saving my life; if I had continued, I would have been heading for health problems. Physically, I feel great, the big stress is gone. Now there are bits of stress when you do a gig, but hit the first couple of notes and it's gone. You're in your element. I'm proud I recognized it was time.

The big plus is the physical, psychological, and spiritual freedom. I'm absolutely more free now than I ever was, even as a kid. The challenge now is to get that band I always wanted. Someday I'm going to do it; knowing everything I now know about energy, directing it to what you believe in.

I've met cranky, narrow-minded older people, and I've met older people that are just rolling right along, comfortable with themselves. They keep busy. You just have to change or shift into mentally and physically constructive, positive activities. I want to keep busy; continue my spiritual development until I die and pass on to the next level. Keep playing music. Hopefully, gigging once a week at eighty-five.

# *"I Have Eighty-Three Years"*

## LOUISA NOBLE DRURY
### Born 1929 – Retired 1991

Shortly after college, Louisa moved to Paris. When she arrived, a new generation of writers—William Styron, Alan Ginsberg, William Burroughs, James Baldwin, and many others—were moving to the city. *The Paris Review* had just been founded, and through her work at the *Review,* she became deeply involved in the literary and artistic scene, and well acquainted with a host of writers and artists, many of whom became well-known.

Louisa met a struggling painter with great promise, and married him. Her three children were born in Paris and spent their formative years there. Louisa worked multiple jobs to support her family, and subordinated her intense and long-standing desire to express herself through writing. After sixteen years in

**Paris, she moved her family to Vermont near two of her siblings, taught, and raised her children.**

**After twenty-five years of teaching, Louisa retired to put her creative energy into developing her own artistic voice.**

I was born in New Haven. My father had been a three-sport athlete at Yale and he went to the law school there. That's where he met and married my mother. He practiced law in New York City for about three years, until he was recruited to teach at Groton, a boys' prep school in Massachusetts. My parents were torn about whether to give up the law and New York. They went back and forth trying to decide. Groton would be a wonderful place to raise a family, but the pay would be so much less. So they wrote two letters in response to the recruiter—one accepting the position and one rejecting it—and then flipped a coin: Groton!

We lived on the campus in a large house, with lots of room for me, my sister, and two brothers. Life was idyllic, lots of sports. In addition to teaching, my father coached football, hockey, and baseball, and taught tennis. There was lots of reading the classics and writing. My mother insisted that we keep journals to work out our thoughts on our lives, friendships, and feelings. My parents were not concerned about material things, and I became even less concerned.

I went to an all-girls' grammar school and an all-girls' boarding school for high school. When I returned to Groton for the summer, much of the student population had gone home, so there was little opportunity to meet boys. I dreamed of marrying someone like Byron or Keats. I remember wishing that I had lived in that romantic day and age. I don't think I ever got over that dream.

In college at Barnard I majored in French. I knew very little French and wanted to learn it. After college I taught at a girls' school in New York. I loved teaching, and still do, but, on a ski trip, I was up on a lift and looked down and saw my life in New York: going from city street to city street, back and forth, home to school to home. I had second thoughts as to whether that's how I wanted to spend my life.

About that time my father went on sabbatical through Europe and my parents offered me a trip to Paris. They probably thought I'd stay for the summer and figure out what I wanted to do, but I stayed for sixteen years. They weren't too happy about that.

As soon as I got there, I started looking for jobs. Paris felt like a place where I'd like to live and work.

My first jobs were at *The Paris Review* and at a bookstore on the Left Bank owned by the grandnephew of Walt Whitman. It was all his family's books. He later renamed the bookstore, Shakespeare and Company, recalling the 1920s bookstore that Sylvia Beach owned, and Hemingway and Joyce frequented. The renaming worked: PhDs and tourists flocked to the store, believing it was the original. Several movies made the same mistake. Both jobs paid poorly, so I got a third job at the *New York Herald Tribune.*

This was an exciting time on the literary scene. A new generation of writers and artists was entering the tradition of Hemingway, Fitzgerald, Pound. I worked with and played with many wonderful artists and writers: William Styron, Ed Naughton, Peter Mathiessen, Donald Hall, George Plimpton, Art Buchwald, Richard Wright, William Burroughs, Ginsberg, Corso, and Ferlinghetti. It's impossible to describe the scene without sounding like I'm name-dropping. It was so alive.

I met my husband, Harry, a painter from New Zealand, at the bookstore. He was brilliant. He was in Paris on a grant. We went for a drink at the Café Dome in Montparnasse. I was twenty-two or twenty-three, and he was twenty-five or twenty-six. We got talking, talking, talking. That night I went home with Harry and was still with him when he died fifty-one years later.

He was dedicated to his art, but painting pictures in a studio is not a paying job. We had three children, and my decision to stay in Paris came in bits with the birth of my children. I worked to support the family as a teacher, translator, typist, and secretary, sometimes two jobs a day. I taught at the American School of Paris. I loved that job. Teaching is performance—like acting. But I kept taking jobs that paid slightly more. Harry hardly ever sold any paintings, and we were frequently broke.

In 1968, I concluded it wasn't working. Life in Paris had become tremendously expensive, even with two jobs. The jobs available to women, especially American women, were low paying. Anti-American sentiment arising from the US War on Vietnam was increasing. I wrote my parents that I needed to return, but they declined to fund the return. They didn't approve of Harry. They thought that I had made my own bed. They didn't approve of my politics, thinking that I was left wing, when I was simply antiwar and otherwise apolitical. So, my brother funded the return for me and the three kids. He helped Harry to get set up in London, where he got a job, an apartment, and supported himself. Harry later joined us in the States.

Leaving Paris was hard, a big adjustment. I loved the city. It was so free—you had freedom to live your life your way, not wasting time on others' expectations. I remember family friends visiting Paris, taking them to a Left Bank café, and being repeatedly asked, "Louisa, what are you doing in Paris? What will this lead to?" And, for the first time in my life, I responded, "Nothing." *Il dolce far niente.* The pleasure of doing nothing, just living in the present—living day-to-day, absorbing, loving every minute of the day as much as possible. The rebelliousness, you could say what you believed. I had been raised such that you had to explain what you were doing, and why and how it's going to better you in the future. In addition to the freedom, we were friends with so many talented, interesting people, including many who never became famous.

I settled in Vermont and lived for a while with my sister until I got established as a schoolteacher in Stowe. I taught in the Stowe public schools for twenty-five years and loved it. Over time Vermont became the center of my social and family network. I spend time visiting my grandchildren. I love it! We do puppets; we do French; sing songs, cook, and play the piano or listen to my grandson play the guitar. He's very good. I'm teaching myself Italian. I have a passion for foreign languages. I've learned eight, but only know three of them well.

I retired from teaching in 1991 at sixty-two because I wanted to write. This is supposed to be my writing time, but I'm not good at having a writing routine. When someone told me I had to be at a job at a certain time, I was there. I'm working on it, getting myself more disciplined, but I find that loneliness makes it difficult to concentrate. I write poetry, and I've always kept journals, especially of those days in Paris. I want to put them into the form of a memoir because, looking back, I realize that it may be a life worth writing about. My daughter tells me don't think of it as a huge project, just do it bit by bit.

Completing a memoir appeals to me as a study of why I chose a different path in life, and also as a study of Harry and our friends who never became famous, even though they were just as interesting and talented as those who did. I think a memoir would provide a way to explore important life questions, such as who defines success and by what standard. In their time, neither Mozart nor van Gogh achieved financial reward.

Among our Paris contemporaries were many excellent painters, poets, sculptors, and artists whom no one has heard of. They lived lives filled with what they loved doing, had a passion for doing. Doesn't that alone make them successful? I lean toward the view that living a full life of devotion and dedication to your work is success. Yet, people who live their lives that way are often scorned and ridiculed for not earning money. But can someone who gave up his or her passion to comply with public bottom-line expectations ever be considered successful?

I always did and still do love teaching, but Paris...Paris for sixteen years was my big adventure. I haven't told my children much about it.

I want it to be fresh when I write it. I don't want it to be secondhand. If you think about something too long, you write not about the experience, but about what you thought about it. I don't want to overthink it.

I'd love another big adventure. That would be wonderful. In 2005 I rented an apartment in Montparnasse near the Café Dome, which many artists used to frequent. It's all been gentrified. It was wonderful to be back in Paris for three months—an adventure of its own—but none of the artists we had known were still there. Some were dead; some had moved. People I had worked with were still there, and people from the US and England came to visit. So that was like an adventure.

In the summer of 2006, one of my friends invited me to house-sit on the outskirts of Paris. That was kind of sad. No one around, especially in August. What I love doing in Paris is going back to the old haunts, museums, galleries, and sit and wonder. But there was no point in revisiting the old spots by myself. Been there, done that. So I don't have any desire to go back to Paris; I just want to write about it.

My goal is to get the book written. I have writings galore in the house. I just want to get it into a form that can be published, at least for my children and grandchildren. It's my main goal in life now. My frustration is that I often spend a whole day not doing anything about it. Just sitting there, doing something else to avoid delving into the big story—my life and my stories. Sometimes I wonder if the memories of the more difficult times are polluting what I want to write for my children and grandchildren. Should I write one book of the good times? And one of the bad? I need to be able to answer why I stayed before I can write the rest. Of course, the answer is I was in love. I know I need to find and write the truth.

Age is interesting because I feel all of my ages—even the pigtailed kid who monitors my poetry, my teenage self, my twenty-year-old self, and all the ensuing decades. The age I know the least is eighty-three because I've only been eighty-three for a few months. It's interesting that we say, "I *am* eighty-three years old." But in French,

Italian, Spanish, and other languages, they say, "I *have* eighty-three years," suggesting that I am composed of all the experiences and life that went before. You have all the years you've ever lived. I can feel all those other ages. They are more a part of me than eighty-three. In fact, eighty-three is barely a part of me yet. I don't know what eighty-three will be like. Inside our soul or essence; in there, there is our whole being, all our experiences. They stay with us.

# *"Do It While You're Living"*

## DICK ELLIOTT
### Born 1925 – Retired 1973

**Dick retired at forty-eight from Sears to pursue his lifelong desire to be an actor. At the time, he had a wife and three kids to support. Since then, he has been in over eighty films, and numerous commercials and television shows. For the last twenty-five years, Dick has portrayed Ben Franklin in historical reenactments and lectures throughout the United States and abroad. Today, at eighty-seven, Dick dons his costume, rides the train to Boston, and greets and engages visitors on Boston's Freedom Trail as Ben Franklin, speaking in the dialect of the late 1700s.**

M y dad was a jeweler and my mother was a housewife. I had two sisters and three brothers, only one of whom is still alive. After high school I served two years in the army in the occupation of Japan. I married in 1950 and worked as a salesman for Sears. I have three boys, four grandchildren, and five great-grandchildren. My wife is eighty-two. My kids have followed their own paths. One became an engineer, another started his own HVAC business, and the other works for the government.

But all along I had this unfulfilled desire to get into acting. It goes back to when I was at the Benjamin Franklin Grammar School. I won the speaking contest for the whole school. My oldest brother saw it and said, "You're going to acting school and I'll pay for your lessons." So I went to a local place, The Anderson Sisters School of Dancing and Dramatics. The three sisters taught tap, ballet, and drama, and their mother played the piano. I was in a musical production with them and got the lead in the high school's senior play. I got a job as an usher at the local theater so I could see the movies and study the actors. I wanted to be a movie actor. I worked with the USO shows in Japan when they came over.

Even while I was working for Sears, I worked as an extra in movie productions, but my time was limited and I wasn't as available as I needed to be. So after twenty-three years, at age forty-eight, I left Sears and worked in real estate so I could be available for acting jobs. I wanted the freedom. I had been getting some calls as a character actor, but just wasn't sufficiently available.

I joined AFTRA—American Federation of Television and Radio Actors—and posted a headshot and a resume. I started getting calls for auditions for commercials. I did a lot of TV and billboard ads for the *Boston Herald* and the *Globe*. One was set on the beach, and I was reading the *Globe* and it gets blown away, to the song, "Boston Moves to *The Herald*." Then the *Globe* hired me to promote its paper. The posting of the headshot also led to movies. I started as an extra, and they kept calling me more and more. So far, I've been in eighty-seven movies.

The first was shot in Boston, *Billy Galvin*, with Karl Malden. I was an extra; it was about a steel worker who wanted his son to be a lawyer.

Then one thing led to another, *True Lies* with Arnold Schwarzenegger, where I played a tango-dancing Russian duke. I am an expert in the tango. From my early days I knew how to tango, but I perfected my skills when I was in the service in Japan. I took about six months of lessons and put in a year of work on the dance. It turns out no learning is ever wasted. Tango expertise was a requirement for the part in *True Lies*. I was also in *Housesitter* with Goldie Hawn and Steve Martin. Frank Oz called me. I played the part of the bartender in the house scene. The scene ran twenty-five minutes. Kate Hudson and Kurt Russell showed up.

I was in *Blown Away* with Jeff and Lloyd Bridges and Tommy Lee Jones. I was on the balcony with Lloyd making a toast of Guinness to the bride and groom. Then Lloyd and I did sort of a dueling Irish jig. I played the official timekeeper in *Celtic Pride*.

I was in *Tough Guys Don't Dance*, a book and screenplay by Norman Mailer, with Ryan O'Neal. I was in eight *Miami Vice* episodes. I played a wide range of characters, from a drug-dealing lowlife to a sea captain. Don Johnson's a very funny guy. I was in twenty-five episodes of *Spenser: For Hire*, the series based on Robert Parker's novels. That was great; it was based here in Boston.

I started playing Ben Franklin twenty-five years ago for the City of Boston's anniversary of the signing of the Constitution. Acting is in your mind because you're controlling your thoughts to project what you want, but you have to look the part to play the part. I was too short to be Thomas Jefferson; Ben Franklin was a better fit.

I love to come downtown as Ben Franklin and greet people on the Freedom Trail at some of the historical sites like Faneuil Hall. I don't get compensated for it, but I love what I do. I get exercise, probably walking three miles a day. I come to Boston about three days a week. I drive to a train station and take the subway in full dress. I talk to visitors and meet people.

Over the years, I have lectured to schoolchildren in thirty-four states and overseas about the life of Ben Franklin. I've even lectured at air force base schools in Europe. At times my wife participates in the lecture or presentation as Mrs. Franklin. She makes our costumes. For elementary through high school kids, the presentation is about an hour long, in large auditoriums. For little kids, it's a bedtime story about how he discovered electricity. For older kids, it's more in-depth about his role in the Revolution. Over a period of time, I researched, developed, and wrote the material myself. By now, of course, it's all in my head.

I still make myself available for work in movies. I'll never retire from acting or from playing Ben Franklin, but I don't come in on inclement days. I love what I do. I love the whole thing; I was a born actor, starting right there in the fifth grade. I enjoy the process of acting; I enjoy teaching the school kids. The kids tell me that they learn more from me than they ever did from books. That's a source of satisfaction. I want to do more schools and more movies.

I do have other interests. I paint, and I'd like to spend more time doing that—pen and ink, acrylics, watercolors. I love music, and my wife and I still dance. But acting is it. I retired to do what I wanted to do, but now I'm never going to retire. I could only do it after I had fulfilled my obligations to raise my kids. I would have left Sears and started acting earlier if I could have. My fellow workers couldn't understand when I left. I wanted to do what I really wanted to do. You have to have faith in yourself, the determination and tenacity to go out and try to do what you want to do. Life is only once. We don't come back again. At least I've never met anyone who came back the other way. So do it while you're living.

Have confidence in yourself, but know you don't control everything. So you have to ride with the tide. Everything has ups and downs, highs and lows. You have to believe in yourself to at least try. Enjoy. I fell in love with acting and I pursued it because I wanted to. For a while I needed a job, but it was always in the back of my mind. If I hadn't become an actor, I'd have been a salesman, which in itself requires acting skills. If people don't like you, they won't buy the product. You have to get people to like you. I think that means you have to like people. To be likable you have to like people, enjoy people.

# IV. ENJOYMENT

# *"I Just Decided to Live That Way"*

## SUSUMU ITO
### Born 1919 – Retired 1991

*Sus at Camp Shelby, with Minnie on their wedding day, and with the Congressional Gold Medal.*

**Sus is a retired Harvard Medical School professor emeritus who still spends large parts of his days in a laboratory working with high-tech microscopes to view cell specimens. He's been associated with the Harvard Medical School Anatomy Department since 1961. His research centered on the study of the gastrointestinal system, and for his efforts he became world renowned.**

**Before his career as a research biologist, Sus was a forward artillery observer and a lieutenant in the all Japanese American 442nd Regimental Combat Team, which consisted of a regiment of infantry, a battalion of field artillery, a company of combat**

engineers, and various support units. The 442nd received more awards than any military unit of its size and length of service in US history. In October 1944, Sus participated in the rescue of the Texas Lost Battalion in the Vosges Mountains of France. Two hundred and thirty men were surrounded and under siege by German forces. Two early assaults on the Germans were turned back. The third attempt was led by the 442nd. In five days of battle, the 442nd suffered over eight hundred casualties. On the fifth day, two infantry companies, Sus, and his three crew members were ordered to charge the hill. This charge has become known as "The Banzai Charge." Of the 371 men who went up the hill, all but twenty-five were killed or wounded. Sus was one of the uninjured. For its service, the 442nd earned the nickname "The Purple Heart Battalion."

A Congressional Gold Medal, the highest civilian US medal, was voted on by the House of Representatives and the Senate, and awarded in a November 2011 ceremony at the Capitol Building. House Speaker John Boehner presented the award to representatives of the 100th Infantry Battalion, the 442nd Regimental Combat Team, and the Military Intelligence Service. It was followed by local ceremonies in California, Hawaii, and other states. Sus was chosen to receive the medal for the 442nd. Minnie, his wife of sixty-six years, attended.

My memory is good but not perfect. About a year ago, my wife and I went to a ceremony in Washington. Congress gave my old regiment a medal for our role in a rescue mission that took place in 1944. The ceremony made some papers and, when I came home, some of my friends had heard about it. They wanted me to tell them all about the mission. I had to apologize—to explain that I don't have any memory of it. Well, I remember certain things about it—the atmosphere of it, sensations that I experienced and that I still associate with that time. And, of course, I'm familiar with historical accounts of what happened. The story is that, on the last day of the mission, my fellow soldiers and I—all of us Japanese Americans—made a cry of "banzai," surged through the German lines, and rescued a group of trapped soldiers. I have no recollection of any of that, none. And, as I said, I have a good memory. I remember so much so clearly—so much about the war and about my life. It's strange. That's how the mind works, I suppose.

I had a very happy childhood. My parents started out as farmers, and so I grew up mostly in the country, in the San Joaquin Valley, which is very fertile land. My father and mother had both left Japan for California. My father arrived first. He was from Hiroshima and from a prominent farming family. As the oldest son, he stood to inherit the whole operation. He gave it all up, thinking he could do even better in America. A few years later, my mother arrived. Theirs was an arranged marriage, which was customary.

Farming was more difficult than they had anticipated. My parents made four or five attempts at it, always in and around Stockton. They were tenant farmers. The setup was simple. My father managed the farming, which involved thirty or forty field hands, and my mother managed everything else—keeping the place running, making three meals a day for the family and for all of the hands. It wasn't easy. We all lived together in tarpaper shacks, with no electricity and no privies. Still, I was happy. I spent a lot of time outdoors, fishing and hunting and running around.

Because my parents had difficulty establishing themselves as farmers, we moved around a good deal. I attended five elementary schools, I think—one of which was segregated. All my classmates were Asian. In most cases, a single teacher taught eight grades of students at the same time, with all of the students cramped into a run-down, one-room schoolhouse. By third grade, I'd fallen behind. My teacher decided to hold me back and sent word of her decision to my mother. Now, my mother was an optimistic, aggressive woman, and she knew that I was not unintelligent. So she decided to pay my teacher a visit—and also to offer her a bribe. She gave her a pair of silk stockings and a bar of chocolate. And it worked, by God. She passed me. From that day on, I always kept up.

At sixteen, I finished high school and was admitted to the University of California at Berkeley. I wanted to go, but my parents had doubts. At the time, because of segregation and discrimination, there were relatively few professional opportunities for Japanese Americans. My parents were uncertain of the value of a university education. They thought it might prove to be a disadvantage. I'd be locked out of professional positions for being Asian, and locked out of skilled labor for lacking the necessary training. So, instead of sending me to Berkeley, they sent me to a school for auto mechanics. This wasn't as strange as it may sound. You have to understand it from their perspective. They'd struggled for so many years. First, they hadn't been able to make it as farmers. Then, they were forced to work on someone else's farm, helping with cooking and the upkeep. Later, they scraped together enough money to open a traditional Japanese bathhouse, which they made a success by force of will. Every day, they started working at five and ended at midnight. They wanted something better for me. I think they dreamed that, one day, I might own my own service station and live happily ever after.

Also, I was mechanically inclined—always taking things apart and putting them back together. I did want to go to college, of course, but I was young and unsure of myself. So I took my parents' advice and went to mechanic's school. I finished my training in about a year and then spent a few years working different jobs around the Bay Area—at a frame shop in San Francisco, at a service station in Stockton, at a Ford dealership in Lodi.

In late 1940, I turned twenty-one. One month later, I was drafted into the army. That was exciting. I'd never left the state of California. Anything further than a hundred miles from Stockton was an adventure. The army represented a chance to experience a new kind of life.

In Japanese culture, soldiers are very much admired. After my friends and I were drafted, the Japanese community in Stockton arranged a large, elaborate banquet in our honor. All the draftees sat together at a table on a makeshift stage. Throughout the night, we were given little envelopes filled with cash. Many people lined up to greet us and to give us these gifts and to wish us well. Many of them, I'd never met—many of them, I knew, had very little to give. In all, I received thirty-seven dollars that night. That impressed me and moved me greatly. It also frightened me, because the banquet took place on the night before our first physical. I'm flatfooted and nearsighted, and so I was worried that I wouldn't pass and that I'd be barred from service. I didn't want to fail and disappoint the entire community.

The next morning, my anxiety deepened. When my family and I arrived at the train station, it was thronged. Everyone who had been at the banquet was there, along with many more people. It was overwhelming. In fact, it was so crowded that, after that day, the station issued an order barring Japanese from the station during future deployments. Well, it took a long while to board the train, because everyone wanted to wish me and the other draftees good luck. And the ride seemed to last forever, because all the other draftees were talking, saying how excited they were. Meanwhile, I was rehearsing what I would say to the army when they found out about my flatfeet: "I'll do all the marches. I'll do everything you need me to do." At last, we arrived and were directed to our physicals. I was probably shaking by the time my turn came. First, the doctor asked me to read a test chart, with and without my glasses. Next, he asked me a few questions about my eyesight and inspected my eyes. And then, just like that, it was over. I couldn't believe it. He never even looked at my feet.

I was inducted into the army in February 1941. At first, I was thrilled. Soon, however, I discovered that in many ways army life isn't too different from civilian life. My first assignment was to a maintenance shop where I repaired cars and trucks. We were stationed near Riverside, in a semi-integrated camp with a population of about eighty thousand. Now, I was living and working with Asians, Whites, and Latinos, although Blacks were still segregated. I got along well with everyone. I felt accepted by everyone. I was enjoying myself. I had a car and, when I was off duty, I could drive home to Stockton, or to Riverside, or to Los Angeles. Months passed like this. I settled into a routine. Army life began to seem as natural and as ordered as civilian life.

On Sunday, December 7, 1941, I was in my tent listening to the radio. I had a day pass, and I was getting ready to go see my girlfriend in Riverside. At about nine or ten, we heard that there was an attack on Pearl Harbor. At first, the details weren't entirely clear. Word got out that nobody was allowed to leave camp. My sergeant was a good guy, an old World War I vet. I can still picture him. Well, he didn't mind bending the rules. He told me to go ahead and use my day pass, and that if I were caught, to say that I hadn't heard the order to stay on the base. So, I left the camp and went into Riverside and spent the day with my girlfriend. It was a strange day, a sad day. We sat together and listened to the radio. We went to church. We walked around the city, which seemed empty. When I returned to camp, I was directed to report to headquarters. I thought that I was going to be punished for leaving, but that's not what happened.

Instead, they asked me to interrogate a group of local Japanese American leaders. The army had found them in Riverside and brought them to the camp. My commanding officers had been waiting for me all day. They wanted to see what I could get out of this group—if I could get anything in the way of military intelligence. I refused to do it. I didn't think it was appropriate. Of course, I was patriotic and completely supportive of the war effort, but interrogating Japanese American civilians who had just been picked up off the street wasn't my idea of fighting a war. I wanted to be a warrior, to go all-out for my country, to serve bravely and honorably. These interrogations didn't fit with that idea.

I had the same reaction to all the propaganda, which told us that we should all hate, hate the enemy. I didn't see that. I thought, *Those guys are just like us. They're fighting for their country and we're fighting for ours*. Anyhow, that night I told my commanding officers that my Japanese was extremely limited; that I knew only a few words. This wasn't entirely true. My Japanese was not excellent, but I'd taken language lessons back in Stockton and, of course, my parents were native speakers. Anyhow, that day I was excused from having to participate in the interrogations. A few days later, however, I was asked to attend language training, which would have prepared me to conduct future interrogations. Again, I declined. They asked a few more times, but my position didn't change.

Three months after the attack, in March of 1942, my parents were directed to report to a local assembly center, allowed to take with them only what they could carry. Next, they were shipped to an internment camp in Arkansas that housed about ten thousand. There, they lived behind barbed-wire fences, in twenty-foot-by-twenty-foot cabins. The conditions were primitive. My father was sixty-four when he was interned. My mother was fifty. For more than a year, I couldn't visit them and they had no access to phones. The internment caused my parents to lose their little business. Everything they'd fought so many years to build just disappeared.

After Pearl Harbor, the army didn't seem to know what to do with me—really, with any of its Japanese American soldiers. We were asked to turn in our rifles. We were no longer allowed to have access to any kind of weapons. Our travel was restricted. I continued working as a mechanic, working in motor pools. This lasted for about a year and a half, until the spring of 1943, when I and some other Japanese American soldiers were shipped off to Camp Shelby, Mississippi. We went not knowing where we were going or what it was all about. When we arrived, we learned that we were joining a newly created regiment—the 442nd Regimental Combat Team, which was to be comprised of all Japanese Americans. I was happy about it. I thought it would be exciting and it was. This regiment was bound for the front, and it included men from all over the country. Many were from Hawaii. Some had been drafted directly out of internment camps. Most were assigned to serve in the infantry division. Because of my mechanical background, I was assigned to the artillery battalion. This was fortunate, because many of the infantrymen in our regiment would later die in combat.

During our training in Camp Shelby, the army lifted the special restrictions that they'd imposed on us after Pearl Harbor. Now, we were training with weapons, and we were freer to travel. Because I was stationed in Mississippi, I was able to visit my parents in their camp in Arkansas. I remember driving there on a number of occasions. After so long, it was wonderful to see them. Also, during this period, we exchanged letters frequently. My mother wrote to me in Japanese. She would tell me how proud she was that I was in the army. She would also tell me to avoid any hazardous duty, to avoid it at all costs. She told me to go to jail, if necessary, and that I should become a conscientious objector rather than expose myself to danger. Her warning was always in my mind. I thought about it constantly.

One day, I learned that there was an opening in our battalion for the position of forward observer. A forward observer is part of the foremost advancing infantry, in the front lines scouting for targets, enemy troops, and installations. It's among the most dangerous positions available. In spite of that, and in spite of my mother's warning, I volunteered. Afterwards, I lied to her about it. I said that I didn't volunteer but that I was assigned. I hated to lie to her, of course, but I did want to be a forward observer. I wanted to see action. As a forward observer, I underwent special training, which was intense. But I knew what I would be in for, and so I worked like mad to prepare myself.

In May and June of 1944, our regiment sailed the Atlantic for Italy. We traveled in a huge convoy, turning and twisting to dodge German U-boats. After twenty-six days, we landed on the Adriatic Coast, in open territory. We took a train to Naples. From Naples, we took a landing craft to Anzio, which had already been taken. From Anzio, we went to Rome. At the time, Rome was an open city. It was undefended and seemed relatively untouched by the war. I remember when we rode through in our convoy very early in the morning, and there weren't too many people out. The city seemed to go on and on, like we were riding through in slow motion. After Rome, we followed the coast north, which is where we had our first battle. I remember the first time we came near German forces, and the shells they fired at us. You could hear them before you could see them. In the distance, they sounded like freight trains.

Many people write about war. But I don't think it's possible to describe it. You cannot know it in the abstract. You can only feel it after you've been through it. Then, it becomes real, and it becomes a part of you. On one of our first days in battle, we walked into a trap and my friend was killed. He was someone that I'd known since I was boy in Stockton and that I'd been to school with. We took a wrong turn and we were attacked and then he was gone forever. With that, war became real.

In spite of the danger, I don't remember any situation where our group was reluctant to expose itself or to enter into combat. I kept thinking about my parents, and about my mother's warning. I didn't feel invulnerable. I wasn't. None of us were. But, all that time, it never occurred to me that I might be killed or wounded. Somehow, even in situations where there were tremendous casualties, where people were dying all around me, I held on to this positive attitude. To this day, I don't understand how I was able to maintain that feeling, that assurance. In every situation, no matter how dangerous, I always told myself: "I'm not going to be one of the victims."

As I explained, I do not remember much of the rescue of the "Lost Battalion." I can only remember certain things—sensations, the darkness of it, the darkness and the thickness of the forest, and that we were under constant fire. I still get goose bumps when I go into dark places. As I explained, I do not remember anything about the last day of the battle, or about our final charge. That's not uncommon, I don't think. That's how memory works.

Months later, we were advancing on the retreating German forces when we came on Dachau. This was in the spring of 1945. According to the Holocaust Society, our group liberated a subcamp at Dachau. I cannot begin to explain what I saw there. I remember listening to a young prisoner of the camp—a teenage boy, emaciated, draped under that gray uniform. He spoke about what he had survived. He translated for the other survivors. I cannot describe it.

A few months later, I left the army. I was home in time for Christmas. Today, I wonder how I made it through and made it back. Sometimes, I think it was a matter of fate. My own decisions had nothing to do with it. I volunteered for dangerous duty. I put myself in dangerous situations. I don't know—it just happened—I just survived. I can't offer an explanation for why I'm here, more than seventy years later, talking about it. I was so fortunate. I don't know why I was so fortunate. Even now, so many years later, I'm still grateful for the time that's been given to me. I'm still trying to make the most of it.

I do know this, however. I don't regret any moment or experience that I had during the war, no matter how tense or awful it might have been. What I experienced and lived through is invaluable. It's a matter of pride for me, pride and satisfaction, that I lived through all that—that I got through it all and that I'm still here and intact and relatively happy.

My parents were released from internment after V-J Day, in August of 1945. Because they'd lost their home and their business, they had no place to go. They ended up in Cleveland, where some other family members had settled. I joined them in December. After the war, thousands of Japanese Americans settled in Cleveland. There was an active social life. One of my friends worked as a caretaker at a Jewish funeral home. The owner allowed him to have parties on occasion, right there in the funeral home, with all the corpses lying about. That's where I met my wife, Minnie. She was raised in Oakland and interned in Utah. (One hundred twenty thousand Japanese Americans were confined behind barbed wire in ten segregated camps for the duration of the war.) We started talking and found that we had many things in common. A year later, we married. We remain happily married to this day. She's wonderful. She's always been very patient and supportive and loving.

One of the last things I did after I left the army was to take an aptitude test. I wasn't sure what I wanted to do. I knew that I wasn't excited about going back to being a mechanic. Also, I knew that I didn't want to be a door-to-door salesman. I'd tried doing that. I only lasted a few weeks. It was horrible. I was horrible at it. Anyhow, the counselor reviewed my test results and suggested three professions. First, engineer, because of my mechanical background. Next, social worker, because he said that I had good people skills. Last, he suggested that I might try something related to science. He thought I might have an aptitude for it.

First, I started a college engineering course. I hated it. Right from the start, I knew. And I dropped it. I didn't have an idea about what I'd do instead. So I decided to follow my instincts. Here, I should make a confession. Ever since I returned from the war, I've only done things that I enjoy. I just decided to live that way. My decision to drop engineering was the first instance of it. Since then, it's been a guiding principle. Pretty much everything I choose to do, I do because I think it will be fun or interesting, not for security or money or recognition. It's one of the most important decisions I've ever made. It changed the direction and the quality of my life.

So, I quit engineering and began taking courses in biology. I found that I loved it, and so I decided that would be my life's work. I told this to one of my teachers. He said: "Why don't you just go into medicine or dentistry? The pay's much better." He was against it, and he was a biology teacher. For me, it was a natural choice. I was excited about it.

At first, I didn't have a clear idea of where my studies would lead. I finished my undergraduate degree and moved on to my master's. One day, I read about Woods Hole, the institute for oceanographic sciences. What they were doing out there didn't have direct bearing on my research, but I was fascinated by it. And so I followed that instinct. I arranged to spend a summer there, studying marine biology and working. I met so many scientists from all over the world—from Japan, Europe, South America. Woods Hole was like an oasis, an academic oasis. It deepened my love of science and broadened my view of what was possible, of what I could accomplish with my life. After that, I won a fellowship to continue my research in Germany. I spent about six months there, researching genetics. I finished my PhD in 1954.

After that, I was hired by a man who would later become a life-long friend, Don Fawcett. He was a world-renowned expert in cell biology and had just become the chairman of the Biology Department at Cornell Medical School in Manhattan. After five years at Cornell, in 1959, Don decided to go to Harvard to become chairman of the Anatomy Department. He asked if I'd like to join him on the Harvard faculty. I agreed immediately. By then, my wife and I had three kids, and we were all living in Queens, in a miserable two-bedroom apartment beneath the Triborough Bridge.

Harvard was wonderful. I had limited teaching duties and was free to spend most of my time pursuing research that interested and excited me. Much of my research involved electron microscopic studies of the gastrointestinal system. In particular, I became interested in how the stomach secretes acid, and I looked at this process and thought: *Some cell has to do that. What cell? How?* I was absorbed by what I was studying. It may sound arcane, perhaps, but to me it was fascinating. I worked in other areas as well. I did research related to Legionnaire's Disease and to the HIV virus.

I retired in 1991. I did so because, at the time, Harvard imposed a mandatory retirement age. But I continued working after my retirement, researching and teaching. So, the change didn't cause me any significant anxiety. At first, my life didn't change very much. I'd always kept long hours. That didn't change. I'd still get to the lab at around six in the morning. I kept going at my own pace, pursuing what I liked.

Retirement did give me more freedom. In those first few years, I did a lot of traveling. After retiring from Harvard, I spent two years working in Africa. I lived and worked in Kenya, at the International Laboratory for the Study of Animal Diseases, where my research focused on parasitic diseases. I traveled all over Africa, and to many other places. Sometimes, I traveled for work—for special projects and funded scientific exchanges—sometimes, for pleasure. Some of the trips would last months. During this period, I went to Japan six or seven times. Once, my wife and I stayed for three months.

It was wonderful. I went to Australia, India, Europe, Africa, South America. I traveled all over America. I've made it to all forty-eight continental states. I enjoy road trips. Since turning eighty, I've driven across the country four times. I always went alone, because my wife doesn't like to be in the car with the way that I drive. Once, I went coast to coast in three days' time. That's driving. On these trips, I'd visit old friends, from the war and from my academic career. And I'd visit places where I used to live, California, the Midwest.

Today, I'm ninety-two and reasonably healthy. I wake up very early, before the paper is delivered. When it arrives, I read it in bed with my coffee, thinking about how I'll spend the day. I do most of the cooking now. Minnie got tired of it. So I get to cook whatever I like. I do the shopping now, too. I don't exercise, but I do work. I fix things, cut trees, chop wood, move things around. And I still do all my own auto maintenance and repairs—so that early training is still paying off. Last year, I painted part of the house. Not too long ago, I shingled the garage. Also, we have a second home, a small house on the beach. I keep it open year-round and do all the upkeep. That kind of work keeps me healthy.

Our children still live in the area, except for one son, who lives in California. We have five grandchildren. They all visit us, which we love. Our five-year-old granddaughter just visited. We spent the afternoon decorating our Christmas tree. And I still keep in touch with so many people from my life, with army buddies, with friends from all around the world, with colleagues from the world of science. In fact, I still enjoy doing science. I'm not trying to make any earth-shattering discoveries. I do it just because I enjoy it. I like the feeling of participating in scientific inquiry, of making contributions to work that may expand our knowledge of the world. I work at the labs at Harvard and at a lab that we've set up here in our home. Right now, I'm working on three different research projects. Two of them have told me that they want to put my name on the papers. I explained that it wasn't necessary, that I'm not working to gain recognition. I'm just enjoying myself.

I no longer have any immediate goals or long-term objectives. In my life, I've done more than I ever expected. And now, I realize that I may not have much time left. My father died at seventy-six. My mother lived to almost one hundred. Sometimes, I wonder if I'll reach one hundred. I'd love to live that long if I could still be myself—if I could live and not be too tied up.

I had a very close friend from my days in graduate school. When I'd drive cross-country, I'd visit him and stay at his home. And he used to visit us and to stay at our home. After his wife died, he took his own life. Physically, he was still fine. But he'd grown discouraged. He no longer saw any purpose to anything. He wrote me a letter. I still have it. It began: "By the time you get this letter, I won't be here." I don't think that I could ever do something like that. I don't think I could ever think like that.

And so, here I am. These days, with all that behind me, I often find myself asking: "What should I do?" It's a difficult question. Sometimes, it seems like an impossible question. Still, I ask it over and over: "What should I do? What should I do?" Sometimes, I find an answer by reminding myself of the promise that I made to myself after the war, when I swore that, for the rest of my life, I'd only do things that I enjoy. That changes my perspective. I stop asking: "What should I do? What should I do?" Instead, I ask a different question—a better one, I think, one that's far healthier and much more productive: "What do I want to do?"

# *"I Want to Come Back as Zip Cahill"*

## JAMES "ZIP" CAHILL
### Born 1939 – Retired 1972

**Zip had been a motorcycle policeman in a city near Boston. He was injured on the job and forced to retire at thirty-two. He has been retired forty years, longer than anyone else interviewed.**

The injury was the last day I worked as a motorcycle policeman. I was doing a school crossing on an icy morning and this six-year-old comes sliding down the hill out onto the roadway. I reached out and stopped him, but he spun me around and *click*—and that was it. I was in and out of the hospital with surgery...The second-opinion doctor said, "Sooner or later you're going to come to a halt." Three months later I did. I couldn't roll over in bed. They removed the disc and fused my spine.

I was thirty-two and had been on the force for eleven years, and on the motorcycle squad about three years. I loved it. I couldn't have had a better job. I wasn't keen on getting out. The chief called me in and told me, "Put your papers in. I can't have so many people on light duty. I don't know what I can do with you."

I wasn't concerned, at that point I made my mind up—the chief was going to do what he was going to do. When I learned that I was off the force, I concluded that I'd move to Maine to a house I bought years before, up in the Rangley Mountains, about sixty miles from the Canadian border. I originally was attracted to the area because of the hunting and the fact that, going back to the '40s there were a lot of people from my hometown with places up here. So I knew folks. I used to come up to hunt and to get away for the summer.

The house I bought is 240 years old and there's constant upkeep. A lot of the stuff I've redone over the years. I measure three times before I cut, but I'm pretty good with electrical and plumbing. I never got antsy or anxious. I always had enough to do around here. I have the house, a barn, a lake house, and some land. So there's always plenty to do.

When I was forced to leave the job, I wasn't worried about what I was going to do. My attitude was I was going to let things slide. I'd spend half the year up here and half in Boston. I'd go back and forth, but now I am not actually interested in Boston anymore.

In 1990, I was approached by the town to do their code enforcement. Now, I have three towns. I don't make any money at it. I've never taken a pay raise—ten dollars an hour and mileage. I set my own time. We don't have zoning here, so the inspections relate more to distances from lakes to brook streams. When the lumber companies do harvesting, I make sure they don't cut in the buffer zones. Lumber companies are very active up here. Smaller operations have these wood lots and they scull the lumber downstream right to the paper mills. At one time there was a toothpick factory that would take all the lumber, but now there are wood pellet factories, and they take the brush and everything. They use the whole tree now, all the tops and the branches. The pellet factories don't give off any odor, but if you get down near a paper mill, you'd see a white foam on the river. And if the clouds were low, you'd get an odor. The locals used to call it "the smell of money."

The code enforcement work pays for my liquids—my gas and my beer. I haven't hunted in recent years. There's a lot of work to it. When you shoot a deer, you have to take out all the sacks, and you got to let it hang and skin it, and make sure there's no hair in the meat—it's so fine it's real hard to get rid of it. I said, "To hell with that." I kick around with hunters, but I don't actually bother with the hunting.

Since 1963 I've been going to Florida, the Clearwater area. Only missed one year in all that time. Used to go down for a week or ten days, but now for three and a half months.

I've enjoyed retirement. Everybody says, "I want to come back as somebody else." Not me, I want to come back as Zip Cahill. I got a good deal. I live frugal and can get along on little money. What I have. I'm not geared for big spending or gambling or anything like that.

I've done what I've wanted to do. I don't deny myself anything. I go where I want to go. Been back to visit the relatives in Sligo three times. Had a grand old time. I drank beer in the most northern pub in Ireland, up in Donegal. I'm not keen on going to any other countries.

I fill the days because there's always plenty to do around here. I get out, chew the fat with people. Go over to my lake camp and use the pontoon boat.

No concerns or anxieties about retirement. I've enjoyed it fully—get out, drink some beer and move around. See people. Mingle with people; it's the best thing in the world. I like the *craic* (enjoyable conversation, gossip), talk along, that's it.

Jesus, now I don't hold grudges. I have no stress. I just don't worry. If I am doing something and something goes wrong, I just mop up the mistake and move on. I think it's the secret to good health, a blood pressure of 102/58. I still watch my back, but I don't have any ailments. I take a couple of maintenance drugs, but that's it. I'm blessed, I'll tell you.

# *"Enjoyed It to the Max"*

## PAUL RAYBOULD
### Born 1942 – Retired 1992

Paul started working right out of high school in a local department store. He was considered "executive material," sent to training school, and became a buyer. He later joined a national discount retailer. In his thirties, Paul opened his own business as a manufacturers' representative selling to all active discount retailers. He had it "made in the shade." In the early 1990s, however, many national discounters went out of business and Paul lost all his customers. Many declared bankruptcy and his commission checks "grew wings and flew away." So, he closed his business and went golfing. Paul marks this as the beginning of his retirement.

Paul has peripheral artery disease, which he believes was caused by his frequent air travel to Asia. He also has COPD and

**an aneurysm on his aorta. He still smokes a pack of cigarettes a day. He is twice divorced, unmarried, and has four children and two grandchildren.**

After seven years in the department store, I took an interview on a lark. When I got offered twice the money I was making, I said bye-bye to my old employer. Man, oh man, the new job was great, I got to travel the world. Hated Europe, but loved Asia. I made twenty-six trips to the Far East: Japan, Singapore, Hong Kong, Kuala Lumpur, Thailand. The Thai women are the prettiest in the world.

I was first married in 1969. It lasted about two hours and seventeen minutes; actually from 1969 to about 1975 or '76. Wonderful kids.

I remarried, twenty years later, in 1989. That lasted about half an hour. I think we got divorced in 1991. No other marriages. No chance. I'll tell you, before my second marriage I had been divorced for many, many years, and I used to say, "I'll get married the day after the Pope." So it went on, and on. So here I am twenty years later at my second wedding. A few of my friends showed up at the reception with a copy of the *New York Post* headlines: "Pope weds! Secret Vatican ceremony."

My social network before I retired was very limited. I had my family, my kids, co-workers, and then I had a couple of very close friends. Outside of that there were people you'd put under the heading of acquaintances, people with whom I wouldn't share my deepest, darkest secrets. But they were also a lot of fun to be with. I've met a lot of people throughout my life with whom I've had a lot of laughs, but I wouldn't consider them if I was in dire need of something. They'd say, "Paul who?" That has not changed as a result of aging. No, just different people that you hang out with. My core network hasn't changed.

When everything fell apart in the early '90s, thank God I had some money. A friend of mine, another manufacturers' rep, was in the same boat. We decided we'd go on our own golf tour. So at the age of fifty that's what we did. We spent a year and a half touring the country, all the PGA Tour courses. We started at Pebble Beach and then played the north and south courses in La Jolla. We played the Ocean Course at Kiawah, home of the 1991 Ryder Cup. Johnny Miller was in the group following us. So we had quite a fun time with him in the clubhouse afterwards.

Then, we played the TPC at Sawgrass in Ponte Vedra. The following day we played the Old Course at Sawgrass. That was just very interesting being in the locker room and seeing all these great names: Palmer, Nicklaus, Trevino, Johnny Miller again...we were in their locker room. From there we played Doral, in Miami. Man, that is one bitch of a course! After that, all sorts of courses...a year and a half of traveling and sliding in some golf and just enjoying ourselves. That was the real retirement!

Since then I've done just a bunch of odd jobs. I became a limo driver in '92. The fringe benefits there were phenomenal. The guys who owned the limo company flatly refused to take bachelor parties to the strip joints in Rhode Island. I happily volunteered, "I'll do it." And that's what I used to do, every Friday and Saturday night. And it was, like, phenomenal. Oh yeah, I'd be in there, for crying out loud, and I'd behave myself, sitting at the bar drinking Coke, and after the girls danced they'd come over. I had more fun and met more of these girls. It was incredible.

I did that for four or five years, until my father got really, really sick. He broke his hip and never recovered. He was just starting into full-fledged Alzheimer's. So my sister arranged to get him around-the-clock nursing. I moved to Cape Cod to be near him.

One thing about being my age on the Cape: women were wonderful. They were discreet and grateful as hell. My father lived a few towns over, which was good, except he thought I never needed to work. So if he decided that he and one of his cronies wanted to do something, he'd call me at seven on a Monday morning. After my father died in 1998, I left the Cape and moved near my daughter, where I've been ever since. I've picked up part-time jobs. I took a job working for a courier company and did that for about five years.

A while back I sold my condo, and took some of the proceeds and helped my daughter get her beauty salon started because she wanted her own business. It's a good arrangement. She has her salon in a house with a pool, the whole nine yards, and it has in-law quarters. So I gave her the dough, the down payment, to buy the place, and I've been living there ever since, and doing as little as possible. Just totally relaxed. About six months ago I picked up another job where I work a couple of hours a week. I pick up a developmentally disabled guy from work two days a week and take him home. Lately, we're developing a good relationship.

I was lucky that retirement occurred as it did. I did what I wanted when I was young. I have an acquaintance who just turned sixty-six. I feel bad for him because he is now doing what I did thirty years ago.

The biggest plus of retirement is that I'm not anxious and worried on Sunday nights, which I was for years. Sunday nights were a bummer. I'd be running through my mind everything I needed to get done on Monday. I don't have to do that anymore. It's totally relaxing. You know what I'm consumed with now? The Red Sox.

I don't play golf as much I used to. I didn't have any goals when I first retired, nor do I now. I've pretty much gone through life without goals. I think about the only goal I ever really had when I was a working stiff was how much money can I make. I was always very lucky that I was in a position, or put myself in a position, where I could make lots of money. Now I'd like to live to see the Sox win the World Series again.

I have come to one conclusion: I was much better looking thirty, thirty-five years ago. I keep looking in the mirror and that's what it tells me. But I have finally figured out the cure for this decline in appearance. I started buying lottery tickets twice a week for Mega Millions. If I hit, I will become instantly handsome and all the young women I'm drooling over will come running.

I've enjoyed every single job that I've ever had. Enjoyed them to the max. But got to the point with each one of them: time to move on.

I would like to be as healthy as I was thirty years ago. I have some health problems now, peripheral artery disease for which I have had surgery. They did a bypass on me all the way from my crotch down to my ankle. I have an aneurysm on my aorta. I also have COPD. I'm not sure about the aneurysm, but the PAD and the COPD are strictly my fault, because I've been smoking cigarettes for over fifty years. Still smoking, about a pack a day.

Occasionally I have wondered why the good Lord has left me here past my expiration date. There has to be a reason. And I'm not sure what it is yet. I was a very spiritual person until the priests' scandal. It impacted me tremendously. Before that, Mass every Sunday. I took my kids to Mass every Sunday. Was really into that. And then I got to the point that I did dwell on that a little bit and I got really pissed.

I've been very lucky. I have enough to do what I want. If I decide to go to Florida and visit my granddaughter when it gets cold up here, I can do that. A lot of people aren't able to do that. Over the last seven or eight years, I've been to Jamaica about twice a year.

I don't think old relationships ever really go away. Honestly, don't think they ever do. There is always that tie there somewhere, and especially if you have children. But the whole thing depends on how you want to handle it. I was very bitter, where I shouldn't have been bitter. For crying out loud, when my first wife and I got divorced, I got to keep the house and I bought her one the next town over. I wanted to make it convenient to pick up the kids on the weekends.

The worst part of retirement is the worse part of life. Getting old. And like I said to a nurse the other day, "Do yourself a huge favor, don't get old." Old sucks. Because you can't do what you did thirty-five years ago. Don't look as good.

At this point in my life I prefer retirement to work. But going back twenty to thirty years ago, absolutely work. I used to thrive on that. Loved working. I used to love to get out there, especially when I had my own sales company. I loved the challenge of going out and selling somebody something.

One thing I'd like to do, am absolutely going to do, is write about some of the things I've done over the years with my friends. Some of it is just hilarious. I could keep you going for months. I'm going to. Absolutely I'm going to at some point. But, like, six more people have to die before I can write it. If you wrote down half the things that I was involved in over years...Oh my God, it was funny.

# V. SPORTS

# "It's All Connected"

## NAT GREW
Born 1937

When I first asked Nat to participate in this project, he was unsure of what he could offer. He viewed his life—family, work, and sport—as fully integrated, and the concept of retiring from one seemed to him a kind of death. At seventy-five, the ranch owner, extreme-endurance athlete, philanthropist, and expatriate New Englander lived a life of adventure, sport, and environmental activism on his vast tract of Costa Rican beachfront. Days after my request, he competed as the oldest athlete in an Olympic-distance triathlon (one-mile swim, twenty-four-mile bike ride, six-mile run). Two days later, he suffered a serious accident while riding his bicycle through the rainforest near his home. His injuries required surgery and threatened to end his athletic career. For Nat, this was a dire prospect. It was also an object lesson in what he believes to be one of the guiding principles of life: that crises mark every stage of our development, and that we must view them as opportunities to reflect, learn, grow, and change. In this spirit, Nat began writing his life history and, a few days later, phoned to say that he would like to be part of the book.

Nat was raised in a wealthy Massachusetts family that had lost a significant part of its fortune during the Great Depression. At thirteen, he was sent to a military academy in Maryland. During his summers off from the academy, Nat lived and worked on a large ranch in Wyoming. Influenced by this experience, he decided to become a veterinarian.

After college, Nat decided against a conventional career path. Instead, he moved to Haiti to work in a community development program. Though he planned for a two-year tenure, he was fired after only six months. Stung, he returned to the United States, enrolled in graduate school, obtained a degree in epidemiology and virology, and married. At thirty, after the birth of his first child and a brief tenure in a veterinary practice in Kentucky, Nat won an NIH grant, permitting him and his family to move to Costa Rica, where he planned to spend two years researching tropical diseases. Again, after a year and a half, Nat lost his position: his funding was cut and he was once more left to face an uncertain future.

It was at this point—in the midst of the greatest crisis he had ever experienced—that Nat decided to change his life. He purchased a large, isolated ranch, hours from the closest town and accessible only by barely passable roads. The ranch was successful almost immediately, and Nat's business interests began to flourish. Soon, he acquired a five-thousand-acre ranch on the Nicoya Peninsula and a coffee farm near San Jose. In later years, he also acquired extensive real estate holdings throughout the United States. As he transformed himself from a fledgling man of science to a flourishing man of business, exercise became a foundational part of his life. In 1983, he participated in his first triathlon. Since then, Nat has been a fixture on the extreme-endurance competition circuit. For example, he competes in one-hundred-mile ultra-marathons and in bike races through La Rut de los Conquistadores, a punishing three-day trek across rainforest roads and over eleven-thousand-foot mountain passes. In 2007, at seventy, he won the Xterra Off-Road Triathlon World Championship for his age group. In 2012, he repeated the same feat in the over-seventy-five category.

In recent years, Nat has deepened his commitment to the environment. In conjunction with his alma mater, Cornell University, and the Costa Rican government, Nat and his family established a nonprofit organization, CIRENAS, dedicated to the preservation of marine ecosystems, as well as to various educational and community outreach initiatives.

L ife demands change—it's the only constant. And before we can change, we need to pass through a period of uncertainty and vulnerability. To move on, we have to shed our protections.

In one sense, retirement may seem like a crisis. To let go—to take a new step—it takes a lot of courage. As my own life has unfolded, I've experienced crises before every new stage of development. These were times of great vulnerability and spiritual dilemma. I had no answers. I was forced to question the meaning and purpose of everything, and to examine and adjust my values. It's been a constant, unending process of exploration. I was raised as a Unitarian, but I've found comfort in Taoist principles—trying to stay detached and positive.

From birth to death, I think that we're all essentially alone. I was on my own when the umbilical cord was cut. I was on my own when I got on that train and went down to military school. It was a harsh place, and not by any means a prep school. I was also on my own in my teenage years, in the summers, when I lived out west and worked on a ranch. For me, adolescence was a stormy time. Some of that inner turmoil has stayed with me.

After college, professional achievement became the most important thing. I wanted to be someone so badly. At the same time, I wanted to explore and to experiment—to be someone by being different. So I didn't take the traditional path. I went to work in Haiti. Later, I went to work in Costa Rica.

I lost my job twice during that period. Back then, that was the worst experience of my life. It affected my well-being. I remember being on a plane back to the States after losing my job for the second time. My self-esteem was zero.

Soon, reality dawned. I realized I was trying to do something that I was never really very good at. Trying so hard to be someone by being different had led me astray.

Buying a ranch changed my life completely. It was hugely successful and paid for itself almost immediately. Suddenly, I was doing what I loved and it was paying off. Being close to the land, the physical activity of the ranch, combined with the surfing and training, it brought my mental and physical health to new heights.

But, after a few years, I lost that balance. I started thinking of myself as a master of the universe. I'd become oblivious to certain warning signs in my family life. My wife asked me to move out. Separation, isolation, loneliness, divorce—it surpassed any crisis I'd ever known. Once again, my protective structures had all fallen away. I felt raw, wounded, defenseless.

Three years later, I married again. It was a blessing. After that, the years flew by.

I found another balance. I began participating in triathlons and extreme-endurance competitions. Again, my physical and mental health improved and expanded to new levels. Today, my lifestyle is holistic. Family, work, sport—they're all integrated.

Ranching has been my occupation for forty-three years. Not too long ago, my son took over the operation. Family businesses can be rough. I can't completely let go. I try to be diplomatic and helpful, but

I'm constantly looking over the shoulders of the new managers, giving them ideas.

Our nonprofit venture, CIRENAS, has also been extremely successful. We've got a semester-abroad program going, with students from different backgrounds, all set up in a beautiful, untouched environment: five thousand acres of pristine ocean beaches, bordered and sheltered by two huge river systems. Working with young people is the best thing. And there's nothing more satisfying than trying to improve the environment and to make the planet a better place. It's amazing what that type of work does for you.

It's hard to explain why I do the endurance events. It's like asking why you love something. I think it goes back to having a strong sense of individual identity. When I went to military school, I had to get tough or I would've ended up in a straightjacket. It starts that far back. It builds. You start doing things that make you tougher. You keep doing them and your capacity grows. Today, I do what I can when I can. I don't have a schedule, but if I don't do something physical, I feel it. Most days, I like to get out early in the morning, alone, and be out in nature.

These events aren't "competitions," not really. They're about preparation, participation. The experience of participating in something like that teaches you so much. You stop thinking. You get into a meditative state. The little monkey on your shoulder stops jabbering away, so to speak. It's very healthy. The intensity of that type of exercise involves your whole body, of course, but also your whole mind and spirit. It's taught me not to think of the body and the mind as separate. That principle applies to other aspects of life, too. For example, I don't entirely separate my marriage and family life from my business life. If I did, one of them would fail. It's all connected.

[*At this point, Nat was asked what guidance he would offer to people who lack his level of financial security.*]

Why think that way? Why compare? Just get out and live in a way that matters to you. Also, that question misses a big point. Like Willa

Cather said, there are only two or three human stories and they go on repeating themselves forever. We've all got the same genetic makeup. We're all just going through life with the same feelings of vulnerability and anxiety. I ride the roller coaster, just like everybody else. I try not to, but I do. I'm high, I'm low—it's tough.

Some people our age think that their worlds are shrinking. But they're not. Our worlds are expanding, always. There's always opportunity around us. If you don't like your situation, change it. The right frame of mind is everything. Believe that anything bad that happens can turn out to be something good. Believe that. Don't fear it. Change.

If my knee recovers from the accident, I hope to participate in a hundred-mile run to benefit an adaptive-sports organization, which provides opportunities for people with handicaps and disabilities to participate in outdoor sports. The athletes involved in that organization demonstrate the importance of having the right frame of mind. They face unbelievable physical challenges, but they keep going. It's incredibly inspiring.

I've been close to death eight times, but I'm not afraid of dying. My grandfather died at seventy-seven. My father died at seventy-seven. Today, I'm seventy-five. If I've only got another two years, I say let's get this thing done. It's like Gabriel Garcia Marquez wrote: "Death did not matter to him, but life did."

I'm living in the moment. My recent bike crash and injury brought that to the fore. I'm going to do everything possible to recuperate fully. The stakes are high. I want to maintain my lifestyle, which I love. But, yes, there'll be changes. I know that. That's the way it is.

I'm not trying to ignore the future or disregard the past. Like I said, it's all connected. How you live today flows from how you lived yesterday. So, yes, I'm focusing on the present. And I'm in love with it, with this moment—with right now.

# *"Tide's In, I'm Out"*

## GEORGE BOSSI
### Born 1935 – Retired 2003 – Unretired 2011

George Bossi was born in Brockton, Massachusetts, known locally as the "City of Champions." The home of Rocky Marciano and Marvin Hagler, it is famous for producing legendary fighters. Bossi embodies the spirit of the city, and today, at seventy-seven, still looks ready to take on all comers. Perhaps more remarkable than his physical bearing is his booming voice. "You've reached the mouth of the Merrimack River," he announces on his answering machine, "tide's in, I'm out." In its strength, clarity, and authority, George's voice recalls thunder, rumbling waves, earthquakes. His handshake suggests a wrestling match—he goes in strong and stays in until achieving a decisive pin.

Sports have always been at the center of George's life. He was an accomplished athlete, excelling in football and track. In college, he discovered a passion for the sport of wrestling. In his senior year, he began working as an assistant coach, helping to train his more junior teammates. After graduation, he earned a master's degree at the University of Illinois. There, he served as an assistant football and wrestling coach, taught classes, and helped the athletic department with recruiting. Though he loved his life at the university and enjoyed the Midwest, he missed being close to the ocean and decided to return to Massachusetts.

Around this time, wrestling was a new sport in the area: only sixty secondary schools in New England offered programs (today, there are more than five hundred). In 1964, George was hired by the large blue-collar city of Lowell, Massachusetts, as a teacher and football coach, and was asked to establish a wrestling program. Starting from nothing, he created the dominant public high school wrestling program in the state, and served as its head coach from 1964 to his resignation in 2003. During his coaching career, he amassed more than 611 victories, was elected to the Massachusetts Interscholastic Athletic Association Hall of Fame, and was recognized by having the preeminent wrestling tournament in the region named in his honor.

After retiring, George remained involved with the team and with the larger scholastic wrestling community. In large part, he spent his time focusing on other pursuits. He is divorced and lives alone, but loves being around his three sons and eight grandchildren. George's house sits beside a system of tidal marshes, at the confluence of four estuaries, within yards of where the Merrimack River empties into the Atlantic Ocean. It is a fisherman's paradise and, since childhood, George has been the consummate fisherman.

His retirement was proceeding according to plan—fish, spend time with family, fish some more—until the coach who succeeded him left the program. Now, at age seventy-seven, George has been rehired as head coach. He is the subject of a soon-to-be-released documentary, *Bossi.*

I'd been looking forward to retirement, but it just hits you so suddenly. I didn't understand what a change it would be. I'd always been a real go-go-go type of person and then, suddenly, a lot of those day-to-day responsibilities are gone. That first year I retired, right after wrestling season ended and before saltwater fishing season began, I kept saying to myself, "What am I going to do? What am I going to do?"

I started fresh-water fishing. Soon, I was fishing almost every day. Those years, my routine was two or three hours in the boat, then the gym, then projects around the house.

Now that I'm back to coaching, my routine is different. During the season, I'm on the phone in the morning quite a bit, arranging things for the team. I go to the gym around noon, and practice goes from two to six. We also practice on Saturday. I probably lose a lot of kids because of that, but that's the way the sport is. You've got to give something up if you want to grow.

One of the reasons I decided to come back to coaching was to revitalize the program. I have no ego as far wins and losses, as long as we do our best. I just want us to be competitive, to say that our program is back. So we're reestablishing our feeder system, getting the sport going in the middle schools. It'll take about two or three years to see results. I don't know if I'll still be involved when the changes start to happen, but I know they'll happen.

We start the season with fifty kids and end up with thirty. I don't cut anybody. Kids drop out, but I don't cut them. If they miss practice, they don't wrestle. If they have problems, they have to see me. Everything's up-front. I'm a disciplinarian. I have to be. And the kids, they have to conform. Show up at practice, put the hours in, stay in shape, watch what you eat. They have to learn the discipline along with the technique.

I've been coaching for so long, it's second nature. I've developed a system, which is a big part of my success, that, and my drill-sergeant delivery. I bark the orders; they follow.

But I'm not just an SOB, I'm also a teacher. I like the kids; I do. And you can really make an impact on their lives. That's one of the big reasons I came back to work as a head coach. At this point in the year, I'll start making sure the kids' grades are good. I get on them, let them know I'm interested. I want to talk to them, eye to eye, make sure they're on course.

Right now, there are a few kids that I'm concerned about. A few have been caught smoking pot, stuff like that. I'll change that. Once I get them hooked on wrestling, they'll straighten out. Some of these kids, the ones who start off in trouble, they turn out to be my best wrestlers. That's a great, great satisfaction.

I've got a good rapport with the kids. I can make them listen. My biggest reward is to see how my coaching helps them to stay focused and accomplish their goals. By doing that, the kids become better people. No question about it. We can change lives. These kids can become better students, stay focused on their education, and do the right thing.

When I look back, I feel I've made an impact on a lot of people. That's the most gratifying thing about teaching and coaching for such a long time—fifty years. I get cards, calls. We have a reunion. I get kids from the '60s that come back. From New York, New Jersey, all over. They stay in touch.

These days, if I could, I'd increase the amount of time I'm involved in the school. I'd come in a little earlier, substitute teach a bit. Spend more time, accomplish my goals as mentor a bit quicker. Now, my biggest challenge is to see how I'll hold out with the rigors of coaching.

If I'm not active, I force myself to go to the gym. Physical well-being sets everything else up. Exercise cleanses the mind, gets you focused. If the body feels good, the mind will be active. Sometimes, I come out of the gym feeling like I could walk on water. Still, other times, the hardest part is just getting out of bed and getting there. So I discipline myself. It's like anything else. If I don't get up at five thirty in the morning, if I'm not the first one out on the water, I'm not going to catch any fish. I'm going to miss the big one.

What do I love most about fishing? Being out on my own. Being in the wilderness, in a foreign environment that can turn hostile. Also, the serenity of it. Getting out there and watching the sun rise in the morning. It's remarkable. You're communing with nature.

I never thought about retiring and going off to some island. Instead, I'll just cut back a bit and still do what I like. If I gave up coaching, I'd probably go south and get a job being an assistant coach or something. Of course, I'd still fish. Not going to change that.

Retirement has given me more time to think about religion and purpose. I'm a Catholic and I want to practice my religion as well as I can. I go to church often, but I'm not like some, who might feel they're getting near their time and preparing themselves. I haven't reached that point.

Also, I like opera and I like to cook. And I've always liked dogs. My own dog died not too long ago. At first, I thought about getting a young pup. Lately, I've decided against that. I'll go to a shelter. I'll get myself an older dog.

I want to keep going. I'm lucky that I still have wrestling and fishing. I don't know how I'll adapt when I'm forced to slow down. I'll just take it as it comes. Maybe I'll start traveling, stuff like that. I've been to Italy twice, to Milan, where my family is from, and to Florence and Rome. But travel is not a real goal for me. I'd rather be doing things.

Actually, all my travel dreams relate to fishing. I've fished on the Keys, for bonefish, snook, sea trout, small tuna. I've been to Alaska six or seven times, to the Kenai Peninsula to chase salmon. I'd go every year if I could find other people to come along.

You know who I envy? Those guys on TV, on that show about deep-sea fishing. They're out on that ship, way off the coast of Alaska. I'd like to try that.

# "Off to the Races"

## TOM AND ELEANOR GALLAGHER
### Born 1936 (Tom), 1943 (Eleanor) – Retired 1996

Tom is a retired corporate lawyer and Eleanor a retired PhD marine biologist. Before retiring to a horse farm in Southern Pines, North Carolina, they lived in New Hampshire, Minnesota, and Massachusetts. Eleanor made family, career, and lifestyle choices to support Tom's career. For years, Eleanor would volunteer, working with ophthalmologists, to bring vision care to poor villages in Latin America. These efforts often involved living in politically turbulent and dangerous conditions.

Tom and Eleanor shared interests in exercise and sports, particularly in tennis and skiing. Their interest in skiing has waned—"it's too cold"—but their other interests have flourished.

Initially, Eleanor's energies were devoted to rebuilding and remodeling a ramshackle farmhouse and horse barns into living space. She lived on the construction site for two years until the project was completed. The finished project reflects her artistic vision as well as the couple's roots, family, and passions: pictures, artwork, antique furniture, and architectural elements salvaged from courthouses, churches, and mills in their hometowns.

They have eight children and nine grandchildren, most of whom live in the Northeast but visit frequently. One grandchild lived with them until going off to college. They also have Roxie, a very affectionate boxer, who has the run of the farm.

**Tom and Eleanor found Southern Pines and their retirement home by chance. Eleanor long had an interest in horses and the equestrian sport of combined driving. (The sport involves driving a four-wheeled carriage with a single horse or teams of two or four horses. It has three events: presentation and dressage, cross-country marathon, and obstacle cone driving. The carriage team consists of the horse, driver, and groom. The groom serves as a navigator and attends to safety concerns. He has the task of using his strength and weight to keep the carriage balanced and upright over rough terrain.) The opportunities for involvement in the sport were limited in Massachusetts. On a trip to Florida, they stopped in Southern Pines for a horse show and a combined driving event. The show was exciting and the area was a hotbed for equestrian sports. After the event, they asked to see some properties.**

ELEANOR: The realtor told us there was a barn for sale, but it's not a home, just a barn. We drove up on a rainy day. The horses, twenty of them, were in the stalls, all looking out their windows as we came up the driveway. The minute I saw that, I said, "Oh, Tom, we're going to buy it! We're going to buy it!" And Tom said, "Oh no, not this again!" The realtor said, "You know it's not a house. You can't live here!" I said, "We'll buy it! We'll buy it! This is it! We're going to buy it!"

TOM: I said, "Wait a minute! How much is it?"

ELEANOR: We bought it the next day. The stalls or wings of the house were like huge arms extending out to welcome you.

TOM: This was Nirvana for horses. Plus, once we finished the restoration of our old home in Massachusetts, we were ready for a change.

I first started thinking about retirement as the company and industry were going through layoffs. They're not fun. The company was evolving away from its roots. Then, it dawned on me that I've got all the numbers I need for retirement. I was as financially ready as I was ever going to be. I loved what I had done for work. I enjoyed going to work every day. It was challenging, fun, and I enjoyed the people, but there was nothing to be gained by staying. That combined with an attitude, "Hey, let's see what Southern Pines has to offer..."

The other side of it was that I had had my career and Eleanor had been very supportive of that, and maybe it was time for her to have her turn. Neither one of us knew how much we were getting into with her turn. But we found out!

ELEANOR: I thought the weather is wonderful, it's a beautiful area... I was tired of the ice and snow in New England. It was difficult caring for a horse when you're trying to put the water in its bucket and it's frozen.

TOM: Pushing wheelbarrows in two feet of snow is no fun.

ELEANOR: It was a new project. I was going to get a chance to do another restoration project.

TOM: We were not yet into the ultracompetitive horse carriage stuff. That was to come.

ELEANOR: Nor, at that time, did we intend to become so intensely competitive. It was the house...I knew what I wanted to do...it was another project that would occupy me.

TOM: And there was tennis and golf. We were both avid tennis players, and this area is huge on golf.

ELEANOR: It was a dilemma because Tom was not a horse person and the area didn't have any indoor tennis courts. It was a good thing he had a chance to go back and forth to Massachusetts while he got adjusted.

TOM: The town was beautiful and the climate was superior to New England. It was a retirement, a chance to do things we hadn't done before. It was working on a farm. It's a whole new adventure.

ELEANOR: He hated the farm. It took him a while. My primary interest was working on the house and getting a horse. I had asked a friend, who lives in the area and was a seven-time national champion and who had been to the World Championship fifteen times, to help me find a horse. After about a year, he called and said, "I found a horse.

I've got a video." The minute I saw this horse, I said, "Oh my God!" I couldn't believe it. But he was pricey. My friend suggested we go to Europe to look at the horse before deciding. I said, "No, we'll just buy him." He said, "You can't do that." I said, "No, we'll just buy him. I feel it in my bones; this is the horse for me."

TOM: This was a spectacular horse, absolutely spectacular, the Michael Jordan of horses.

ELEANOR: His name was Kashmier and he was shipped over. The day he came, everybody came over to see this magnificent horse. He was black, with white markings on his face and legs. He was gorgeous, gorgeous.

TOM: The horse had just got off a ship from New York and was keyed up.

ELEANOR: I thought he would want some grass from that pasture and to move about. I started out with him. He kicked me and knocked me down. I thought, *If I don't get my breath I'll die, but this horse is really beautiful.*

TOM: Over her objections, I insisted that she go to the hospital. She had severed her liver and there was danger of internal bleeding. She was kept immobile in the hospital for seven days and then spent several months at home recuperating.

ELEANOR: Then it was "off to the races." We had the horse, and a past champion to teach me to drive and make me a champion, and he did!

TOM: For years we spent every day out in that field with the horse... seven to eight hours every day for ten years, practicing all the events... learning to guide the carriage through the obstacles and how to take the turns.

ELEANOR: The body that governs equestrian sports selects three individuals to represent the US at the World Championships. To be selected you have to compete for over a two-year period. Those with the best scores are selected. Then they compete against one another to get down to five or six and from that they pick three. After two years we were selected.

Tom: During that two-year selection period, we'd go on competitive tours. Beginning in January, we'd go on tour. We'd have to trailer a horse, carriages for the dressage and marathon events, and supplies to international shows in Ocala, Florida, then home; then to Georgia, then home; and so on, to shows back here in Southern Pines, and then on to Pennsylvania and New Jersey and up to Quebec. This is the spring show season, six or seven shows from January/February up through June. So, you're always on the road, packing, unpacking, and training. In the fall, it starts all over again.

Eleanor: In 2002, we were selected for the World Championships in France. We were third in presentation, and had won the dressage test. But on the day of the dressage event, Kashmier got thrown off his game by reflected sunlight, which caused him to see many reflections of himself, and he would not go near the judging booth. The dressage was technically perfect but only done in three-quarters of the area.

Tom: After 2002, we kept doing it. Eleanor was driving and I was helping with balancing the cart and actually moving it by lifting and shifting weight in the turns, shouting directions, and keeping track of obstacles over the courses. It's strenuous.

Eleanor: We got our granddaughter involved. She's the youngest driver to ever compete at a national event.

Tom: It really provided a great way to bond with her...doing something together.

Eleanor: Our event, the singles, was coming up again in 2006, and we were selected again to go to Rome.

Tom: They go to school for this in Europe—driving, eventing, horse handling—they make a living doing this. This is a sporting activity for us, but a business for them. Their trailers are covered with logos, just like NASCAR, and there's prize money. They televise it everywhere. There's a formal closing ceremony in a grand stadium every day. It's loaded with spectators waving handkerchiefs and cheering.

Eleanor: What I love about the sport is the people. They're so compassionate. Anybody who competes at this level...has an empathy for their horse. You have to be able to read your horse, or you're dead. These are big, strong, sometimes nasty animals.

What counts with folks active in the sport is your ability, your empathy for your animal, and your involvement in the community that matters.

Here, the neighbors are open and friendly. Up north, I didn't know my neighbors. Here I know everybody. We've made a lot of friends, and got to know them very well, who are good sports and good people with animals. It's very hard to make such friendships in your sixties, even just one.

Tom: It's the shared activity and shared community. The community does so many charity events. It's all about how you feel about your neighbors and how they feel about you.

When you work so hard to get the horses ready for events, it's grueling. Only folks who are doing the same thing know how hard you work, and that's a bond.

Eleanor: Never in my life did I think retirement would be so good.

Tom: More so, more so! The climate is hugely beneficial for outdoor activities...but it is the community.

Eleanor: In addition to the people, I love the oneness with the horse. Taking an incredibly large animal and training him. When you go into a hazard...you're really focused. I don't hear anything. I don't see anything. All I do is see my horse. You could get killed. That's part of the attraction. It's not the winning. I mean, I'm very competitive. If you have seven hazards and you do even one perfectly, you can remember that and think about it the next day.

Tom: The danger is not an attraction for me. That field is not where I want to die. The groom is balancing the carriage, sliding it, telling the driver instructions and directions, navigating and keeping time, because there's an overall time goal for the marathon.

The hazards are set up only a few inches wider than the carriage. Getting a horse to pull a carriage through them at speed is a challenge, and if you do it right, it's an accomplishment. We're constantly talking to each other and yelling encouragement to the horse. It's teamwork, and it has all the excitement of any competitive sport.

After the 2006 World Championships, we decided to scale back our level of competition. We retired some of the larger horses and got five Welsh ponies. Eleanor has started to learn to drive a four-in-hand, which is the most difficult driving activity there is. That is, four horses pulling the carriage. We'll compete here, but international competition is over.

ELEANOR: As you get older you don't want to compete at the highest level, because it would be foolish not to recognize that aging takes your abilities down a notch, but you can still compete at an intermediate level and have fun.

With the ponies, we've won everything we've been in. We've had them for six years, but we've not gone to the highest level. And we haven't needed to. It's been great. We've cut back and focused on involving our granddaughter. She drives them and she competes and we're involved.

TOM: We get a lot of satisfaction and fun going to a few shows a year.

ELEANOR: That's the truth. Any sport can bring you and your kids and grandkids together, but this is a lot more exciting.

[*Eleanor leaves conversation.*]

TOM: I made the decision not to go into legal work of any kind. I had opportunities. But I did that. Loved it. Time to do something else. I've been fortunate. This community is open and I've been able to get involved in a lot of activities. Some promote the sport, some environmental things. For example, I have been active in the Sand Hills Area Land Trust. We try to preserve land from development over a seven-county area.

Most satisfying, though, has been the volunteer work. For the last thirteen years, I have been volunteering at the hospital in the transportation department, taking patients from their rooms for tests. I found that when I first started, the patients were older, and I said,

"Well, I'm making a contribution and it makes me feel good." Now that I'm older, I find that most of the patients are younger than me. I feel good about that, but I think, *Aren't I lucky*. I've developed friendships at the hospital with the co-workers and with some patients. I find I'm a much nicer person as a result. Maybe I've been hardnosed, dealing with others at other times in my life, looking back at things...I find I'm nicer. I like myself much more and I'm doing something that benefits people and it's making me a better person.

I've gotten to appreciate my co-workers and their backgrounds so much. The area and the people have been the most broadening thing in the world for me. These are wonderful people.

[*Eleanor returns.*]

ELEANOR: They always call you "honey" and "dear" down here. You almost think they mean it. I think they do. One of my kids went to the local food store and couldn't believe it. The clerk talked to each customer in line and no one objected or asked them to hurry. Just the pace and the friendliness.

AUTHOR: Tom, at the start of our talk, you said that you approached retirement as a time for Eleanor to do her thing. Do you still see it that way?

TOM: Well, now that she's had her turn, my question is: Is it my turn again?

# *"Take the Time to Figure It Out!"*

## GERALD B. MOSES
### Born 1946 – Retired 1975, 1996, 2008

Jerry was born in Yazoo City, Mississippi. His dad was a baseball scout and his mom stayed home to raise Jerry, his brother, and two sisters. Jerry and his brother were very athletic. Jerry was a High School All-American quarterback and standout catcher in baseball. He was recruited by top college football programs and was scouted by Major League Baseball teams.

After receiving four or five offers, Jerry signed as an amateur free agent with the Boston Red Sox for a bonus of $50,000. He became one of the few in the majors at eighteen, the youngest Red Sox to hit a home run, and, in 1970, the starting catcher and a member of the American League All-Star team. The following year began a series of trades that took Jerry to California and then to five other teams. In all, Jerry played nine years, appeared in 386 Major League games, hit twenty-five home runs, and compiled a .251 batting average. He retired at twenty-nine.

He then began a successful career as an entrepreneur and executive in the food-service business. He retired about three years ago when he was diagnosed with progressive aphasia, a degeneration of the front temporal lobe that is characterized by a disorder of language, speech, and memory.

Jerry has been married forty-three years, has two children, and six grandchildren, all of whom live within a mile. He is also close to his mother, his siblings, and some of his old teammates. Today Jerry teaches hitting four to five days a week and, with an occasional assist from his daughter, coaches his grandkids' baseball teams.

When the pros were trying to sign me, my dad set the ground rules. It wasn't going to be an auction. He told them the price, and said we'd pick the best opportunity for me from the teams that met the price. He rejected some efforts by teams to top any other team's bid. I probably could have held out for more, but we, my mom and dad, were happy, so that's how it happened, and I'm not crying. Whatever I did or became was because of my mom and dad, how I lived my life all the way through.

Two days after high school graduation, I was playing in the New York-Penn League, living with four other players. I couldn't understand anybody up in New York or Massachusetts. The next year, because of rules related to free agents, the Red Sox had to play us or risk losing us in the next draft. So, I appeared in a few Major League games when I was eighteen. I was a raw kid with some talent, but wasn't ready for the majors. Jim Lonborg and I came up together and shared an apartment for a while. He was an unbelievable person, very savvy, out of Stanford. Here I was from Mississippi, but we melded pretty good. After those brief required appearances, I was sent down for seasoning and played in North Carolina. I was young, and there's a lot of knowledge and experience that goes into being a Major League catcher.

It took a long time to be able to catch and do what other guys did in other aspects of the game, but there was never a time I couldn't hit a baseball. It was a God-given talent. But the thing that hurt me the most was I had two all-time greats as hitting coaches, two baseball guys I admired more than anybody, other than Mickey Mantle. They took me and tried to change me. Ted Williams said, "Swing up." Bobby Doerr said, "Swing down." I was stupid enough to listen and they basically made me into a line drive hitter. If I had just listened and done what I wanted, well, that's shame on me. I didn't understand anything when I got to the big leagues.

I got married in 1968. We met in that Impossible Dream season, 1967, when the Sox won the pennant for the first time in over twenty years. We've been married forty-three years. It's wonderful. She's a stronger person than I am in a lot of ways. I'm glad I met her. This is the road I wanted to go and she tolerates me, so...

I left baseball in 1975, but started thinking about leaving the year before. A local business guy was the CEO of a national food-service business, including the local racetrack. He said, "Whenever you're ready." He gave me an opportunity. I spent eleven years with that company, learning the business, managing locations like the racetrack and the Superdome, and getting into sales. Made more than I ever did in baseball. During this time, I developed a real good relationship with local concert producers and had their venues.

About this time, an old Red Sox connection, a guy who was an entrepreneur, and I were going to open up ten fast-food chicken franchises. I told my boss and he was very supportive. He told me if it didn't work out, I could come back. Then he said, "If you want that concert venue business, you can have it, because we won't be doing it without you." The concert promoters said, "Sure, Jerry," and the entrepreneur put up some cash. That's when I said, "Oh, my God!" We made money the first year.

My first money partner left and another guy came in his place. We had a good run for seven years. We grew to twenty-eight concessions at different venues. That's a pretty good number, but margins are low in food service. Anyways, we sold out, and I made some money, but had to work through a transition period. I was a salesman. I used to do pretty well.

I did that for a while, and then retired again. I was about fifty. It was great. I played golf on my home course for about a year, seven days a week. Then I got antsy and went back to work in food service, first with my old company and then with my old partner, until about three years ago. I was sixty-three.

I knew something was wrong. I had a terrible time remembering names. That was not like me. Once I ran a baseball camp with over three hundred kids and I knew every name. So something had happened and I knew it was wrong. I had to leave the business.

I went to Brigham and Women's Hospital. They gave me a CAT scan, an MRI. They were thinking that maybe I had concussions from getting hit a lot in football and baseball. But I didn't have any signs of concussion damage. So they sat me down and gave me a three-hour test. It had an easy part, a medium part, and a pure torment part. The easy part was they'd put a star in front of me, take it away and tell me to draw it. That was OK. Then they gave me some numbers, "three-one-four," and I'd say, "three-one-four." Then they'd say, "four-two-five-three," and I'd say, "four-two-three." I couldn't get it, the five was gone. When they got to the torment part, I was frustrated because I couldn't do it.

I went back two weeks later with my wife and kids, and got the diagnosis: progressive aphasia. I had never heard of it and didn't know how to spell it. They don't know how I got it. I've since learned that there's Alzheimer's, then there's dementia, and there's aphasia. They're all different and about 80 percent of those with aphasia get at least a good ten years. I'm about three and one-half into it now. I take Aricept, so that's part of my life now...The Aricept helps. Without it I'd be a babbling idiot right now.

I have a great relationship with God, and I don't care if I die right now. My parents always went to church. I never miss Sundays and generally go four to five times a week. Spiritually I'm fine and whatever comes to me, I'll take. I'm not a preacher. I don't do that. I just know something better is coming.

I'm happy. I have a great wife and great children, and six grandchildren and another on the way. They're great kids. They're close and we spend a lot of time with them. The only regret I have is I feel like I let them down. I was doing very well, had a lot of money, but relied on some advice and lost a lot, a lot of money. I gave my kids some help, but I had wanted to pay to send my grandkids to college. I had wanted to do that for years. I just felt like...

When I understood that I couldn't get a job anymore, I just relaxed for a while and let it sink in. As it did, I figured if I were going to die, I'd want to die doing something good. So somebody asked me to help kids with hitting. I spend five to six hours a day, five to six days a week helping the kids. I feel really good about it. I'm doing something good. But I think now I owe my wife more time. I think we'll travel a bit, maybe Italy...Alaska, just take a boat ride on one of those cruise ships up the coast.

Right now I'm going to do stuff with my kids and grandkids. Maybe go down and see my mother.

I feel blessed. I've done most everything I wanted to do. I don't have many regrets, other than maybe I wish I'd kept my mouth shut when I was in baseball. I thought I knew more than I did. I don't think I ever tried to hurt anybody...I don't remember having any fights. Maybe in high school I'd act like I would fight, but I wouldn't. I was afraid I'd hurt somebody. I think I've been humble—got that from my mom and dad. Mom is the sweetest woman I've ever known.

The doctors told us that pressure is not good for me, but hell, I wouldn't have done anything without pressure. Sometimes, it's a good thing.

The baseball life, when I was playing, was the most important thing, plus I enjoyed it. But when I left, I left. I didn't miss it. I was looking for something else. Then business filled part of my life.

The only people who remember us are guys fifty, sixty, or seventy years old. When the Red Sox had their hundredth-year celebration and they brought all the players back to Fenway, there were probably forty-two thousand people, six thousand over capacity in the park. They didn't know who we were, and we didn't know who they were, either.

What hurts me so much about this disability is that I used to do a lot of public speaking, and I was good at it, I enjoyed it. But now I can't do that, even if it were written in front of me. It's not sad, it's not sad. I don't feel sad about it. I have a lot of friends from the old Red Sox and get a lot of support from them. We go away for a week and play golf. They are a source of comfort. We stay in touch. We call each other for nothing.

Prayer also helps. All you got to do is close your eyes. Nobody has to know. I'm not trying to make anybody else do what they don't want to do. I don't get down. Every day something good happens, but you got to take the time to figure it out. I make a point of doing that every day. I put up on the wall: God, family, something I can't remember, business. Ask yourself what's the most important things you want to do, and how much time you have to get them done. Concentrate on those things that are important. Pursuing my priorities is how I find meaning, and it leads to happiness. You can't get everything done all the time.

This interview hasn't been so bad—just like confession.

# VI. FAMILY

# "An Incredible Privilege"

# HON. RAYMOND L. FLYNN
Born 1939 – Retired 1993, 1997

*Ray Flynn (back row center) and the 1958 all state high school basketball team.*

Ray Flynn was the mayor of Boston from 1984 to 1993, after which he was appointed as the US ambassador to the Vatican by President Clinton. He served as ambassador from 1993 to 1997. Since leaving the ambassadorship, he has served as the president of two advocacy groups, the Catholic Alliance and the Catholic Voice. In addition, he has authored two books, *The Accidental Pope: A Novel* and *John Paul II: A Personal Portrait of the Pope and the Man.* He is a regular contributor to newspapers and magazines, and a popular and frequent public speaker.

During his political career, Ray developed close personal relationships with, and was deeply influenced by, Pope John Paul

II, Mother Teresa, and Nelson Mandela. These influences, combined with those of his faith, family, and neighborhood, continue to inform and drive Ray's character and activities.

Ray was born and raised in South Boston. His father, a longshoreman, was stricken with tuberculosis, and his mother provided for him and his siblings by cleaning offices nights in downtown Boston. His youngest brother died as an infant because the family, without health insurance, was denied care.

Growing up, Ray worked at a variety of jobs to help the family. He also relentlessly devoted himself to developing his athletic skills and earned a basketball scholarship to Providence College. There he became an All-American and the MVP of the National Invitational Tournament. He pursued his dream of being a professional athlete until he was the last player cut by Red Auerbach from the World Champion Boston Celtics.

He continues to live in South Boston with his wife, Kathy. It is a very close-knit neighborhood and Ray knows everyone. Ray and Kathy have six children and seventeen grandchildren, all of whom live close by and he sees often. Ray and Kathy frequently care for their grandson, Braeden, who was born with a small cerebellum, which impacts his physical and mental development. They focus all their energy on trying to help Braeden. This includes taking him to physical therapy, as well as praying, researching, speaking, and writing about the subject, meeting with doctors from around the world and the National Institutes of Health, and raising awareness of the condition.

W hen I was young, my goal—the biggest thing that I wanted from life, my ultimate dream—was to be a professional athlete. That was it. That's all that mattered. I had no interest in anything else. Certainly, I had no interest in politics. None whatsoever. Yet, here I am, "in politics."

Anyway, back then I put all my energy into athletics. I wanted to be the best that anyone ever saw. And I believed I could do it. I did. I was serious, committed. And I got pretty far, all the way to Boston Garden.

I'd done well in college ball and got a tryout with the Celtics. I played with them all through the preseason. Before I knew it, the preseason was over and I was still there. I started thinking—daring myself to think, really—that I'd actually made it. All that time, since I was small, I'd been dreaming of that one thing. The old Garden—the court and the banners and the crowds, the way it all looked and sounded. It was all right there in front of me.

But, of course, we're not here to discuss my career as a professional athlete, and so you can guess how the story ends. On the last night—the very last night before the season opener—Red Auerbach comes down and finds me in the locker room. He just looks at me and says—he was very plain about it—he just says: "Ray, its over." That was it. Last one cut. I'd run out of road. I thought, *If I stop at not becoming a Celtic, my life is over.* Suddenly, it was time to find something new. So, I adjusted. I had motivation and determination, drive.

Of course, I moved on. And, of course, I put all my energy into the next thing, and into the next thing after that, and so on and so on. And now, as I look back on it, I see that not making it was not the end of the world—far from it. It was the start of something new, something that I hadn't been able to see until then. It was an opportunity to change—a chance to adapt.

Which isn't to say that it wasn't difficult. At first, it was a real struggle. But, in the neighborhood where I grew up, I saw a lot of struggling. I saw people living lives that they didn't like and didn't want and never imagined for themselves. Putting off their dreams. Forgetting who they were. Feeling lost. Not seeing a first step, much less a finish line. Just never knowing how to get out of it. It's hard, God knows, having a dream, coming up empty all the time. Trying to carry on.

What I'm trying to say is that those kinds of experiences have helped me to think about aging and change. You could say that, in my life, I've retired multiple times. I retired from my life as mayor, from my life as a diplomat and as an ambassador. And, even earlier in my life, at each different stage, I retired from one thing and moved on to the next. Basketball is an example of that. A time and a season, you know. And also a time for what follows—a time to move on and to find out what's next.

I think that so much of your life—your priorities, your values, how you relate to others and to your community—I think that so much of that is determined by your childhood. Certainly, that's true in my case. My father was a dockworker. When I was a boy, he got sick. He was in and out of the hospital for about five years. Because of my father's illness, my mother was forced to work. We had a big family. And so she cleaned offices downtown.

What my mother did for our family was amazing, absolutely amazing. It's also amazing that, for her and for the rest of my family, that's what life had been like for generations. My grandfather was an emigrant. He'd tell us about life over there in Ireland. They were really up against it—terrible poverty, terrible oppression. Growing up in this neighborhood, I saw so much misery—people drinking too much, suffering from mental illnesses, struggling in silence and not getting the help they needed. That type of suffering rarely gets any attention. It's not addressed in the media. And, in the political arena, it's not addressed sufficiently—not as deeply and as substantially as it needs to be.

I also saw a lot of people holding on to grudges. One thing I've learned is to patch up any kind of bad relationships you might have had over the years. Don't wait until it's too late.

Anyhow, all of that—those experiences and stories and memories— all of that made me who I am. It formed every single part of me. It gave me my sense of drive, and it directed my sympathies and my focus. So, my drive and energy haven't changed, my basic priorities haven't changed. How could they? They're part of me. All that changed was my specific focus.

All my life, I think, I've been trying, in one way or another, to help the less fortunate. My mother and father always emphasized that. They'd say: "Treat everyone you see like the most important person in the world." That really stuck with me. I remember, one time when I was a kid selling papers over at Braves Field, I gave my bus fare to a stranger. He was really hard up, and I figured he needed it more than me, and I could just walk. So I was a couple hours late coming home. At first, my mother was angry. Then, I explained to her what I'd done. She said, "Well, all right, but remember that's the only excuse that'll work around here." Those instincts were planted right at the start—charity, good works, social responsibility. My circumstances have changed. But who I am and what I care about has always been the same. Like I said, it was planted in me, right here in this neighborhood, right from the start.

Of course, my background shaped my service as mayor. When I got some power and visibility, I made a point of going over to play ball with kids in Roxbury, or grabbing a beer with guys who'd just finished their shift, or standing in line with striking workers, or stopping on a training run at 4:00 a.m. to thank city workers for cleaning the streets.

My background also shaped my thinking. I've always approached policy issues, not just from an intellectual perspective, but also from an emotional perspective. Take health care. When I was young, my father lost his job and our family was left with no health insurance. Around this time, my younger brother died. He couldn't get the health care that he needed and he died. That always stayed with me. And so there's no way that I can listen to anyone talk about health care without thinking about my little brother. For me, the health-care debate isn't just a policy issue for me. It's an ethical issue, an emotional issue.

These days, one of the best things about my life is that I have more time to do the things that I want. I have the time to focus on issues like health care—issues that I care about and that I think are important.

I no longer hold public office. And yet, I feel that I have more power than ever to effect real change. I'm able to look at life and know what is really important. Any mayor can fill potholes; that's what they're supposed to do. But not everybody can make people feel good about themselves. I always had part of that in me, but I now have a deeper understanding of how important that is.

Today, I am frequently hired to speak to large audiences, and I take these engagements as opportunities to influence their thinking on important social issues. I do so by recounting some of the experiences I've had—building homeless shelters and soup kitchens, my interactions with Mandela, Mother Teresa, and Pope John Paul II. The stories are fascinating to the audiences and affect them deeply. The unifying message in all these stories is that every individual is valuable and should be valued—it's a powerful, uplifting message. Once the audience absorbs this message, they feel better about themselves. So, I get asked to speak year after year, even though the audiences have heard me before and even though they could well afford to go with someone from the world of sports or entertainment.

When I was mayor, I was dealing with day-to-day issues, and of course, those issues were critically important. But now that I've left office, the causes I'm working for, I think, are fundamentally more interesting and more consequential. Certainly, they're more personal.

For example, not too long ago I wrote a piece about my five-year-old grandson, Braeden, and about his medical condition. He was born with a small cerebellum, which makes it impossible for him to speak or to walk. We spend so much time with him. We love taking care of him, love just being around him.

Well, the piece that I wrote about him was published in the op-ed section of the *Boston Globe*. After it ran, I was told that it had the most online "hits" of any op-ed ever published by that paper. Of course, publicity isn't important, not in and of itself. What's important is what publicity can sometimes accomplish. As a result of that op-ed, I was invited to speak all around the world—Florida, California, Ireland,

South Africa—they saw the piece and asked me to come talk about my grandson and about his condition. I didn't expect that kind of reaction. Speaking in all those different places was a good experience—Braeden enjoyed it, too—and I know that we did some good. But I couldn't keep up with the invitations. I just couldn't. I don't want to just travel around talking about my grandson. I want to help him; I need to help him. And traveling and raising awareness isn't going to do it. I need to stay here and roll up my sleeves.

These days, I feel so driven, more so than ever. I've always been a determined person, but in these past few years I've found a new gear. I've become relentless. I need to help my little grandson. I'm constantly reviewing medical journals and articles and corresponding with research organizations about his condition. We need to help him get better. We believe in the power of prayer and we pray. But, it's an incredible challenge. But it's also an incredible privilege, to be able to work for him, to focus all my energy and attention on him. Working with the best doctors in the world, with renowned scientists, with the good people at the National Institute of Health. Taking Braeden to physical therapy. Just spending time with him. Getting to be here and getting to know him and to love him.

Every day, I walk down Broadway with my grandson. It's the same street in the same neighborhood that I used to walk when I was a little boy. Last night, it took us almost three hours to walk just three miles. We stopped and spoke with everyone. We met so many different people. When I was mayor, I never knew so many people; at least, I never knew them in the same way, with the same depth of connection and feeling.

These days, I feel like I know more about people than ever.

Sometimes—not too often, but sometimes—I think what it might be like to live my life over again. Don't get me wrong, I've been incredibly fortunate. I have my family and my faith, and because of that, I consider myself the richest man in the world. I do. And all the rest of it is just icing on the cake. I'm incredibly grateful.

If I had the chance to do it all over again, I wouldn't try to do different things. Instead, I might try to do the same things, only in a different order. For example, I'd like to wait a few years before becoming mayor. First, I'd spend a long time walking the streets of the city and talking to people and getting to know them. After about five years of that, I'd work for those people. I'd try to know them as well as I could so I could serve them as well as I could. That would really be something.

# "Nostalgia Isn't What It Used to Be"

## JOHN F. BURKE
Born 1936 – Retired 1993, 2009

**John has been married for fifty-two years and had eight children. He has twenty-seven grandchildren and one great-grandchild. Most live nearby. He sees them regularly and frequently takes care of them. After law school, he served as a judicial law clerk and then worked in the administrative office of the state supreme court. In this capacity he dealt with the press, all internal court matters, space and court requirements, broad personnel issues, the relationships among the various courts, as well as the relationship of the judiciary with the executive and legislative branches.**

I'm only the second person in my family to ever retire. My great-grandfather was a tenant farmer and he could not retire. He might reduce his workload on the farm until death or feebleness prevented him from working anymore, in which case his children would support him until death, sort of a charge running with the land. Sometimes children who had emigrated would send US dollar bills to help. They were known as "American letters."

My grandfather retired as a teamster for the Department of Public Works. He enjoyed that time accompanying his son-in-law, Danno O'Mahoney, a well-known wrestler, to matches in Montreal, Liverpool, and Ireland. My father died at forty-seven and never had a chance to enjoy retirement.

My first job was in the seventh grade for the public library, putting books back on shelves. I thought I was a big shot. I was getting forty cents an hour, but when I retired it was creditable service for pension purposes. They prorated it because I was only working two hours a night.

I had two retirements. The first was not a very happy one. I had worked for the state supreme court for more than twenty years and had very good working relationships, particularly with two successive chief justices. But that changed with a change in personnel.

So when the state offered an early retirement plan, I said, "The hell with this." I took the early retirement more to sever a relationship and to get some relief. It was premature; I wasn't sixty. So I understood that I couldn't sit around for the rest of my life. I had to do something gainful, whether for financial or mental health reasons, although mental health turned out to be the bigger one.

Shortly after this first retirement, I was asked if I'd come back to work on specifically assigned projects for the trial court. That was all right by me. I didn't have to put up with some of the tedious problems that I encountered before. I'd have specific projects. To some extent I could set my schedule. Also, I started teaching history and government to immigrants in a community college two days a week—something I found especially satisfying. All in all, it was an enjoyable arrangement. I felt useful. In addition, I started taking off more time than before and did some traveling. I visited relatives in Ireland a number of times, and took some trips to London, Mexico, Canada, the Southwest, what have you. So it was quite enjoyable, between the work for the court, the teaching, and the traveling. I did that from around 1993 until two or three years ago. During this period my wife's health was declining. She didn't travel; she didn't like to travel. At that point the real retirement set in.

The second retirement was mandatory because appropriations to the courts were running short, and they had to lay people off. From my point of view, the only fair thing, and what I proposed, was to start laying off the part-time people who already retired and had pensions.

The second retirement was inevitable, foreseeable. As I approached my second retirement, no, I wasn't really looking forward to it. But I wasn't anxious about it, either. I suppose you get to a point when your time has come and I was, what, seventy-three, seventy-four then, which is beyond the average retirement age anyway.

With retirement, you wake up the next morning and it's still the same as it was the day before. If you're healthy the day before, probably you're healthy the day after retirement. If you have a problem the day before, you'll have it the day after retirement. It's a continuum. There is no sharp change as far as I can see, except that your source and amount of income has changed and you don't have to go to work. And that's about it. Some, working at a reduced pace, may glide quite serenely into retirement without knowing it, or admitting it.

I think the tendency to identify yourself by your work gradually diminishes during retirement. The early restlessness fades. You have steadily less and less contact with the people you used to work with. You stop by the old office less frequently. You look at trade publications less frequently. You drift away from the old work-related material. Whatever prism you had before your professional life, whether hereditary or religious, you'll continue to have...but I wouldn't go around defining myself by my former profession. Some people are so caught up in their job status that when they're retired, it really shatters them. I can remember when mandatory retirement came in for judges. That really shook some of those guys. One judge wanted to be recalled to serve past his retirement; we wouldn't recall him; he was bordering on senility. So he called me up one day and he saw that there was an opening for a special master, who can do things like set bail. He wondered if he could be recalled to do that. I said we'd think about it. Then he asked, "If you call me back for that, could I wear my robes?"

Same thing with a lot of people in the military. Many have spent their lives with people at their beck and call. Everybody saluted. They have been kingpins. Facing forced retirement and the uncertainty of what to do caused one of my army battalion commanders to commit suicide. I don't think anybody cavalierly sheds the whole job over-night. And there is always some regret, especially if you think that things could be done better. You can't hang around forever. You can't be the boss forever.

There is no rhythm to the day. You get up and ask what is it that I should do, or would like to do today, and arrange your schedule ac-cordingly. I noticed, for the most part, that my time is unscheduled, but constantly subject to a variety of interruptions. Then I have to ask myself: What is being interrupted? What would my time be like with-out interruptions?

When I was working I really didn't have an organized hobby in any formal sense. Between work and family there was not much time for hobbies. Like, I never became a golfer. There were things I did. With the kids, I liked to take them camping in the summer; did a fair amount of fishing, but haven't done that in a few years. I caught eight stripers one day just off the beach nearby.

Some people have developed more connections or hobbies while working so it's easier for them to continue them. The person who kept his nose to the grindstone and had no contacts, no activities, then he's suddenly left in a position of having to invent a life for himself. And those are the people who can't say I want to continue, and play it by ear, and add and subtract as I go. That person is really stuck with noth-ing; he would have to invent a life. It's kind of late.

Now I'd say my social network is mainly my family. That has in-creased since retirement. Most of my time is spent on family situa-tions. Until a few years ago, all my kids and grandkids lived in this area. I see them frequently and deal with them.

Yesterday afternoon I spent babysitting for four of the grandchil-dren. A situation came up where my daughter needed somebody to watch the four kids for an afternoon and it fell to me. There is more of that relationship now and not work-related things...more in the role of caregiver to the grandkids and others. Grandchildren, that's one of the total changes. Entirely. You do have the opportunity to deal with them; watch them grow, maybe help them grow, and that can take a lot of time. It can be enjoyable. It can be annoying upon occasion as well, but you can't come in and just start lecturing them, "When I was a boy..."

There's more expanded activity within the family, and with a family this size it's only natural. You get to the point where just the normal course of events, the usual things that come up in families—the weddings, the christenings, first communions, confirmations, graduations, funerals, and so forth—that there is just more and more of those. It's not going to be a full-time occupation, attending wakes and things like that—unless you're a politician from the era of *The Last Hurrah*.

I had some objectives having to do with travel, places I would like to go and see. One place I would like to go, and I've been there before, is Italy, Rome, Assisi, Tuscany, up in that area. I like the scenery and the people, the food, the architecture, the history, the religious sites. It's a fascinating place. When I travel, I like to take a plane to a destination and then be scheduled to take a plane back at a certain date, and no fixed itinerary in between. Just go from place to place. I like the independence of being able to drive. Retirement has probably increased my appetite for doing such things, but commitments, especially to my wife, who has some health problems, have limited my pursuit of these things. Retirement is not a free ticket to go roaming the world.

There are the events that you witness in retirement and there are things that happened long ago that you reflect on in retirement. You see events in a different light now that you've had more time to think and reflect. It's because you're older and you've learned more, experienced more. I suppose the word is mellowed, somewhat. Could be wisdom. I'm more patient, I think. You adopt a more "to each his own" attitude. Anyway, I understand people see things from different perspectives. When you have had eight kids, you look at things differently.

Becoming a recluse and doing nothing is not healthy, which a number of people I know have done. I've seen it. One relative had to retire early because he had a couple of severe heart attacks. From that point on, his life was sitting at the kitchen table. You can't withdraw into a shell and become a recluse and not do anything. But it's not one size fits all. Everybody's in a different situation, but there are some general things that I suppose apply to everybody. Keep busy, keep active. Keep healthy; watch your investments; things like that. But beyond that, so much is going to vary with the individual. Some people enjoy travel, sports, charitable organizations, family. Different things that not only take up their time, but allow them to do something entertaining and, I hope, useful.

When I hear people talk longingly about earlier stages of life, I think of that old line: "Nostalgia isn't what it used to be."

# "A Spiritual Being That Needs to Be Nurtured"

## JAMES SHELDON
### Born 1935 – Retired 2004

Jim is seventy-six years old and has been retired seven years. He retired from a forty-year career in data processing for large commercial banks. He has been married to Prudence for fifty-two years. They met as kids in church-related activities in their small hometown in Michigan. Prudence has had Alzheimer's for fourteen years. They moved to a Methodist Church-sponsored retirement life center three years ago. Jim lives in a cottage on the facility's campus and Prudence is a patient in the nursing unit. Jim devotes his time to visiting Prudence and volunteering in numerous community and church service programs. They have a daughter, a son, and four grandchildren whom they see frequently.

I started thinking about retirement when I started working at First National Bank in Chicago. I was fifty-four. The company's program permitted you to retire at sixty-five, with at least fifteen years' service. My plans were to rent or buy a small motor home and travel. I envisioned coming across the Northern states as far as Massachusetts and down the East Coast to Florida, and over to Texas, Arizona, and Oklahoma to my brother's, just making a round of it, visiting family and friends, in a big circle. It was just a conception.

When my wife was diagnosed with Alzheimer's I didn't know what to think. I talked to some people just a few months after she'd been diagnosed. I had anticipated maybe two or three years she'd be in a nursing home. I had no idea what it would mean. But I learned. Some people survive twenty years after a diagnosis. Now she's in the nursing unit here at the retirement facility. But I took care of her in our cottage until last year. She's been in the nursing unit for a year now.

When she was first diagnosed, I was still commuting into Chicago and I'd have to leave her alone. I'd call her twice a day. I determined whether she had taken her medication by asking her to shake the pill bottle near the phone. If it rattled, I knew that she hadn't taken her medicine. I'm still surprised we got by. She was very complacent and cooperative and that helped. If I went to church meetings, Prudy would go with me.

It was just the way it was. She didn't complain at all. She enjoyed being out and doing things. That's what we did. This went on for seven years.

Retirement didn't turn out as anticipated. It changed because I had become my wife's principal caregiver. By the time I retired she was to the point where she needed me at home. And so, yeah, it's been somewhat of a disappointment. But, I keep busy, being with her and doing work in the church. I try to stay fit by being active. Every month they have a committee here that selects someone as being, displaying the spirit of service to the community and the church. I got that award back in May. I counted up seventeen volunteer jobs I am involved with—seventeen of them.

The most rewarding aspect of retirement is the time to do things for others, the time to do all the volunteer things that I do, the time to be active in the church. I had a reputation for being active in the church for years, but my calendar is even more tightly scheduled now. I do so much volunteering there is no question that I am fulfilled. My sense of optimism and well-being is fine. Retirement hasn't changed me in that regard.

My future goals and plans depend on Prudy's health. She seems to be doing quite well where she's at. She eats everything on her tray at mealtime, but since we've been here, I have seen some deterioration, but not much at all. So as long as she is still with me—and sometimes I do think about which one of us will go first—but as long as she is with me, I'm gonna be here. Sometimes, I'll think about what I'd do if Prudy were to pass away. I'd probably travel a lot more, probably to Tucson. Tucson is nice in the wintertime. I'd probably not get a camper at that point, just myself and a little red car.

While taking care of my wife, I read a book called *No Act of Love Is Ever Wasted* by Richard Morgan and Jane Thibault. It's about caring for people with dementia. The crux of the message was that no matter how out of it people with dementia seem, there is still a spiritual being there that needs to be nurtured. It helped me understand that and relate to my wife in that way.

She doesn't talk anymore. So our primary communication is that I go up and lean down where she's sitting in her wheelchair, I kiss her, and she responds to that, she kisses me right back. One time I was sitting next to her, on a Sunday afternoon, watching a movie on TV, and I looked over at her and she's sitting there with her lips puckered ready for a kiss. That's our basic form of communication, those kisses. The experience of caring for my wife has deepened my view of each person as a spiritual being.

# *"Sorry, Babe, I'm Booked"*

## STEPHEN KANDEL
Born 1927 – Retired 2001

Stephen Kandel has devoted his life to his family and to writing. The son of writer parents, he was raised between New York City, where his mother and father were active among a set of prominent Manhattan literati, and Hollywood, where his father enjoyed great success as a writer of feature films. Stephen's own career as a screenwriter and producer spans six decades—an almost unprecedented stretch of time in the entertainment industry. By some accounts, Kandel has written more television programming than any other writer. His list of credits reads like a history of American popular entertainment in the second half of the twentieth century: *77 Sunset Strip, Sea Hunt, Gidget, Batman, I Spy, The Wild Wild West, Mission: Impossible, Mannix, Star Trek, Barnaby Jones, Hawaii Five-O, The Six Million Dollar*

*Man, Charlie's Angels, The Dukes of Hazard, CHiPs, The Love Boat, Dynasty,* and *MacGyver.* Kandel also writes fiction, and has published several well-received short stories and novels. In addition, early in his career, he authored a comprehensive history of the Yiddish theater, which, in his words, "sold at least a dozen copies." Throughout his career, Kandel has placed primary emphasis on his family. In that regard, it was family that finally convinced Kandel to leave Hollywood. In the late nineties, he and his wife moved to the East Coast to be closer to their children and grandchildren.

I never wanted to be a writer—at least, not when I was young. My parents were both writers, so I fought against it. A natural reaction, I suppose. Teenage rebellion.

My father started out as a novelist and occasional playwright. Warner Brothers purchased the film rights to one of his books and dragged him out from New York to work on it. This was the 1930s. At that time, if you were working in the motion picture industry, you were toiling in a blessed Eden. Writers were earning $2,000 a week when many Americans were lucky to see that in a year. And writing for the pictures was like being on a very long, very well-paid holiday. Each week, your sole responsibility was to turn in five pages—five pages, that was it. And if you didn't submit those five pages, the studio would just say, very gently: "That's all right. We understand. Next week, please do try to finish those five pages." Hollywood isn't like that anymore, but it's still its own little planet, with its own peculiar customs and rules. It's an improbable world.

I'm thinking of one of my father's stories about that early period. In 1935, he was working on a film, *The Lives of a Bengal Lancer,* starring Gary Cooper, about a group of British soldiers in India during the Raj. During preproduction, the studio hired one of the original soldiers to work as a consultant—a very proper former officer of the British Army. He touched down in Hollywood, took one look at the production, and politely informed the studio that the whole thing was absurd: "Your facts are inaccurate, your story is preposterous," etc., etc. The studio thanked him but refused to make any changes. And so he spent all his time holed up in his office on the lot, collecting checks. After weeks of being ignored, he quit and went back to England. Now, a decade later, the studio decided to remake the same film. And they asked the same officer to be a consultant. Out of curiosity, I suppose, he agreed. The studio gave him a warm welcome and directed him to his old office, where, to his surprise, he found everything just as he'd left it. Everything was the same except for a tall stack of paychecks on his desk—one check a week for the entire ten-year period since he'd quit the original production and left Hollywood.

In those days, movie studios were profligate, and my father enjoyed profligacy as much as any man who ever walked the earth. On the other hand, my mother was a purist. After he finished a few movie projects, she'd remind him of his obligation to do serious work, at which point we'd all pack up and head back to New York. Then, before too long, we'd need money, at which point we'd all pack up and head back to Hollywood. So I grew up shuffling between the coasts. It was kind of like being an army brat—always the new kid.

I think those early experiences left me with a bit of a restless streak. For example, I decided to skip my last year of high school. I finished all the work in advance and spent what would've been my final year at a job in the city. I worked as a machinist, operating a turning lathe and machining military parts. I liked it and was good at it. Near the end of that year, I was accepted by Harvard and by Dartmouth. I remember going to the shop foreman to tell him the good news. He said: "College? You're going to college? Don't do it, kid. You could really be a good machinist." I took it for the compliment that he intended it to be.

Anyway, I chose to go to Dartmouth. At the time, Dartmouth was a bit conservative and I was a bit rebellious. So, at first, the school and I did some head knocking, which continued until we both agreed on our respective positions. After that, I found that I liked Dartmouth a great deal. My time there was interrupted by the war. I was drafted in my second year. When I came back, I began working on the student newspaper. I was the editor on the night that Truman beat Dewey. All we had for photos was a small picture of Truman and a large picture of Dewey, who'd been the anointed winner, right up until the eleventh hour. So what I did was to position the large photo of Dewey upside-down, with the small photo of Truman set above it, as though Truman were looking down over the toppled Dewey. The headline read: "Upset." We sold something like eleven thousand copies, which was unprecedented.

My experience on the paper helped me to get a position as a stringer for local newspapers in New Hampshire and Vermont, writing short articles on spec, which I did as a way of helping to work myself though college. As a stringer, I didn't get a salary. I'd write something and, if the papers liked it and had room for it, they'd pay me. After I graduated and moved to New York, I made a deal with a few of those papers to work as their urban stringer.

So now I was out of college and earning a little money as a writer, the job I swore I'd never do. I hadn't been able to shake my youthful aversion to writing—rather, my aversion to the idea of falling into the same line of work as my parents. So I tried my hand at a few different things. More than a few, actually. I almost went to law school, for example. Cooler heads prevailed, thank God. I even tried selling insurance. I was a terrible insurance salesman, just terrible. I was too sympathetic. My allegiances were in the wrong place. I cared more about the people than the company.

After a year or two of this, I'd become very eager to find something new. One morning, I happened to visit my parents' apartment. My father was working on a television series and the studio had sent him a sample script. I found it, leafed through it, and told my father what I thought of it—that it was a piece of garbage. His response was: "You think you can do better, go ahead and write an episode." So, after lunch, I went back to my apartment and wrote a complete episode in four hours. And the studio bought it for two hundred dollars. Back then, that was real money. Two hundred bucks for an afternoon's work—it didn't seem legal.

Around this time, I married a nice, middle-class Jewish girl. And we moved into a nice, rent-discounted apartment. And every morning I'd wake up and make her a nice, handsome breakfast and watch her out the window as she went off to work. I'd begun to write fiction and to have a few stories published. So, for a few months, I didn't have a job, and after my wife went off to work, I'd spend my days in our apartment, writing. After about four or five months of this, she said: "Honey, if one of us is working, the other should be working, too." That was the end of my honeymoon.

First, I got a position as a researcher on a television series. I don't remember the name of the show. Nobody remembers the name of the show. It was on the fringes of the fringes. Anyway, the whole time I was there, I kept sticking my nose in on the writing staff. Finally, I bugged them to the point where—like my father—they threw up their hands and said: "You think you can do better, go ahead and try." So I did, and, before too long, I began earning a small amount of money as a television writer. Soon, I was hired to the writing staff of another show. I found that I enjoyed it. I liked the pace. Television is quick. That agreed with me.

At one point, I was told that I've written more television than anyone in the history of television. I'm not sure that's true, but I have written a great deal. You name the show, I wrote for it. And I've written even more if you count everything that I wrote using a pseudonym, which I did from time to time. Actually, I had two pen names, one for drama and one for comedy. It was a way of keeping up appearances. For example, if the company that you're working for sees that you're working on three other projects at the same time, they tend to suspect that they're being shortchanged. I remember, under a pseudonym, I once wrote an entire series for Brazilian television. It was a crime thriller that took place in Rio. I'd never been to Brazil, and the studio wanted to send me down there. But I didn't want to be away from my family, so I went to the local library and studied up on Brazil, on its history and culture. In the end, I wrote forty-six half-hour episodes. I did them all in English and later worked with a translator. That was a fun project.

Although I've written a great deal, I don't necessarily consider myself prolific. When I was young, I had a facility because I was young. When I got older, I had four kids, and so I had a facility because I damn well had to. Anyhow, when I'm writing, if the words don't come, I can be hard on myself. I don't go out for a walk. I sit there until it starts to flow. I just sit and talk with my inner writer. His name is Schmuck. I say: "Listen, Schmuck, it's two in the morning. Neither of us has had any sleep, and neither of us is going to have any sleep, not until we get this done." Schmuck hates me, but I always get him to cough it up. And I've never been blocked. Yes, I've had difficulties. It can be very difficult work, but I don't allow myself to become frozen. I just don't let it happen.

Difficulties aside, when my kids were young, writing was a kind of ideal occupation. I wrote at night, and so I got to spend part of every day with my kids. That was incredibly important. I didn't have to rush away to an office every morning. Instead, I started every morning by having breakfast with my kids. In Hollywood, breakfast business meetings are big, but I'd turn them down every time. I'd tell producers: "Sorry, babe, I'm booked." When you get busy, it becomes very easy not to accomplish anything. It's paradoxical. Instead of getting things done, you spend all your time just filling time. The little things add up. You stuff your days with trivia, like breakfast meetings with Hollywood producers.

Family was always the first priority, always, even later on, after my kids had grown up and started families of their own. When our kids moved east, my wife and I decided to come east. That was about fifteen years ago, and it sort of precipitated my gradual exit from the business. After we made the move, I kept on working, but I was working more like a raider. I'd parachute into Hollywood, take care of business, and fly out.

Over time, the work dwindled. It was gradual. Entertainment is an odd business. There's a certain amount of ageism in Hollywood. It was never too bad for me. I always stayed active and got along well with younger people. I never made a point of defending my age. I didn't feel that I needed to. But maybe ageism was part of what caused things to slow down for me. Also, screenwriting is unique in that it's an externally driven activity and business. For the most part, it's not about a writer going off to create something wonderful on his own. Instead, it's driven by assignments, by projects being developed and by writers being assigned to work on those projects. After I left California, I was somewhat cut off from that process.

But, more than anything else, things slowed down because I chose to shift my focus. My wife and I love traveling, love visiting our kids and grandkids. It's a lifestyle for us. We love it and we won't commit to anything that might interfere with it. I enjoy working hard, but I'll only do so within the strictures that I've created for myself—one wife, four children, eleven grandchildren. These are lives in which I'm deeply involved, and I don't want to do anything to detract from that involvement. I could direct my energies into some grand, all-consuming project, but that would risk interfering with my relationship with my family. If I took on something consuming, I simply couldn't spend the necessary amount of time with my family, no matter how hard I tried. And I refuse to do that.

Right now, I'm writing a novel and an opera—well, technically, a libretto for an opera. What's great about writing the novel is that I get to write it in bits and pieces, interposing that work with other activities. I focus on it for a bit, and put it aside when my wife and I go traveling and when we're spending time with our kids. For example, this afternoon, I'll take two of my grandkids to lunch. Afterwards, I'll go home, work for a bit on the novel and, later, go to the gym with my grandkids. We all go work out together.

I'm not going to give that up. I'll try to finish the book. I'll try to get involved in other projects, but never to a degree that threatens or inhibits what I'm doing with my family.

I think that, at a certain point, you have to correlate what you're going to do with what you've already done and with all that you've accumulated along the way. Listen, I'm eighty-five years old—I've reluctantly given up my hopes for Wimbledon. I've also given up mountain climbing—I can get down the mountain but I can't get up. These are things that my body just won't do. I'm quite aware of what's happening. Like everyone, I'm equipped with a body that can only hold out for so long. I catch myself struggling to do things that used to be simple, thinking: *Jesus, this used to be a lot easier.* I hate that, the inevitable physical decline. When I started to teach my kids tennis, I was the best tennis player in the family. Then, one day, I discovered that my son was better than I was. Then, not too long ago, my son and I both discovered that my grandson is better than all of us. The little peanut. I hate that, but, of course, I love it, too. So I'm trying to hold on, to stay as active as possible, and to postpone debility for as long as I can.

I'm not entirely without regrets. I can think of some, but they're mostly of the either/or kind. It was either do this or do that. There were things that appealed to me and interested me that I didn't pursue. In most cases, I didn't pursue those things because doing so would have meant sacrificing something else—giving up on some other part of my life that I deemed more valuable. And so I made my choices, as we all must. And I'm happy with my choices. My life has been very good. Today, it's all still very good. It's all very gratifying. I'm a very, very lucky person. My marriage, my children, my grandchildren—I am incredibly lucky.

Still, there are some things that I wished I'd had the sense—no, that's the wrong word—not the sense to do, but the urgency to do. Sometimes, I suspect that I may have lacked the requisite sense of urgency. I'm thinking of one friend in particular who, after achieving a little success in Hollywood, gave it up to work in the theater. In certain moments, I think that I should have done more and done better—that perhaps I could have written better. I would've loved to have written something that turned out better than anything that I could've ever expected to write—to have surprised myself—to have astounded myself with my writing.

Of course, I fully expect the book that I'm writing now to become a best seller. And why not? It would be a surprise, sure, but my entire career as a writer was a surprise. I never expected to make a dollar with it. And, if there's one thing that I've learned in a lifetime of writing, it's that human beings are surprising. That's one of our principal qualities.

# VII. COMMUNITY

# *"You Have to Put Yourself Out There"*

## ESTHER MAY PARSONS
### Born 1922 – Retired 1979

*Esther and late husband George on their wedding day.*

In 1944, twenty-two-year-old Esther May Lee—who, in the pre-ceding year, graduated from nursing school, left the upstate New York farm where she was raised, joined the service, and complet-ed basic training—arrived in Fort Dix as a second lieutenant in the US Army Nurse Corps. At Fort Dix, she met George Parsons, a private first class recovering from shrapnel wounds sustained in North Africa. Four months later, they were married. Shortly thereafter, she was transferred to England. There, she trained in preparation to support the D-Day invasion and treated burn victims returning from the Battle of the Bulge. On one occasion, she was caught in a German V-Bomb attack in London and spent a sleepless night listening to the rockets screaming and exploding in the surrounding area.

Soon after arriving in Europe, Esther discovered that she was pregnant. Army regulations dictated that she could no longer serve and she returned to the United States to live with her husband's family. George was discharged in 1947, and the couple settled near Boston. George worked as a truck weigher at a chemical plant, while Esther worked as a surgical nurse and, later, as a school nurse. They had five children—one of whom, a daughter, passed away—eleven grandchildren, and seven great-grandchildren. George passed in 1999. Today, Esther lives in the same home that she and George settled in after the war.

I've always enjoyed life. Wherever I was, whatever I was doing. I like to be with people. I have a lot of friends and a lot of interests.

I retired at fifty-seven because my mother had dementia and could not be left alone. My husband retired a year later at age fifty-nine. Even after I retired, I worked part-time for the local Visiting Nurses Association and for a local nursing home. I loved nursing. I miss it. I also volunteered with the Bloodmobile. I enjoyed that work, too. I got to meet all the people in my town and the people in the surrounding towns.

Before we retired, we bought a travel trailer and joined a camping club. Our camper was small, seventeen feet. We bought what we could afford. George pulled the trailer and backed it up. I directed him.

While my mom was with us, we'd take her camping, mostly around New England and down to Florida. After my mother passed away, we asked my youngest daughter to stay in our house for a year while we went on the road. We were on the road for fifteen months. We'd drive two to four hours a day and stop whenever we wanted to. No marathon sessions. That's what retirement is about. Relax. Enjoy it.

First, we went down the East Coast to Florida and spent three months there. Then we headed west to Texas and hooked up with a Good Sam's Safari. There were forty trailers and travel homes in the caravan. We crossed the border into Mexico and put our car and the trailer on a flatbed railroad car. For ten days, we lived in the trailer on the flatbed. Sometimes, our railroad car would pull into a siding and we'd find ourselves stuck among cattle cars. That was different.

We went to the Copper Canyon in the southwestern part of the state of Chihuahua, Mexico. It's larger and deeper than the Grand Canyon. Every night we'd get off the train and visit villages with different Indian tribes. Some were living in mountain caves. We went down as far as Mazatlan, where we got off the train and started driving with the caravan. The roads were so narrow, two lanes, and often just dirt. As we went through some of the villages, we encountered kids begging. I remember one who tried to sell my husband a set of false teeth. Not sure if they were used or new.

We were in Mexico for three weeks, and then drove back up to Nogales, Arizona. We did Arizona for a month then headed west, up the California coast, visiting friends, and then up into Western Canada. Then, back into Wyoming, Montana, visited friends in Salt Lake City, and then across South Dakota and that way home. I have no idea of the number of miles. When I was headed home at the end of that trip, I wasn't thinking, *The fun's over.* Oh no, the fun is still going on!

I took a lot of photos during that trip, but never look at them and have never taken photos since. I just can't be bothered. Maybe I should look back through them, but I haven't.

In addition to camping, my husband and I always enjoyed gardening, dancing, and, of course, we did a lot of other traveling, too. For example, we took a cruise up the Mississippi from New Orleans, and another along the Orinoco River in Venezuela. I still remember that trip, and how we tried all those strange native dishes.

In 1999, after my husband died, I gave the camper to my youngest son. My husband and I had a wonderful twenty-year retirement. We just enjoyed life. The time just flew. Oh, he was a real catch—he was. He was a lot of fun!

I still do the same things I did with him. I have wonderful friends and family who helped me through his passing. They allowed me to keep going the same way I had been, the travel, the camping, but now with friends.

These days, I usually spend ten days a year with younger friends at Scusset Beach on the Cape, and then go to campgrounds in New Hampshire. I still love to travel. Each year, I go to Florida right after Christmas and stay with friends until the end of March. I play bridge three times a week, sometimes for points and sometimes socially. I'm still driving, so it makes it possible for me to do all this.

I typically get up between 6:00 and 7:00 a.m., and do stretches and some strength training. I can't do much walking because I have spinal stenosis, a buildup of calcium in the spinal column that puts pressure on the spinal nerves. It's painful. Otherwise, I'm in good health, although I've had two complete knee replacements. I wore them out.

Retirement hasn't impacted my self-esteem or my sense of purpose. I've enjoyed my family and friends, and life is good. The only way I could improve retirement is to make the days longer. But I'm fortunate, and I appreciate that not everyone in retirement is as happy as I am. Whatever goals I've had, I've fulfilled. I have no big plans, but the fun goes on and on. My priorities have changed. I wanted to travel and see the world and I think I have. So now my priority is to enjoy each day.

I've kept a daily log of what I've done for over forty years. It takes about five to ten minutes, just recording the events of the day. I never look back at the logs, other than to check whether an event occurred on a given date. In fact, I don't look back very often. I look to the future more than the present. I'm planning ahead. My husband used to say that I'd get to some places a week too early.

My advice is to keep making new friends because your contemporaries die. You make new friends through activities. You have to put yourself out there.

## *"A Cultural Movement"*

# CHARLOTTE BENEDICT
Born 1929 – Retired 1997

# JAMES JORDAN
Born 1926 – Retired 1996

Charlotte graduated Phi Beta Kappa with a degree in chemistry from the University of Rochester and was admitted to medical school, but deferred for a year. She then began a series of science-related jobs that evolved into her career, and medical studies were forgotten. She moved to Europe, met her husband, and married at age twenty-eight. She and her husband settled in San Rafael, California, and raised three sons, and now have six grandsons. They shared the usual family activities as well as an interest in motorcycle touring. Together they toured the California coast, the Canadian Rockies, and she took a solo trip to the Grand Canyon. In addition, she traveled frequently, and when her husband lost interest in travel, Charlotte traveled with friends. She has visited all seven continents. After retirement, she and her husband led increasingly separate lives. About ten years ago, Charlotte, separated but not divorced from her husband of forty-five years, moved into a retirement community of about four hundred near Sacramento and continued living on her own.

Jim was born and raised in a small town in Oklahoma where his dad built and ran a restaurant. Through Jim's early years, he worked in the restaurant. He also worked as a laborer for the Santa Fe Railroad, as a stevedore, and as a navy seaman. His family was quite close and religious. Jim won a football scholarship to Oklahoma State University, and earned degrees in architecture and engineering. He married Louella, his now deceased wife, and had three sons. He has seven grandchildren and four great-grandchildren. Jim worked as an architect in California, and authored several articles on California building codes and architectural and engineering practice. In retirement, Jim continued writing and is the author of a trilogy of religious-themed books. Jim and Louella, his wife of fifty-eight years, moved into one of the cottages in the retirement community about five years ago. About a year later, Louella passed away, and he dealt poorly with the resulting loneliness. His sons urged him to find another mate.

Jim met Charlotte and, after dating for almost a year, they participated in a "ceremony of commitment," went on a honeymoon, and have been living together ever since.

CHARLOTTE: I moved to the retirement village in 2002 and Jim moved in 2007. I didn't know Jim when he first moved in.

JIM: My wife passed away November 20, 2008, and I wasn't doing well. I was alone in the cottage we had shared. My sons suggested that I look for companionship. Here in the village, it's easy to meet new people, especially women—the ratio is easily in the man's favor. Plus, we have a dining room where you can share dinner and get to know one another. I had begun doing that. But I was also involved in the community's theater group. Charlotte and her buddy were the leaders of the group.

CHARLOTTE: I hadn't been active in theater, but when I came here, I was just separated from my husband. So I jumped into activities with both feet rather than sit around and feel sorry for myself.

JIM: I joined after my wife passed. I decided to try out. We have two productions a year and notices are sent out to all residents.

CHARLOTTE: About four years ago, Jim showed up.

JIM: Charlotte was the director and an actor as well. It's probably the first time we noticed each other. The play was *Five Nuns in Vegas*. I was a casino manager and Charlotte was assistant mother superior of a convent that moved to Las Vegas from the Midwest.

CHARLOTTE: We didn't immediately start seeing each other. It wasn't until after the anniversary of Jim's wife passing. Jim didn't start to entertain ladies until well after that.

JIM: I hadn't dated for more than fifty-eight years. You could sit at a table and have dinner, but I'd call ahead and arrange to have dinner with a lady. It was relatively easy.

CHARLOTTE: In a place like this there are two distinct social groups, the couples and the singles. Not that they don't interact, but the couples and the singles tend to socialize among themselves. We have cottages with patios and garages, and apartments. The couples are concentrated in the cottages and the singles in the apartments. The apartments have a concentration of women.

JIM: In the play Charlotte was the top nun. I was attracted to her. She is the hardest worker in the community. She does ten different jobs and does them well, very active and outgoing, high energy level. We started dating in spring 2010.

CHARLOTTE: I wasn't looking. I was fine. I had friends. I traveled a lot. You have the community living and you can retreat to your home and have privacy. Jim was developing courses for the community to be taught three days a week. He was sick with a kidney infection at one point and asked me to cover for him. So I went out to his cottage to pick up some material, and for some reason, we started to talk about football. I admired his dedication to the courses and his intellect. Those are things that attracted me to him. Then we found out we had this common interest in football. And that's how things started to blossom.

He invited me to watch football, and then we started talking about life in general. He indicated that he was lonesome, and then the dinners became more consistent, like once a week or more. There was a period where he disappeared for a while and I wondered what I said wrong, you know how it goes. Then it became pretty much every night.

JIM: I started to believe that I needed companionship like my boys said. I was concerned about whether they thought I would be able to marry again. They thought it was a good idea, and I began to look. It finally came down to two women. Both of them are...it's amazing... the two women I had selected both ended up being nominated to be president of the community's membership council. I thought that was amazing. Of all the women I had to select from, both had the qualifications to be president of the council.

The proposal and engagement? Oh, yeah. Well, there are people here who have just decided to live together and don't make any bones about it. They just move in together and that's it. We talked about that possibility, but I told Charlotte that I could not. The apartment we're in belongs to Charlotte's family trust and my cottage belongs to my family trust. So our monies are tied up in family trusts that our children will inherit someday. Once my wife died I was sole owner of my trust. Charlotte's husband is still living. I told Charlotte that I couldn't live with another man's wife. As much as I loved her, I couldn't just move in with her. It's not the way I am. I suggested that we ask her husband if he agreed with our going through a ceremony where we dedicated ourselves to each other. Would he put something in writing that he was OK with it?

CHARLOTTE: I respected Jim's feelings on that. So we worked on this letter to my husband for a couple of weeks and finally sent it off, and my husband called the next day and said, "I am so glad you found somebody." He wrote a little affidavit sort of thing that my relationship with him was only financial. Otherwise, we hadn't been together for close to ten years. There's never been a divorce. I looked into a divorce, but it was going to devastate both of us financially.

I had been completely independent for many years, even while I was still married to my first husband. We lived separate lives. It's been a little hard for Jim because of his close relationship with his first wife. I've had to learn to defer to him, or at least discuss things with him a little more than I was used to doing. I'm used to making my own decisions.

Financially, of course, we do our own thing. We divide up the household expenses. What I worried about, really, was the family. Jim's family was already on board.

JIM: At least the boys were.

CHARLOTTE: We got engaged just before Thanksgiving and didn't break the news to my youngest son until about Christmas. I was a little worried about that one. My concern was that they would not be accepting of the idea because I was still married to my sons' father. But it turns out they were OK with the idea. I was concerned about the grandchildren. My middle son was a confidant and advisor during the decision-making process, having just gone through divorce himself. My oldest son lived two thousand miles away so I wasn't as worried about that family.

JIM: I was concerned about my grandchildren, too.

CHARLOTTE: They all came to the wedding, although the family in Minnesota didn't because of the distance.

JIM: The minister to bless the ceremony of commitment was no problem at all. I had a close minister friend, and for years, he and I would go fishing. He was the minister here at my old Methodist

Church. I asked him, knowing that he would do the marriage. We also had the Presbyterian Church here. The assistant minister was a wonderful young lady and a friend.

CHARLOTTE: I knew the lady minister because we started talking about things and we became close. I started going to church with Jim.

JIM: The associate minister agreed to join with my friend the minister. The two of them would marry the two of us.

CHARLOTTE: There was no marriage license, but we exchanged vows. Oh yes, we wrote our own vows.

JIM: There were 150 people at our reception, big reception here in the auditorium. We each wanted old friends, family, and people from the community. Two of my sons took part and Charlotte's friend was the maid of honor. Her middle son gave her away. Reaction? Everybody here was all for it.

CHARLOTTE: I had a few questions because some people knew I was still married, and I think there was a bit of buzzing in the background. There are several other couples here in the same situation.

JIM: Some of them have gone through a ceremony, some haven't.

CHARLOTTE: Our invitation referred to it as a ceremony of commitment, rather than a wedding ceremony. Actually, people thought other such ceremonies were marriages. You really can't tell the difference.

JIM: For our honeymoon, we went to Okinawa and Japan to visit my son and grandson.

CHARLOTTE: We haven't received any overt negative reactions. After the local newspaper article about our ceremony, the story was picked up by other newspapers and the Internet. There was only one negative article, "Seniors Shacking Up." All the rest were respectful and talked about the elderly going through commitment ceremonies.

JIM: It is really a cultural movement. In the ten years I've been here there have been six to eight such couples. Sometimes with formal ceremonies, and sometimes with just a big reception to announce they're joining together. It's becoming fairly common, largely because of family concerns and financial planning.

CHARLOTTE: Challenges, there have been some. We've had some tearful sessions. Jim had such a wonderful and close marriage. He believed that once we went through the ceremony, we were one. I still have some difficulties with this because I've been alone so long. Even as a child, I was a loner. I was an only child.

One of the biggest problems is where to live. I still have my apartment and Jim has his cottage. We tried splitting our time between them, living in one for a few nights and then the other. It's exhausting. I couldn't do it. Stocking two refrigerators, having medications in both places. So now I'm living out of the cottage and use my apartment in the daytime. I have my financial records, my computer, and all my library work in the apartment.

JIM: We call the apartment near the center our city home, and the cottage our country home. It's out at the far end of the grounds, near a park.

CHARLOTTE: My biggest challenges have been clothes and transporting stuff back and forth. I go to get dressed and my clothes are in the other spot. Essentially, I'm living in someone else's domicile. I haven't attempted to redecorate or anything. It's not my main interest and I don't want to decimate the apartment. Most of the things in the cottage Jim and Louella had set up. In the last few months we made some changes in the furniture and so forth.

At times, it's been difficult for me to accept that. At other times, it doesn't bother me at all. Every once in a while, if I get stressed or I get low, then some of those things begin to bother me. It's been a challenge not having everything where I'm used to.

JIM: The biggest challenge for me was gone as soon as we got the writing from Charlotte's husband that he was OK with it. He agreed to the whole arrangement. That relieved everything because I could just...that had really bothered me.

The second thing is my grandkids. It's more difficult for them. My sons were no problem. Their wives had a bit of resistance. But the grandkids were difficult; even Charlotte's grandkids had some issues.

One of my granddaughters didn't like the idea, and it took her parents quite a while to convince her of the truth that my being married to Charlotte had nothing to do with lessening a relationship with their grandmother. As long as they understood that I was still honoring Louella's memory and Charlotte was not going to be weakening that at all. Charlotte was somebody to share my life with, rather than being alone. I think they finally agreed.

CHARLOTTE: Jim is closer to his grandchildren than I am to mine, just family dynamics.

JIM: Our families are quite different. Mine has always been closer. The biggest reward is having somebody to be with, somebody that I love, somebody that thinks pretty much as I do about things, although we have our differences. The fact is that we seem to be very amiable. We just fit; everything seems to be right.

CHARLOTTE: For me, it's a whole new marriage. Once I moved here and was on my own and found I could function on my own, it increased my self-esteem, which has always been a problem for me. Now to find somebody who tells me several times a day that he loves me. Just the closeness, I'm soaking that up.

I wasn't ever looking for another relationship. Some women come into a place like this searching, looking for a relationship. I wasn't. I was adapting to the failure of the former one. So it has been a real upper for me, to find somebody who cares for me and about me. When I get in one of my little moods, he brings me around real fast. He won't let me get away with it.

As to the future, and practical things such as medical instructions and so on, we both have revised our advance directives so we have full access. The families could be here in two hours if something happens.

We've made our final arrangements and have that control within our individual families. If something happens to Jim, I can make immediate interim decisions, but the final decisions remain with the families. Same with mine. He's first on the advance directives, but unless it's something immediate, he won't make the final decision on when to pull the plug; it'll be up to my family.

JIM: As to funeral arrangements and such, we've both concluded that all preexisting arrangements will stay in place. I've donated my body to a local university medical school for research purposes.

CHARLOTTE: In this retirement community, no subletting is permitted. So as long as I can afford to, I will keep the apartment. The cottage is so far out, and this is a wonderful location. I would not want to live way out in the cottage by myself. It reverts to his family and I'll just keep the apartment. Had it not been for the economy, we would have elected to sell both places and buy a larger three-bedroom place.

We keep active physically and mentally. Some people come here and say we don't want all the activities a facility like this offers, and then end up in their units talking about the next meal.

JIM: We're identical in that respect. I started giving classes three days a week—religion, science, and history—and now we run the classes. I'm chairman of the barbershop chorus. Interestingly enough, the second lady I had to choose from is now the music director.

CHARLOTTE: The beauty of a place like this is the wide array of classes and activities.

JIM: I can't tell anyone else what to do about the possibility of a new romance in his later years. I can only deal with how I react and feel. I couldn't begin to tell someone else how to feel. I don't tell anybody to believe as I do. All I can do is point out what works for me. People like it, then fine. If they don't, then make their own conclusions.

CHARLOTTE: My advice would be just let it happen. If you come in looking, it shows, and it turns off the opposite sex. Be yourself and see what happens. It depends on the mix of people. You find that most men who lose their spouse are not looking for another permanent liaison; they're looking for companionship. Some couples even travel together, even though they are not committed. Be easy, be yourself, and find somebody you can share companionship with. If it develops into more, great; if it doesn't, then at least you had pleasant companionship.

JIM: I want to make a statement about the "shacking up" business. It really bothers me. We feel good about being with each other. It's not the same thing as when we're eighteen or nineteen, or twenty-four, when I was first married. My wife and I were very much in love, sex was very important. There's still some physical relationship, but it's not the driving force. Although, when we are parting we'll kiss each other or duck into a hallway to kiss each other.

CHARLOTTE: He wouldn't hold my hand in public until after we were engaged.

# *"Here To Build"*

## FR. OTTO J. HENTZ, SJ
### Born 1937

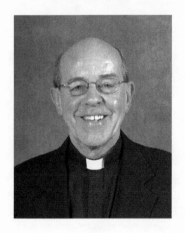

Father Hentz was born in 1937 in Philadelphia. He was the youngest of eight children, all born within nine and a half years. His dad died in an automobile accident a few months before he was born. After high school, he began training to become a Jesuit. He was ordained in 1968, and awarded a PhD from the University of Chicago in 1972.

For forty years, he has taught at Georgetown and resided in its largest student residential village, continuously expanding his contacts and influence on students. His course, *The Problem of God*, is one of the most popular, and he is always among the most highly rated professors. Over the years, he has developed strong friendships and instilled in students the concept of living for others. He did this through his teaching and through outreach programs he started and facilitated in Nicaragua and Peru.

Today, he continues to teach and nurture his network of current and former students to achieve his goal of accomplishing good works for others on a broad societal level.

S ome of the most interesting and important things in my life didn't happen because I planned for them or because I sought them. So much of it, I just sort of backed into.

My mother insisted that I attend a Jesuit high school. I'd been interested in other non-Jesuit schools, but she set her jaw and told me, "Your father wanted you to have a Jesuit education and you're going to have one." So that was that. I was off to St. Joseph's Prep.

At St. Joseph's, I was impressed by my teachers, many of whom were young seminarians. They struck me as very centered—committed to what they were doing, with a good sense for what's important and what's not. Plus, they had humor. They could laugh at human foibles. And they taught us so much. I loved what they did for us. I thought, *Maybe I can do the same thing. Maybe I can get saved.* Now, almost sixty years later, I'm still trying to follow their example, trying to live up to what I saw back then and admired so much. Of course, whether I've gotten myself saved or not is another matter.

I entered the seminary in 1955. The way the seminary was back then, it might as well have been 1855. In graduate school at Chicago, I lived with six other Jesuits and we took turns cooking. I learned so much sitting around those tables, just talking and listening. When I came to Georgetown, I wanted to replicate that experience and I found a way to do that. My residence is situated in the middle of a student village. I talk to students all the time and have dinner with them on a regular basis. In general, there is no agenda. It is informal. It encourages open discussion. Those kinds of interactions are invaluable. Throughout my career, both as a student and a teacher, I've learned as much by surrounding myself with thoughtful people as I've learned in formal study and in classes.

Today, my goal is the same as it's always been: to help undergraduates at a formative time in their lives. I try to teach them theology and, in the process of teaching them theology, to also teach them a certain style of thinking—thinking that's done with energy and purpose, and with a sense of personal investment. As a teacher, you're not just leading the students through the material. You're demonstrating certain habits of mind. The point of an education is not merely to develop a base of knowledge. It's not to prepare you to do the crossword or to appear on *Jeopardy!* The purpose of an education is to foster a critical consciousness. It should encourage you to examine how you think, how you look at the world. I'd like students to leave here as pilgrims—pilgrims of the mind, if you will—and to never stray from that road. This emphasis is particularly so in a Jesuit education, the object of which is to suggest a style of thinking and living that corresponds to a vision of social justice.

Nicaragua is a good example. For nearly fifteen years, I ran a volunteer program in Nicaragua. A group of students came to me with the idea. At first, it was a real mom-and-pop operation. We arranged a brief orientation course—language, history of the region, current political scene. After that, we put ten kids on a plane. This was 1981, when the stuff down there was really starting to hit the fan. But, I knew that our students would be working with local Jesuits. I trusted the Jesuits and I trusted our students. And the program was a huge success. Soon, word got out, and we did essentially the same program every year for fifteen straight years.

The summer after the first year of the program, I traveled to Nicaragua and lived there for two months, staying in the villages where the students were volunteering. After that first visit, I went back every year for a few weeks during Christmas break. The poverty was incredible. Forty families shared one water well, and everyone lived in lean-to huts. I was impressed that our students were willing to live and work in those conditions. I was even more amazed that, in all those years, I never had to recruit anyone. Every year, the students sought it out. They wanted to help. After about fifteen years, we started Jesuit Volunteers International, which is a larger operation, very well organized and well run, more on the model of the Peace Corps. Today, it's thriving and has expanded its work to eight countries.

In particular, I remember one student from the Nicaragua program, Kevin Mann. He went there in the late 1980s and was assigned to work with an Italian priest, Father Fabretto. Father Fabretto had been in Latin America for over forty years, running orphanages. He took kids off the streets of Managua and gave them a chance at life. During Kevin's time, Father Fabretto died of a heart attack. Kevin decided to stay on and to continue the mission, and he's been there ever since. Now, his college classmates have helped him to expand the operation. They've organized fund-raisers and a foundation. Today, Kevin is helping about six thousand kids, working all over the country, revamping impoverished country schools, providing nourishment and development opportunities to thousands of children. Not too long ago, I traveled to Nicaragua to do Kevin's wedding.

It was amazing to see the transformation, to see the scope of all that he's accomplished. I'm so proud to have been there at the beginning of it and to have helped him, if only by saying yes. Yes, go to Nicaragua. Yes, stay on to help. That's characteristic of my life, I think. I've managed to do some good simply because I've been too embarrassed to say no.

I've been fortunate to stay in touch with so many people. I'm always getting together with someone for dinner. I spend a good part of every week on the phone. And, of course, as a priest, I do a lot of weddings and baptisms. I enjoy that, but all the traveling involved can make it difficult. Keeping in touch takes work. And I've been around a long time, so there are a lot of people to keep up with. All in all, it keeps me busy. It's also great fun.

In fact, although I'm older now, I think of myself as pretty much the same. There haven't been any dramatic changes. I do find that I'm thinking about my age more than I ever did. And I've dealt with death in my own family. My mother passed. I lost five siblings. Experiencing loss like that makes age—and time—difficult to ignore. But, one advantage of going bald early is that, for the next fifty years, people will tell you that you haven't changed a bit. Are you kidding? Did you not see the hearing aids? Do you want to hear about my new hip? So yes, in general, I still feel good, just not as high energy. In my sixties and seventies, I noticed myself slowing down a bit. Time was, I'd say yes to everything—alumni committees, hiring committees, departmental committees. I've cut back a bit. That's all right. For years, I was running around like a mad hatter.

I still try to stay as active as possible. That's important. It keeps me alert and in touch with people. I've developed new interests, too. History, painting, they stretch my mind and keep the creativity and the energy at least at a simmer. Also, I follow a regular routine of prayer. It's nothing too dramatic, just some prayers in the morning to keep my spirit lively. When you think about it, it's difficult for anyone not to pray, at least in some form. Some might not call it prayer, but I think that most people spend at least some part of their days wondering about the meaning of their lives and about their relationship to something beyond themselves. The human spirit is always churning, I think. Something is always going on.

Sometimes, I look back at my life and say: "Well, what have I done? Let's see, I've graded ten million papers." I suppose that's a common reaction to a common question. People wonder what they've accomplished. Often, they look back to find a lifetime of modest acts, small victories, persistent difficulties, things that didn't work out. For most of us, our lives don't read like historical sagas.

I think that if you look deeper, however, you'll realize how much we all contribute. I'm reminded of the homily by Archbishop Oscar Romero of El Salvador, "Prophets of a Future Not Our Own." He says that we all give something. Our contributions may appear modest, but, in the grand scheme of things, everything appears modest. What I've done with my life hasn't been perfect or complete. Yet, everything that we do—whether in a day or a lifetime—is imperfect and incomplete. And it all forms part of a greater whole, a whole that lies beyond our comprehension. We all face the same limitations. None of us can do everything. All we can do is to help set the foundation and to remember that we're working to realize something beyond ourselves, beyond even our imagining. It's a difficult realization, but also a liberating one. It frees us to do what we can, to try our best, accepting that we may never see the product of our labor. That's all right. That's as it should be. We're workers, not master builders. We're not here to roam about the palace. We're here to build it. I like to remember that. And so I content myself by taking the long view.

# VIII. SERVICE

## *"From South Central"*

# DENISE JOHNSON
(Pseudonym)
Born 1963 – Retired 2010

Denise grew up in South Central Los Angeles. Her dad was a carpenter and her mom did secretarial work, as well as some catering and other things. She had a sister and two brothers, one of whom passed away years ago. She graduated near the top of her high school class and from one of the most renowned universities in the California system with a degree in mathematics. Denise then joined a large financial services company as an analyst and over the next twenty-seven years progressed through management positions in a variety of companies. Along the way, Denise earned the prestigious Chartered Financial Analyst certification and developed some financial independence.

Recently, she has left financial services and its rewards to teach at a "recovery" high school. The students must be completely committed to recovery from substance abuse. The school is new and will offer a comprehensive academic program leading to a high school diploma, a GED completion, and/or dual enrollment in a community college. It will also offer counseling, family stabilization initiatives, and tutoring.

**Denise has many interests outside of work, notably biking and running. At least once a year she rides a century, a hundred miles in a day. She also has interests in travel and the arts.**

Teaching has always been on my mind. Always. I come from South Central Los Angeles, from a very working-class background. My parents did a wonderful job raising us, but when we were kids, my siblings and I weren't really aware of the kind of opportunities that a good education can provide.

I've wanted to teach in an urban environment. I've wanted the kids to see somebody who looks like them. I've wanted them to understand that you can come from a difficult background and still succeed. Your circumstances don't have to define you. What you're facing right now doesn't have to be your future.

As I said, teaching has always been on my mind, but I started thinking about it more seriously five or six years ago. And so I got my teaching certification in high school math. In the public school system, if you don't have your certification, they won't even consider you for a position. It doesn't matter what your background is.

The public school system is failing—I've seen that firsthand. Right now, I think I can add value to the system by working as a teacher. But, longer term, I think I'll also be able to add value by using what I learned as a teacher about how the system works. Down the road, maybe I'll be able to start a charter school. But, really, I'll do whatever I can to help our school system to succeed, because right now a lot of these schools are failing miserably. In whatever capacity, I'll keep trying to contribute to improving education in this country for the rest of my life. I think that I can keep adding value for years and decades to come. But, all of that is sort of my long-term mission. Although I may not stay a teacher forever, right now I'm totally focused on being the best teacher that I can be.

As I said, there's a strong connection between my desire to teach and my upbringing. I think that you'll find that anyone who came from South Central—or from Appalachia, or from any similar kind of background—anyone who came from difficult circumstances and has achieved a certain level of success recognizes the enormous value of education. That kind of experience forces you to see that your success is about more than just financial rewards.

It's extremely important for me to let others with similar backgrounds know what's possible. I know how many bright, capable people coming from that kind of background end up failing simply because they didn't have the right direction. They didn't have the right adult intervene in their life to put them on the right path.

I'm amazed when you look at the innate abilities that people have. I don't think that where you end up is about your innate ability, necessarily. I've worked with some very successful people. I've also been around some people who've just struggled to get by. The innate abilities at both ends of the spectrum aren't any different. One group got a chance, the other didn't. The difference between them is about the influences they've had in their lives. It's about having parents and peers and other people who care about you.

It's about having people intervene in your life, people who influence you to move in the right direction. Kids need that. It's critical. They need to be in an environment where excellence is expected. It makes all the difference.

There are way too many people coming out of our urban communities that are in prison, or that are mixed up with drugs, or that are wasting their potential. These people could be contributing to society. They could contribute so much. I know that. I've seen it from both sides. There's no question about it. And that's a huge part of why I'm doing this.

So I'd been thinking about leaving finance to become a teacher for some time, and I'd almost made the jump. When I was ready to do it mentally, I had to ask myself whether I was also ready to do it financially—because it's a tremendous hit. [*At this, she pauses and laughs to herself.*] The reality is that I'm not wealthy. Not by any stretch of the imagination. And I do appreciate the finer things in life. I'm not completely selfless.

Needless to say, the compensation that you receive as a teacher is dramatically different from the compensation that you receive as a relatively senior executive in a financial services firm. As a teacher, I don't receive some kind of credit for my business background. I pretty much had to go in at a starting teacher's salary. All joking aside, the money is a serious consideration.

But, one thing that I learned from working all those years in finance is that, if I'm not happy with what I'm doing, money won't balance the equation. No amount of money is going to make you enjoy going into work every day and doing something that you don't like to do.

The past few years, working in finance was becoming less and less fun for me. Thankfully, I could afford to do something like this. I don't live a lavish lifestyle, believe me. But, nonetheless, I had to work to put myself in a position where I'd be reasonably secure—where I'd be all right doing this.

Once I was ready, it wasn't easy for me to make the move. Teachers are being laid off right now. And, when I first wanted to make the change, I didn't have teaching experience. But, I had a reasonably successful business career, a degree in math, and—to be perfectly honest—I'm a person of color seeking to work as a teacher in an urban setting. I thought that the schools would be happy to have me. But that wasn't the case. I applied to a lot of jobs, but I didn't get too many interviews. If you have a nontraditional background, it's difficult to get a job as a teacher. Even if you have really solid credentials, the school systems just aren't interested. Some of the interviews that I did get were intense, even a bit confrontational. One interviewer said to me: "Well, it's hard to imagine somebody who didn't go through a teaching program becoming a good teacher." In this area—and in some other areas, too—the school systems are suffering from a collective mental block.

As you know, I work with kids who struggle with substance abuse. Going into it, it wasn't entirely unfamiliar to me because I know people who've had to struggle with those types of issues. I've been exposed to it. One big difference is that, if you've struggled with substance abuse, in order to feed your habit, you've developed some really unique skills. In order to hide the habit and support it, you've had to learn a certain kind of coping. Many times, if you have a habit like that, you have become very good at manipulating people. I've been exposed to that, unfortunately. I know when someone's trying to game me. I know when someone's being untruthful and making excuses and whatever else.

To be honest, there was a certain prestige associated with what I did in the financial services industry. The income thing—that's what it was. Society puts more value on what I used to do than what I do now. Of course, I know that teaching is an honorable profession. I don't think that it should be held in any less esteem. But, from society's point of view, I've lost a bit of prestige by going from being a senior professional in a well-regarded financial firm to being a teacher just starting out.

I'm the kind of person who goes by the beat of her own drum. I follow my own values. But, to be realistic, I think we're all greatly affected by how others perceive us—there's no question about it. There's a certain part of us that is defined by how others perceive us. I'm probably more aware of it and more immune to that kind of thinking than some. I don't have any question that I'm doing the right thing and that I'm strong enough to make the change. But, I've gotten some strange reactions. People have said things like: "Are you kidding me? You're going to give up finance for teaching?" Some people are incredulous.

My values—my appreciation of what life has to offer—have changed immensely in the last few years. The changes haven't necessarily come from soul-searching. I think that that kind of change—that kind of fundamental change—can only come from action.

I was comfortable making donations to charity and being on a board or two, but that didn't buy the kind of satisfaction I was looking for. In high school, I did volunteer work with young kids. As my work commitments grew, I ended up making more donations of money instead of time. But once financial pressures were less of a concern, I had to ask myself if I wanted to continue to pursue financial rewards even if it's not spiritually fulfilling. The reality is, now that I'm more mature, I have a different outlook.

I respect learning, education, and intelligence—I've learned more and I can appreciate people who've contributed these wonderful gifts to the world. I like reading books about science, especially physics. I've become fascinated by it. Recently, I attended a speech by a Nobel Laureate in physics. I was more impressed by him than by anyone I ever met in finance, even though many of them had incomes that were many multiples of his.

Life expectancy is so much longer now. I don't think that people take significant advantage of the opportunity that living longer affords one to have a second career. It's hard to have a second career when you've achieved a certain level of success in your first. You're not inclined to go back to school. It's hard to get people to see that, maybe even if you don't have the specific background for the new career that you're thinking of, you've done many things that would make you a highly effective performer in that new endeavor. If given the opportunity, I think that a lot of people would want to try for that second career. But, I know how it is, you get so involved with what you're doing...and the inertia of your circumstances and habits and everything else...well, it all kind of works against making a change.

For me, teaching is not only a chance to contribute and to help others; on a personal level, it's a new challenge. It's not that what I was doing before was bad or that it wasn't worthwhile. But, apart from wanting to help others, I also wanted to have the challenge of doing something new, to focus my energies on something that I hadn't mastered.

And I have found it challenging. It's been fun and it's been an important learning experience for me. So, I have a good feeling about it. I feel like I'll be happy and proud and fulfilled by what I'm doing now.

Sure, a part of me is apprehensive. It's a lot to take on. There's a lot of uncertainty. But, that's what a challenge is all about.

When I look at my students, I remember where I came from. I remember myself as a little girl—I think about what it was like for me growing up and trying to get somewhere. It's incredible to think of myself as I was back then, of that little girl sitting in that high school class in South Central. Her world has expanded so much. I can't believe it.

# *"Should I Bring My Ice Skates?"*

## SISTER JUDITH SHERIDAN, SSMSM
### Born 1939

Sister Judy joined the Marist Missionary Sisters at eighteen. After seven years of rigorous training and education she embarked on a fifty-three-year career of service as a nurse, teacher, chaplain, lobbyist for peace and social justice, and administrator. Her service has always been to the poor, the afflicted, the abandoned, and the desperate. She has been a nurse in a leprosy hospital, and has since served as a health-care worker in flood-and war-ravaged Bangladesh, a chaplain to a large hospital's neurological ward, and a teacher in Papua New Guinea. For the last six years, she has been the provincial for the Marist Sisters, essentially CEO for a nonprofit comprised of 104 nuns in North America, Tanzania, and Jamaica. In a few days, her term as provincial will end and she will, at seventy-three, begin a new mission, working at a safe house near the Mexican border with victims of sex trafficking.

I was born in Peoria. My dad worked for the air force as a civilian munitions inspector. We moved nine times in twelve years. My mom stayed home to care for me, my sister, and my two brothers. Later in life she became a nurse. My brothers and sister live in the Midwest and the Northeast. I see them occasionally.

My call to missionary work goes back to age five or so. My mother would read stories of a missionary saint who traveled across the sea. Maybe St. Theresa? I distinctly remember telling myself, *That's what I'm going to be.* The thought was in the background until near the end of my high school days in Portland, Oregon. I thought about going to college and having fun with my friends, but I also thought that I'd be unhappy my whole life if I didn't follow my vocation. So I wrote to several missionary orders. The Marists wrote back and I was attracted to them, but I didn't know very much about them, and never even met one until the day I entered the Order in Lowell, Massachusetts. Before the family drove me out, I had telephoned and asked the superior, "Should I bring my ice skates?"

"Oh yes, yes!" she said.

"Should I bring my tennis racquet?"

"Oh yes, yes!" she said.

"Should I bring my clarinet?"

"Oh yes, yes!"

But I never used them.

The Order was quite strict. The day I arrived I put on a habit. You're a nun from day one. Of the thirteen who entered the convent with me, only three made it all the way through.

We had a superior who was so tough, really tough, we have a "survivors' group." She had served lepers at a hospital at Makogai, Fiji. When she went there, they had nothing. Nothing! So she was going to make sure you were mentally tough enough to serve. Nothing was ever right; you don't walk, talk, or look right—it was boot camp.

After my RN training, my first overseas assignment was to a leprosy hospital in Spanish Town, Jamaica, that the Order had run since 1940. (The Marist Sisters have more than one hundred years of history of serving those suffering from leprosy in the South Pacific.) We had been invited to run the hospital, but were barred from any kind of explicit religious proselytizing. But I don't think you can dispense compassion, care, and dignity without being Christ to the world. It was 1964, and the laws required confinement of those with the disease. There was no satisfactory treatment. Those with the disease were abandoned, neglected, living in slum conditions. The general population was frightened of them.

Over the course of two separate assignments to Jamaica, I spent seventeen years in hospitals, clinics, community health programs, always with the poor. I consider that time and service a great gift.

In 1977, I went to Bangladesh, formerly East Bengal/East Pakistan. The country was formed when India was created, and the Hindu population forced the Muslims to emigrate out and to live in an area about as big as Iowa. It's incredibly overcrowded—160 million people. It's bordered by rivers that flood a third of the country every year, making development impossible. In addition, it's subject to cyclones and drought.

Waterborne diseases are prevalent in the surface water, and the groundwater is polluted. Infectious diseases—hepatitis, typhoid, malaria, dengue fever, leptospiriosis—are common. It was the Sixth World. I thought, *This is the super mission. This is the call, the real call!* It was a Muslim country, and we couldn't wear our habits. We went as nurses. We lived in half of a renovated school. Curtains separated our beds. We had a stove and a kerosene-powered refrigerator for the vaccines. We had a varied diet—fish and rice, and rice and fish. I was in a state of shock for months. Just walking down the street people were lined up begging—malnourished babies, smallpox sufferers, the blind, the lame. I thought, *What am I supposed to do?* It was too big. There wasn't anything you could do. I tried to help one beggar boy who had a massive tumor on his jaw, but he resisted help because he was the principal source of income for his family. His condition improved his earning power. Begging was the country's welfare system.

After a year or so I got violently sick from worms that entered my body from the exposure of my feet to the sewer-like groundwater. They lodged in my intestines and lungs. I had pneumonia, great weight loss, high blood count. They didn't know what was going to happen. I remember crying, "I don't want to die here...send me to my mother." A real big tough missionary!

When I recovered, I was depressed. It was a big crisis for me. I had gone to Bangladesh believing in a God of love. But when I saw misery everywhere, I asked, "Where is this God of love?" I came back to the United States thinking that I had been wrong about my whole vocation. The depression lasted and I went through therapy for more than a year.

I then returned to Jamaica for five years, but continued to struggle with these issues. Midlife stuff. I felt overwhelmed, worthless. Not good enough as a person. These feelings come from childhood. They're inside and underneath. It doesn't matter what you do. Those early messages are there forever. It may be that my decision to be a missionary was trying to prove that I was good enough.

I came back to the States and became involved with an adult children of alcoholics support group. I needed that support and wouldn't have had it in Jamaica. So I stayed and started a program for our Order focused on global awareness, justice, and peace. It was part of our mission to tell the story of what we've seen in the world and to build bonds between diverse cultures. We lobbied for Bread for the World, for welfare. We even lobbied for a national day for peace. We tried for years, but couldn't get it, one day for peace!

I served as an assistant provincial for six years, responsible for about one hundred sisters. I dealt with administration, real estate, insurance, recruiting, everything that kept the organization oiled. Most relevant, I was coordinator of senior services. Because of war or various crises, we had forty nuns coming back to retire. For many, it was the worst thing that ever happened.

There's reverse culture shock coming back to the US, coming from a place with no electricity and limited food. You go into a mall and you get physically sick from the stimulation of the vast array of goods, 450 different types of cereal. You have no idea how to choose. You see all these colors, sizes, types...you just look at it. It would take me hours to shop.

When my mother was in her late eighties, she had serious health issues and I returned to the Peoria area to be nearby. I couldn't get a job in the medical field. Work in the missions does not relate to a modern high-tech hospital environment. I wanted to help because we didn't have much money. I had forty applications out at one point. I was willing to do anything. For a year I taught kids in a huge rural diocese. During this period I took chaplaincy training and began work in a neurological ward. I really had to sell to get the position. But when I did, I was in over my head. I had never been around so many comatose patients before. Some never recovered and went to long-term care facilities. After my mother died, the grace God had given me to do that work evaporated, and I wanted to get back to missions. I wanted to go somewhere with no electricity, no intensive care units.

They were looking for someone to go to a high school in Bougainville, Papua New Guinea. A civil war had just ended, the peacekeepers were still there, and we were returning to our missions. I said, "It sounds good to me!" So that's what I did.

Each village had its own dialect, but for inter-village relationships they speak pidgin. One estimate is that there are over 1,300 languages in Papua New Guinea. We taught in English. It was on the equator and the heat just killed me, but it was a fantastic mission. The Melanesian people have a huge culture gap to bridge from two thousand years ago and the present.

When we arrived, the civil war had just ended and all of the infrastructure had been destroyed. The people were living in grass huts and struggling to get back on their feet, to get a better life, their courage and desire for education, a very smart people. The kids would sit for exams for university scholarships on the Papua New Guinea mainland.

The area was beautiful, but there were land mines and other unexploded ordnance from World War II. Sometimes, if the kids got upset at school, they would get a fire going in the bush and throw the land mines into the fire. The mines would explode and spew all over the teachers' cottage, and you'd say, "Oh, my God!"

The country was beautiful, small gardens were prevalent. I've worked with poverty all my life. If you have a strong culture and natural beauty, despite the lack of material goods, it doesn't seem like poverty. In Bougainville the people color painted themselves like in Africa, wore headgear, did native dances, and recounted mythical stories. A strong culture, and I was with young people.

After my mother and my work in senior services for the Order, I thought my youth was over and I was destined for senior services. And here I end up in high school. I didn't think I'd know how to talk to the kids. I loved the kids! They would drive you crazy, but...That I could help these young people learn about themselves and the world was a wonderful thing. But, I was sixty-seven, and after several bouts of malaria, couldn't take the heat of the equator in the afternoons. By the standards of Bangladesh and Papua New Guinea, I was very old. They would call me "Grandma." Those people don't think about retirement; they think about survival and food for today.

So when another nun asked me if I was going to go to an assisted-living facility, I asked, "What happened to me?" I didn't think I was that old. But I didn't feel young. I felt very tired and in the mode, "I can't do it anymore." But then they asked me to be the provincial for 104 sisters in the States, Jamaica, and Tanzania. I had been away for many years and the issues of finance, real estate, and administration were daunting. The sisters were spread out in apartments and eleven different communities, with many nuns in their eighties and nineties. The average age was seventy-eight. We have some new sisters joining, but in Tanzania and the South Pacific. We have only fourteen nuns under sixty-five. This represents a large problem. Who is going to take care of this aging population?

Now we provide for our sisters in nursing homes, visit them, advocate for them, make sure they have clothes, take them to medical appointments. This declining population is scary. It means we'll be on our own without the support of the community. We have few resources. We were paid little for our pastoral work, enough for room and food. I made seventy dollars a month in Bangladesh. The Order has some investments and is certainly planning, but in some instances we're dependent on the help of other Orders of nuns, the Sisters of Charity, of St. Joseph, and the Carmelites.

My next assignment will be at Mary's Guest House, Chula Vista, California, near the Mexican border. It's a safe house for victims of sex trafficking. They come from all over—Indonesia, Colombia, Mexico, Nevada—anywhere, really. They go to work or training, work with case managers on their immigration status, everything to try to establish a normal life. I don't have the self-image of the super-missionary anymore, but I'm attracted to this work. It appeals to me.

It's a new beginning, and that means I have to find a place in a new community.

At this stage in life I am a much more reflective person. It's natural to shift from activity to contemplation—maybe that's what they call wisdom. I don't have the same energy, and I'm not an "all hours of the night" type. I hope I can be present for them when they come home late and want to talk about life at midnight. Other challenges will be meeting new people, a small community, learning Spanish. There's a delicate balance between recognizing your limits and convincing yourself that you can't do something. What you believe is what you get. So I believe I can do it.

I'm seventy-three, and in seven years I'll be eighty, but I'll stay as long as I can. You just don't go on forever. This is a window of opportunity for me, the right ministry for this time in my life. I've loved every one of my missions and got something important out of each place and people. But it's not about changing the world anymore. Been there, done that. All the work I've done in those countries; they're worse today than when I went to them.

I recognize that it's difficult to offer advice because our lifestyle is so different. We have so many spiritual helps—a prayer life, meditation, daily office, daily Mass. But it's our life, our responsibility. If we're not growing in God, then we've missed the point of our lives. Missions used to be to far-off places, to the poor, but it's all God's work.

I'll never stop being a missionary, even if I'm in a nursing home.

For you, how do you find your meaning? How do you become the person you were meant to be and grow in greater relationship with God? That's where you put the emphasis at this time in your life. It's the goodness you try to do every day, the love you give to the people around you. It's really about making the world better by working on the case you've been given. God's working; we just don't know the big picture.

I've fought depression, and I've seen a lot of suffering in desperate situations. That's God's challenge to me. I've accompanied so many, many people in their dying.

And I know that often aging and physical diminishment are seen as purely discouraging. If we are committed to living life faithfully, then we must embrace the "letting go," the humiliation and bodily changes. They are sacrifices that prepare us for a new life. As we age, our spirituality increases, and prayer and redemptive suffering become our primary mission. We must embrace our new mission using not our physical aspects, but our hearts and souls as part of a neverending discovery of God.

# *"What Would She Want?"*

## JAMES WILLIAMS
### Born 1955 – Retired 2000

Born in Louisiana, James Williams was raised in an air force family and spent much of his youth living abroad before settling in Las Cruces, New Mexico. It was there, as a teenager, in 1971, that he met Sharon, whom he would marry eight years later. The couple attended the same college and later worked for the same company, moving first to Minneapolis and later to Hong Kong. After their children were born, they returned to Minnesota, where James started his own business and Sharon worked for their church.

**In 2000, when she was forty-three, Sharon underwent an elective hysterectomy. After the surgery, she was overdosed with morphine, causing respiratory and cardiac arrest. Deprived of oxygen, she suffered an irreversible brain injury and lapsed into a coma. At the time, their two children were in elementary school. Sharon survived in that state for eight years before passing in 2008, at fifty-one.**

It's not about age, but circumstance. Things change, and you have to reallocate your energies and your focus. It doesn't mean that you terminate all your activities. For me, retirement from the business world has been an opportunity for passion and purpose to intersect.

My best friend...when my wife became ill, my mission in life changed. The most important thing I could do was try to save her. She was my sole focus. I liquidated my business and put together the best team I could, people from around the world. I got a nursing team to take care of her twenty-four hours a day, as many as twenty nurses. Eight years, every single day, it was my life. I did everything I could, pursued every technology that existed. I even flew her and her nurses to the Dominican Republic, where there's a clinic run by an American doctor providing embryonic stem cell treatments. My hope—my expectation—was that treatment would repair and replace brain cells damaged by oxygen deprivation. I was searching everywhere.

In the course of my search, I encountered hyperbaric oxygen treatment. It appeared to help Sharon, and to ease her discomfort. Ultimately, I became interested in building a clinic offering that treatment. The treatment puts 100 percent pure oxygen under pressure. It becomes much more concentrated, so your organs, cerebral fluids, and bloodstream all get saturated. The body detoxifies and repairs cells at the molecular level. Those healthy cells provide an environment for the growth of new cells. We're involved in an important study right now with the National Brain Injury Rescue and Rehabilitation

Project. We're one of thirty-three clinics participating in treating veterans with traumatic brain injury and post-traumatic stress disorder. The first phase has demonstrated a 28 percent increase in brain capacity, after only an eight-week session. (A recent study on autism demonstrated significant improvement in overall functioning in children treated with hyperbaric oxygen therapy. Though available at independent clinics and several hospitals, most medical insurance companies do not cover it for the treatment for autism.)

My only goal now is to keep providing the service. Originally, I got involved and built the clinic to save my wife. Since then we've treated more than seven hundred patients. For the last year we've been treating Iraq and Afghanistan veterans for free. I'm using the limited money I have to subsidize treatments. But I can't do that forever. I have a foundation to raise funds to provide treatments for kids with autism. In the Twin Cities, we have a large Somali population. They have the highest incidence of autism in the US. What is remarkable is that autism doesn't exist in Somalia. I've put together a network of service providers: nursing, nutrition, oxygen detox, etc. The network providers discount their services by 25 percent and my foundation picks up the remaining 75 percent.

I'm also involved in a lot of community programs. I've found one particularly meaningful, One Hundred Strong Who Care. I go to inner-city schools and encourage kids to continue their education. I'm also a member of the Woman's Club of Minneapolis—the gentlemen's section, of course. It's a way to promote the clinic and the network.

When I first began to think about this path, it was exciting. I had tremendous hopes for it. My wife...my baby would do anything to help other people, so I invested a lot in building this clinic to save her and to help others. We weren't able to save her, but we've helped people with traumatic brain injury, post-traumatic stress disorder, stroke, Lyme disease, autism, cerebral palsy, multiple sclerosis.

Something positive, something productive has come out of this nightmare. It was devastating, paralyzing. Absolutely paralyzing.

Once you overcome the paralysis, this becomes your new reality. I've always had high energy, but once the paralysis lifted, my energy went to another level. Since this happened, I'm not looking too far off. I'm thinking about what I'm doing today. Ten-year projections just aren't my reality.

I don't know how I got through those days. A lot of prayer, a lot of support. I always was spiritual, but I've lost my faith. Miracles happen every day, all around us. Why didn't I get my miracle? I was taught to have faith and to believe that God will bring you through. It's shattering when that doesn't happen.

The price I paid was too high. My wife's life is over. That outweighs any good that I might do. I ask, what would she want? A healthy, stable family. But, more than that, the opportunity to be a blessing to others.

Our kids live ten minutes from me, and we have two grandkids. I know how much Sharon would have enjoyed playing with those kids. She's really, really missed. Our family is not complete.

# "I Don't Idle Well"

## TED LEGASEY
### Born 1945 – Retired 2004

*Ted and his father, Roy, at Air Force Academy graduation, and Ted (l.)
and trekking the Camino de Santiago with friend, Charlie Hugo.*

**Ted Legasey is a Distinguished Graduate of the US Air Force
Academy and earned a master's degree from the University of
Pennsylvania. He spent nine years on active duty, worked on
large logistics management systems, and directed software test-
ing and evaluation for the B-1 flight test program. In 1978, Ted
cofounded SRA International, a global information technology
and professional services firm. He helped build the company into
a major player in the information technology industry. SRA went
public in 2002. Ted retired from SRA as executive vice president
and chief operating officer in 2004.**

Today, most of Ted's time is consumed with philanthropic ventures. He is on the boards of a half-dozen academic and philanthropic organizations, including Malden Catholic High School, the Air Force Academy, the Charleston Symphony Orchestra, the College of Charleston Foundation, and Trident United Way. He focuses on educational improvement initiatives in the city of Charleston. For his efforts, Ted was named Charleston's Outstanding Individual Philanthropist for 2010.

He and his high school sweetheart, Tricia, have been married for forty-five years. They have one son and live on Kiawah Island, South Carolina.

"How do you sell thirty thousand blue suits? Hire Roy Legasey." That was the ad campaign Filene's used to run. My dad sold suits in that department store for fifty-two years. He was a driven guy. He had an eighth grade education, but taught himself to read the classics in Greek. He and my mom, who worked in a stationery store, were determined that their kids got good college educations. They had a weekly ritual of gathering the family together and depositing money into our college funds. They instilled a strong work ethic. I worked in a local grocery store starting in the seventh grade and paid my high school tuition.

I retired at fifty-eight. I was one of the two people who started SRA. My partner was the guy with the idea, one of the Pentagon's whiz kids, very smart guy, a fast-track military officer. When I met him, he was the youngest full colonel in the air force. He was kind of a hot rocket. He had watched a lot of the whiz kids start companies—Computer Sciences, CACI, etc.—and had a vision we'd start a company.

Long story short, that's what we did in 1978. He was the chairman and CEO and I was the COO. Those were our roles. I was the operating guy who made things happen day-to-day. He was the over-the-horizon strategy guy. It was a good division of responsibilities.

We were a private company for twenty-four years, until 2002. Post-9/11, the industry got valuable. The public markets realized that these guys are guiding the command and control systems, the intelligence systems, the sophisticated data, all that kind of stuff. So a whole bunch of companies went public, including ours. I was the COO for two years as a public company. My partner was ready to step out of the CEO role and become chairman, and I was to move up to the CEO role. But I was fifty-eight, I was going to have to commit to sixty-five or sixty-six, and it just wasn't a burning desire to do that. I had done the things I wanted to do in that industry. You can't be the CEO of a public company if it's not the most important thing in your life. I said, "This is not the most important thing in my life. I'm going to step back from this." We had done a lot of great things and there was work to do, but it didn't hold the kind of attraction that I needed to motivate me daily.

At that time I had no alternative vision of what to do. I knew there were things I didn't want to do. I didn't want to get on a lot of company boards and hang out a consulting shingle and work in the industry from a different pedestal.

I wanted to do something different. I always had a hobby of woodworking. This house has a thousand-square-foot cabinet shop. We live in a resort on the beach and there are a lot of people here like me. But, they pretty much divide into two categories. Guys who play golf every day and people who do woodworking. There's a subset of a half-dozen guys who have shops.

One of the beautiful things about Charleston is its architecture and the restoration that has taken place. Very quickly emerged the idea that I would buy properties, restore them, and sell them. I would do enough of the work myself—building cabinetry, trim work—so that I could stay busy. I would also volunteer with one or two nonprofits and everything would be hunky-dory. That's what I told people I would do. I was going to focus on historic restoration. We did two properties. The real estate market dried up, and the economics of doing that were no longer attractive. Also, I realized that the woodworking was great and satisfying, but I need people in my life.

I get my energy from people. The solitude of a shop is OK as a sauce for me, but not as a main ingredient. I need to be involved with people. My career has been as an operating guy. I'm a problem solver. I have an ability to lead and motivate people. So as time freed up, I started to spend more time with nonprofits in the Charleston area.

In about 2006, I was being asked by more organizations to get involved because some of the early things I had done had some visibility in town. I won't just sit on a board. I want to put my hands on the organization; I want to help mature the organization to bring the sound principles of enterprise development to these nonprofits, which are organizationally immature. I started to do that. There's no shortage of that kind of work. Quickly, I became involved in things here.

Now I spend my time as a quasi-operating guy in three to five organizations here in Charleston that try to make a difference in the community. Plus, I serve as chairman of the board of my high school. I run a full schedule, forty to fifty hours a week. For these organizations I go to budget, finance, and strategy meetings, and recruit executives for leadership roles.

I drive myself by putting stakes in the ground. The public education system here in Charleston is like any other midsize or major city, where there are some really great schools, and there are some really embarrassing schools. Trying to fix the systemic things that cause these embarrassing schools to continue to be embarrassing is a real goal. I think I can help move them in the right direction and that's something you can measure. It would be a real accomplishment if we can make progress in those schools.

One of the organizations, the Charleston Philanthropic Partnership, is engaged in "social venture philanthropy." The idea is to get people involved who want to do more than write a check; they want to help the organization develop. The way the model works is you recruit partners to the partnership, they guarantee a financial commitment each year. The partnership invests in two or three priorities. They invest at a level that's going to make a difference, but you don't just give them the money. You build a plan and the partners actually play a role in helping the organization grow.

For example, there's a push right now in Charleston around literacy. Several years ago I was part of a group that created Charleston Volunteers for Literacy. This is a program in about a half-dozen schools that works with first to third graders who are not phonemically aware. It enables these kids to read at grade level.

Another project is the Social Innovation Board. It gets the many organizations working on a problem aligned with each other so that there's an overall, cohesive strategy. It's very outcome focused.

I have become a professional community volunteer, with the objective of leaving a mark, creating something in life and making a difference...not just leaving a butt print in the sands of time. So it's very gratifying in that regard. It's somewhat frustrating in that, unlike a for-profit enterprise, it's really hard to move these nonprofits. They're all volunteers.

Insofar as being just a retired guy, I'm having an impact on my community. I'm having a positive impact. I've got the best of all worlds because I meter myself. I decided where and how I'm going to spend my time. It's not constant, but from year to year priorities shift. I fall right to sleep at night; I'm really tired. I get up in the morning and I'm ready to go.

The biggest challenge has been balancing priorities and deciding what's the best use of my time, to make certain that I'm not just dabbling. I want to spend enough time that I have an impact. That's probably been the trickiest thing.

I had prostate cancer in early 2005. When you go through that, you do pause and say: Have I got things sorted out? Do I have my priorities right? Am I applying my God-given skills and abilities in a way that is generating the right return? Am I living life the way I want to live it? Am I spending enough time with my wife, focused on the things she wants to do?

# *"I Just Go and Do"*

## ELIZABETH STEEDLEY
### Born 1943 – Retired 2002

**Elizabeth taught in a middle school in a small Georgia town for thirty years. She retired after the deaths of a son and an uncle, the final illness of her mother, and a divorce. She spends her time teaching in a GED program for the Georgia State Prison System, and relaxing on a family farm, cooking and driving her Kubota 3400 tractor.**

I was born in 1943 in Nashville, Georgia. My mother taught sixth and seventh grades and my dad worked building military bases, in the Brunswick shipyard, and later, as a small-town home builder.

I went to Valdosta State, studied business, and got my master's in education. Then I taught in the public schools for thirty years. I married at nineteen, after my first year of college. I had two boys. I lost my oldest son in an accident, when he was twenty and home from college. He was driving a tractor, mowing, and it turned over. That was a very hard time. I was married for thirty-five years. I'm divorced. I don't think you can have a major tragedy and get through it without becoming closer, or you'll grow farther apart. It's part of you. I've been divorced for nine years.

I have four grandkids. They all live in town. My son is a part-time juvenile court judge and has a law practice in town. My son enjoys being a lawyer. He's a good judge, because he's a fine young man—not a young man anymore, he's forty-four.

I retired at age fifty-nine. I just needed a rest. At that time I had gone through a divorce, my uncle had died, and my mother was not doing well. One of my sisters was in the same town as my mother, about sixty miles from here, and was her major caregiver. I was the only sibling living nearby. I'd make two trips a week to help. It was a thing I needed to do, so that's what I did.

As I've gotten older, I have friends that I enjoy being around. I have girlfriends that we go and do and shop. I have gentlemen friends, too. I have one particular friend who has been very supportive in our friendship, and I have enjoyed going and doing things with him, too.

When you're older, I don't think you feel the need to be attached to someone. I had one long marriage and I'm probably the type of person that's meant to be married for life, like an animal that mates for life. So it's been very hard for me to marry again. I've had proposals; I have just not wanted to make that step. Once you've been married a long time, everything is intertwined, things like credit cards, simple things. When you're married, you got this identity together; when you're single, that changes.

Once you get everything separated, you get your credit card, your debit card, your bank account, your CD, and your whatever. As an older person, this is important, it becomes very hard...You think twice about the different people you meet, and you think, *Could I make it forever and ever and ever with that person, or would I have to go through the same thing again?*

When you're young, you just throw caution to the wind. It really doesn't matter. It's going to be fine. Whether you have the next meal on the table or not, you don't worry about that too much. You're supposed to be struggling a little anyway. You enjoy it. You don't worry about it. As you get older and you go through retirement, you do have to worry about it because you don't want to have to ask your children for anything. You don't want to be dependent. You want to maintain your independence. At the same time, you want to leave your children financially secure. You still think of them even after they're out of the house. You want to make sure you leave your grandchildren something. Not that they couldn't make it on their own.

I talk to other divorcees, and not everybody is like me. Some will say, "That's the person I'm going to marry and be with for the rest of my life." I'm not going to say that's not going to happen to me. I'm just saying that up to this point it hasn't. I think one thing, too, I've been very busy. I lead a very busy life.

As I approached retirement, I was so exhausted. I was just going to rest. I did, and I caught up on things. I traveled a little bit, to St. Simon's, to Savannah, to Florida and different points of interest. Maybe not way off, but I traveled around to Florida, Georgia, South Carolina, Hilton Head, and Charleston.

I like to go up to my farm maybe two, three times a week, just being up there, especially this time of year. The fall colors are so pretty on the Alapaha River. The river has a life of its own, and it all depends on nature and the water coming from north Georgia, feeding into the different streams and then into the main river. The river rises in Georgia, flows through north Florida into the Suwannee River, where five rivers meet.

The farm is thirty miles from my home. In years past, it was a big working farm: livestock, tobacco, corn, peanuts. It's one hundred acres. It was part of a land grant to my ancestors dating back to the American Revolution and was divided on my uncle's death. I let another farmer grow cotton up there. I don't rent it. I just love to see the cotton grow and see the fields the way they used to be. The farm is up in Berrien County. It looks like a step back in time. I have the house, the barn, and all the outbuildings; the tobacco barn, the corn grinder, the syrup boiler, and all the things you'd have on a farm. The syrup boiler, as a small child, it was a big thrill.

When I go up there, I enjoy. I like to cook. Like this morning it was real crisp, so I got up and made blueberry pancakes, with blueberries grown right here on the farm. Putting them up takes a little time during the summer. And I grow flowers. I have flowers. Also, I like to mow the pasture with a Kubota 3400. It will pull a six-foot mower. I simply like to do that, get the fresh air. It's an easy tractor to drive. You push your foot forward and it goes forward. Push your foot back and it goes backward, power steering and all that. So no big deal, and I enjoy it.

I have neighbors near the farm. In fact yesterday, my neighbor—she's an older woman—came and visited, old-time style. You don't see a lot of that anymore. She's lonesome, because until I go up there, there's only one other neighbor she can visit with. So she came down and visited and talked general woman talk. She's near her eighties. She and her husband are getting on in years. It's a remote property, and since its river property, it's good to be in touch with your neighbor. You have to watch out for one another. My next-closest neighbor is about a mile from me.

The other day I had a delightful surprise...a new neighbor has moved in, a retired naval commander, only in his forties. He walked up and introduced himself. I thought, *Well, golly!* He was so young-looking, and he was actually forty-something. That's young to retire.

He bought the place so he would have it to hunt. The deer are very plentiful, and the wild turkeys and all that are very plentiful, then the ducks on the river. If you're into...I suppose you call it blood sport...I'm not, but I do realize the herd has to be controlled because it gets to be a bad thing.

Even when I am not at the farm, I like my flowers, I like to grow flowers. I have a flower garden—daylilies, gardenias, camellias—things you have in a Southern garden. My mother, when she retired, had a nursery, and my sister and her husband have one now.

In my first year of retirement I joined a group over at Valdosta State. We would do yoga, courses on computers, candy making, etc. I also learned dancing, ballroom dancing, and swing dancing with my friends. This was my first year out of divorce and I enjoyed being with a group, rather than just being singled out. It was therapy for me. I like to dance. I've always liked to dance. I think it's good for me, too.

After a year, I got restless and started thinking there is something else I can do. I wanted to be helpful. I did librarian work at the Homerville Prison. I was there for five years until it closed. Then I got a position at Robert L. Patton Detention Center in Lakeland, a couple of days a week. I have been there eight years. I teach all five subjects for the GED program: English, social studies, math, reading, and writing. The students are not there because they missed Sunday school. It's a prison. Sometimes they look at you and tell you something they did, and it's not like they're proud of it. There's a real broad range. Some are as young as eighteen and some appear to be fifty. Prison is not a good thing...it's a very dangerous place.

It's an outlet I need. At this time of life you need to feel as though you're productive. I need to be helpful. I need to be productive; that's just part of who I am. I teach because I've been busy all my life; it's hard to stop. I really like to do this. I've taught all my life, and I don't know anything else.

I love for them to get their GED. It is simply so fulfilling. When you see those prisoners—through their own fault they are where they are at—when you see how happy they are, and their first response is, "Oh, my family is going to be so proud of me! My wife is going to be proud of me! My children are going to be so proud of me!" When they actually see that all the work they put into it, the studying; they got something themselves. You see, I didn't go with them to the test. The only thing I do is teach them. They know it's what they have done. It's not something I have done for them, because it's not. All I have done is teach them.

As a teacher in middle school, I was focused on being goal-oriented. You don't really get to sit back and just enjoy the children. You feel a lot of responsibility simply because the child is young and doesn't have the same motivation you have. Whereas in the prisoner mode, their focus is a little different; they're motivated to do it.

You don't have that much time to enjoy any one prisoner's success, because as soon as this one gets his GED, you fill that space. I teach a class of twenty, but it's specialized to their needs. The majority of them will tell you the reason they quit school is because they were thrown out for being incorrigible, or being disruptive, or some type of criminal activity. Some reason they did not fit into society, and you are going to have that segment that quit because they were not motivated or because of the drug culture. The drug culture has taken its toll. I have twenty students for four hours, two days a week. I have prison aides who help with correcting the tests and tutoring. I have to make sure the material is covered. The students have to make a certain score on the practice test before they're allowed to test for the GED. I don't think I was ever really scared of going into a prison. Remember, I taught middle school.

I think I'll know when it's time to retire. [*Dog barks.*] That's a little Chihuahua, four pounds of yappy, Libby. She's a blond Chihuahua. I don't know why she wasn't named Marilyn Monroe. My granddaughter got her when she went to college and asked if I would take her. And guess what—I did what all goodly moms do. Basically I did not like a dog in the house. So I adjusted. Now, she's so watchful and very generous. I do enjoy her. She's a good thing.

I can't say I don't worry about the future. I do. If I found a companion to go through life with, I think that would be great. I haven't as of yet, and a lot of that might just be me because I'm so hesitant. I'm not an exception; a lot of people who were married a long time find themselves in this situation. I have a lot of wonderful memories. Right now, I find my life very full. I don't see the urgency, maybe I should! I'm having a good time in my life. I am enjoying myself.

I go all the time. Shopping with my friends, trips with my friends, I go out every weekend. I'm lucky as an older woman because I stay busy all weekend long with people. Maybe I am an exception. Maybe there are some lonesome people in the world. I don't have time to get lonesome.

Honestly, I think that making new friends is the easiest thing in the world for me because I'm receptive. I will meet anybody from whatever class of life. I am not saying I will go with them anywhere or do anything with them, but I'll meet them and talk with them, which has always been an easy thing for me to do.

I've become more conscious of my decisions, more conscious of my example, more accountable. I've already lived way more than I'm going to live. You have to face that your productive years, when you can really get out and do, are not as many as they were. So you got to be selective. You have to choose how you're going to spend these years.

I volunteer through church and teaching Sunday school. Now I'll do, but I won't take responsibility for a position. I've met too many deadlines. I'll help you out as much as I can. Just tell me what to do, but don't put me down as responsible for all of it.

Somewhere along the line I hope I've made a difference. And I'm teaching now, I feel sure I'm making a difference, especially when that prisoner has that GED in hand and a chance at a better job, which may or may not be true if they're in that prison turnstile lifestyle. Nothing's more rewarding than seeing prisoners get their GED. All the time they thank me. "You have inspired me. You pushed me." That's very rewarding.

It has nothing to do with money. I'm very hopeful for their futures.

# IX. CHANGE

# *"Five Seconds Changed My Life"*

## GAILMARIE HANNA
### Born 1941 – Retired 1992

Gailmarie's parents were born in Egypt into very large families. They met in the United States and had an arranged marriage. Her father was a career army officer and her family moved frequently. She attended grade school in Georgia, Virginia, Texas, and New Jersey. At her parents' insistence she married right after high school. This marriage lasted four years and produced a son and a daughter.

After her divorce, Gailmarie worked a variety of jobs, from waitressing to air freight at Logan Airport, and went to Boston University full time. On graduation she moved to California and raised her children as a single mom. She worked and continued her graduate education at UCLA, where she obtained an MBA.

**She lived and worked in Southern California for almost forty years, with a two-and-a-half-year stint in Hong Kong.**

**She lives in Gulf Coast Florida and her children live in Wisconsin and Michigan. She talks with them four to five times per week. She has four grandchildren.**

I was inspecting a warehouse for safety and OSHA requirements when it happened. I tripped and fell against some warehouse racks. I suffered a severe neck injury that crushed three discs at C4-5-6 on my left side. I had to wear a neck brace for over four and half years. I wore a halo brace to immobilize my cervical spine. I had surgery to insert a titanium plate in my neck. I was totally disabled and had to retire. I went from making six figures to making exceedingly little. I had to get into a long drawn-out battle with the insurers to get any compensation.

After the accident, I couldn't sustain my lifestyle and I had to sell everything, including my house. I wasn't sure where I would live. It's difficult to decide where you want to go when you grow up when you don't want to grow up. I had been grown up all my life and I didn't want to be grown up anymore. I had worked hard all my life. I had had a lot of responsibility from age eighteen, supporting two children. Once the injury happened, for the first time, I had to be just me. I had four years of getting through the injury to think what I was going to do next. It was an evolving process.

I put my children through private schools and gave them wonderful educations, one at a military academy and the other a private Christian school. They were raised in Southern California, but never became part of that culture. They had really strong value systems. I did that by myself. I'm proud of that. My children think I earned retirement and are appreciative of all that I did for them. The injury also brought home how wonderful my kids were. When I got rid of my house and rented a new condo, I went to pay my rent and found that they had already paid six months' rent.

My children didn't stay in California, and I had thought I'd never leave. The perfect climate, the mountains, the desert, the ocean, but it also has major social issues and a high cost of living, and so I did leave.

When I left, I had an extended visit with my son in Alabama, but decided not to stay in that area when it became clear that my social attitudes were not compatible with the culture, especially given that I'm opinionated and outspoken. I thought it best to move along. I went to Michigan and spent some time with my daughter. I spent a winter in Oakland County, Michigan, and decided that I couldn't live in that climate, although it is beautiful six or seven weeks of the year.

Then I came to Massachusetts and spent time with my family, and met a friend who suggested I try Florida. He was having a new home built that I could house-sit. So I said sure. I figured I didn't have anything to lose. Well, I did like it. I've learned that I can't live where palm trees don't grow naturally, and Florida is closer to my kids than California. Also, I was able to live near the water, something I had done most of my life. So I rented a house in Punta Gorda. It's a great, friendly community.

In 2004, while I was visiting Las Vegas, Hurricane Charlie hit. It destroyed my home and I lost everything, for a second time. So I stayed in Las Vegas for three years visiting friends and trying to recover. I didn't come back to Florida until 2007.

I've lost everything twice in my life. That has impacted my priorities. Those events, plus age, refocused my priorities. You need food, shelter, but other material things are less significant. In the final analysis, what's important is your family and friends. If you can count one person as a true friend, you're fortunate. I count five, so I'm very fortunate. This realization really hit me when I was injured. It was amazing how many people all of a sudden didn't know me once my finances changed.

I'm very competitive by nature, just something that you're born with. But today it is totally different. I just want peace and tranquility in my life. I'd like employment, to feel useful, but not competitive, just to stay mentally alert. I'd rather be working. I miss the social aspects of work, but I wouldn't want to be part of the rat race today. I don't want the sales goals. I don't want the Los Angeles traffic, or the Boston traffic. I like Punta Gorda, this little, small town. Everyone is friendly. They'll talk to you even if they don't know you.

I've had a bout with cancer, so there's been a bit of drawback there physically. I lost a kidney two years ago. I've been fortunate. I've been going every six months and now, after two years, graduated to once a year. I had a left knee fracture a year and a half ago. It hasn't healed as well as I'd like and so I'm not as active as I'd like. Otherwise I'm doing well. Three leaking valves in my heart, but I don't need a valve replacement. So I'm very fortunate there. Health is a major concern. That's what you have to worry about as you get older. It just happens—wear and tear.

I love crafts. I have been drawing in pen and ink for almost forty years. I used to go to hospitals and do drawings of kids. Now I do it for gifts. My son-in-law had been a naval officer and I did drawings of the lighthouses of the places he had been. He was born and raised on the Great Lakes and stationed in Florida and California. That's a lot of lighthouses. Lately, I've been doing caricatures of movie stars. I spend two to three hours a day now doing them. It's fun. I started by doodling and it expanded. I found it fun and relaxing. I always had the ability to draw.

In addition, I'm trying to develop information about my father's service and decorations. I know he had two Purple Hearts. My father left my mother after thirty-seven years. He remarried and relocated to Las Vegas and retired there. Where else but the desert for an Egyptian? My mother had his medals and decorations. I don't know where they are now. So I've got part of his service record. I was amazed at all that he had done. It's important for my children and grandchildren to understand this.

At this point I don't have any major goals or objectives. I want to spend more time with my children. I wish they lived in a warmer climate. They want me to spend the holidays with them, but I live in Florida and they live in tundra country. The idea of going to Michigan or Wisconsin in the dead of winter doesn't thrill me. When they're telling me it's thirty-five degrees below, I say, "Are you nuts?"

I've traveled a lot. I've seen all fifty states. I've been to twenty-seven countries and lived in Hong Kong for two and a half years. All my travels were in the Pacific Rim. What I'd like to see now are the Caribbean Islands.

Aging has had no impact on my sense of well-being. I'm still very optimistic. Any day you wake up is a good day. It's a gift. That's why they call it the present. There are always things you'd like to go back and change about the past, but you can't. There are no do-overs. So I try not to dwell on it, just learn from it. I don't believe in organized religion, but I do believe in God or a higher power. I'm spiritual, but not religious. Spirituality is a way of life, doing things and living your life by your beliefs.

Nobody is ever prepared for tomorrow. Tomorrow is a big surprise. Expect the unexpected. Prepare for the worst. Five seconds changed my life completely at age fifty-one.

# *"If You Don't Like Me, So What?"*

## DEREK SANDERSON
### Born 1946 – Retired 1978

Derek Sanderson was an all-star hockey player known for his versatility, his ability to win crucial face-offs, and his never-back-down attitude. He and his Big Bad Bruin teammates ended a twenty-nine-year drought and delivered Stanley Cups to Boston in 1970 and 1972. For this, Derek was much loved, but he had so much more. He had leading man good looks; he was named the sexiest man in America. He lived the lifestyle of a young play-boy. His companions in the fast lane included "Broadway Joe" Namath and soccer star George Best. At one point Derek was lured to the fledgling World Hockey Association (WHA) and be-came the highest-paid athlete in the world. He owned nightclubs, a Rolls-Royce, diamond rings, and at least one mink coat.

His lifestyle and developing dependency on drugs and alcohol, along with his accumulated injuries, took their toll and brought his brilliant hockey career to a premature end at age thirty-two. When this happened, Derek thought he would earn his living from his nightclubs, but those went bust. His dependency on drugs and alcohol worsened and his fall was of extreme proportions. He found himself sleeping on park benches and seeking shelter in underpasses, stealing wine from stores and sleeping winos, and panhandling to support his addictions. Compounding this, his injuries so hobbled him that he could only get around on crutches.

After burning himself in a grease fire, and after many failed attempts, Derek achieved sobriety with the help of an old teammate, Bobby Orr, and others. He then began to re-create himself. He became a popular TV personality providing analysis and color on hockey. He now counsels students on substance abuse and young athletes on prudent investing. Derek, along with some Boston financial institutions, established a practice providing financial advice to athletes. Although he immersed himself in charitable works, his crowning achievements were marrying and raising two boys of whom he is so proud. He recently published a memoir, *Crossing The Line*, which recounts the inspiring story of a life re-created and resurrected, and his life story is being made into a movie, *Turk*.

M y dream was to be a hockey player, like every kid in Canada. I started skating in the backyard when I was three. I got half good at it because of an extremely dedicated father.

My dad was my god. He was a journeyman machinist for Kimberly Clark, a voracious reader, a self-taught man. He was a genius at machinery, an amazing human being. As a kid I remember an incident when a 410-foot assembly line broke and no one could repair it. After five days, he said, "Give me a shot at it." He got the blueprints and disassembled it. He then got the line up and running, and saved the plant thousands and thousands of dollars.

Later, he declined a better job in Toronto and stayed in Ontario so that I could continue to play on the junior team, the Niagara Falls Flyers. My dad followed the methods of Lloyd Percival, a popular and controversial sports innovator, who wrote about hockey skills, conditioning, and team play. Percival studied hockey as played all over the world. He believed all players should be trained to play all positions, like interchangeable parts. In case of injury or penalties, there would be someone to play any position. He also advocated certain eating habits that would aid in your play, such as eating pasta pregame, not steak. Pasta would have an immediate positive and longer-lasting effect. He also believed in ice baths, and I started taking them when I was ten in peewee games.

After much discussion, my father reluctantly let me leave formal schooling in the tenth grade. I was a well-mannered kid who had good schooling up until that time. My father's conditions were that I must go to the rink daily from nine to twelve. I must learn a new vocabulary word every day. The first was *obsequious*. I would use the words in paragraphs and then put them in a story. Dad said, "If you have command of the Queen's English, then, perhaps, bullshit will baffle brains and they'll not know you're not an educated person."

I played junior hockey at fifteen, six feet, 149 pounds. There were four spots open at the tryouts and 134 kids trying out. I thought I was going to get killed, but I made the team. When I went in to see the owner, Hap Emms, the room was dark. He was behind a desk with a light glaring in my eyes, just like in *The Natural*, only this was before *The Natural*. He says, "So you think you can play?" My father taught me to be well mannered, so I told him, "I just work hard."

I played and did well. I won a lot of trophies, including the MVP and scoring trophies. At that time, Weston Adams, who owned the Bruins, was friends with Hap Emms. Every year, Adams would give Hap's team all the Bruins' year-old equipment and was awarded in exchange one of their players. He chose me. This led me to Harry Sinden, the coach of the Bruins, who told me that all my trophies meant nothing. He said, "We'll look at you; we'll give you the benefit of the doubt. If you don't have balls and you don't have courage, you ain't going to be here very long." I realized that all I've got is hockey. I'm going to work as hard as I can because I'm not going back to the minors.

Even though I made the team, its members did not accept me right away. I had to prove that I was tough. This happened during a brawl in Montreal where I hit everything that moved. There was a rough fight in center ice and Teddy Green, the Bruins' tough guy, and the rest of the Bruins backed me up. Bobby Orr said, "Nobody's in this fight alone." The fight forced the league to institute the "third man in" rule, which attempts to eliminate other players from joining a fight by imposing stiff penalties.

Of course, winning the Stanley Cup was thrilling, but most of us, because we were Canadians, didn't realize just how significant it was to lifelong Bruins fans. Plus, other than me, we were a humble bunch. For me, the difference between winning the Stanley Cup or losing it was like taking a playmate to London or a college chick to Cape Cod. We didn't feel like we owned the city because we weren't from here.

After I went to the WHA, I injured a disc in my back and pretty soon a dispute developed about whether to have surgery. I told them they could operate if they could guarantee that I'd be able to play hockey again, and of course, they couldn't. The management wanted out of paying me. I couldn't skate, but I could work out. They got a German drill-instructor type to put me through really intense physical conditioning—a lot of love/hate in that relationship. They were trying to break me physically, but they couldn't. I just got in great shape. So next they go to the psychological stuff. They got a full-length mirror and made me stand in front of it and look at myself. They said, "What do you see?" I said, "A rich kid you can't break." I loved it. Finally, I got bought out and went back to the Bruins, and then got traded to New York.

During this period I was living high. I had the cover of *Life* magazine of me and my girlfriend in a huge circular bed. Four hundred copies were printed, then J. Edgar Hoover died, so they quickly changed the cover.

After playing for a number of years, I'd had problems with my knees, hips, and particularly with my back. Joe Namath was a friend who had terrible knee problems and he went to see his doctor in New York. I went along and told the doctor I'd had knee surgery when I was seventeen. He looked at my left knee and realized that my back issues were because of this knee. He measured my thighs and my right thigh was four inches bigger than my left. This was because I had been favoring my left leg and had skated for all those years, mostly on one leg. This imbalance had thrown out my back. I had totally dismantled the robotics of my system. Everything was off.

After I finished up with hockey, I owned nightclubs in Boston: Daisy Buchanan's, Scott's, Gatsby's, and Zelda's. Around 1978, I really hit the skids. I was broke and living under the bridges in New York City. I would sleep on the benches in Central Park in the rain. Panhandling, drugs, and booze were consuming my life. I would steal booze. I learned they'll never chase you for a pint. They'll chase you for a quart, but not a pint.

Alcohol creates fear and you don't even know what you're afraid of. You have your worst nightmare come true. Mine took the form of snakes eating my eyes. I think it came from some movie I saw as a kid. I was destitute for two years, in and out of detox and rehab, trying to get sober but always failing. Bobby Orr managed to get me sober twice. My "come-to-Jesus moment" involved a drug deal gone bad and a subsequent grease fire where I severely burned myself, jumped out the door of my home and into a snowbank. I was stuck in the snow. After a long time and many painful attempts, I managed to free myself and get back into the house. The phone was ringing and it was a local doctor calling to ask me to hand out trophies to local hockey players. I told him how badly I was burned. He sent help and they took me to Ft. Erie Hospital. I believe there is a God. For those who don't believe, there's never enough proof, and for those who believe, you don't need any.

One day I was walking down Newbury Street in Boston and I met Senator Joe Timilty, a real stand-up guy. He said, "You need some help." He and Mayor Ray Flynn got me some medical help and a job working in drug and alcohol awareness programs. Why do kids do drugs? They need self-esteem; they need to nullify fear. Fear plays such a big part in drug issues. When I was sixteen, I was shy. I went to a dance and finally got up the nerve to ask this girl to dance. I still remember her name and what happened. We began dancing and, twelve bars into the music, she started laughing at me. I stopped and have never danced since. Fear is real. Fear molds us and fear makes us who we are. It never goes away. You have to let it go and let God. Clarity comes when there ain't no fear.

I was married on December 28, 1986, and now my goals concern my wife and my kids. Success means they're happy. I'd like my kids, when they graduate from college, to own a house with no mortgage. My challenge in the next few years is to make money.

I'm in the investment business. I know what it means to have money. I was the highest-paid athlete in the world. I was a millionaire at twenty-four. It was the worst thing that ever happened to me. I bought a Rolls-Royce the first day I got the money. I was intelligent and I ended up on a junk heap.

I don't miss hockey. The only thing I miss is the gratification of doing something I did best. I was confident inside the boards. Outside the ice I was like a duck out of water.

How do I feel about aging? I don't think any different than when I was twenty-one. I have absolutely no fear of dying. I have no problem with self-esteem. If you don't like me, so what, you're not that important to me. My dad said, "Quit trying to impress the people you're hanging out with. Impress your mother and me and your friends. Why are you trying to impress people who don't like you? Don't give them the ability to hurt you."

The most rewarding thing I have done, other than to raise my family, was to talk to kids in schools about drug and alcohol awareness. I did this for thirteen years, over seven hundred thousand kids in over eight hundred schools in Canada and the US, five schools a week. I'd like to continue this in some form as long as I can. I think a lot of changes that I've already gone through in some ways are similar to the changes people face as they age. Sudden changes in how you spend your time, a period of transition, finding out what is important to you, and getting yourself in a position to pursue it.

I am a spiritual person, although not for organized religion. I know there is a God. When overwhelmed, I say, "God help me." Spirituality is a personal thing. I'm comfortable with Jesus Christ and I believe you move on to a better place. I learned in AA that some people just want to do it their way. I can't control my life. God can, so I'll let him.

# *"Change the Narrative of Your Life"*

## HON. JAMES E. MCGREEVEY
### Born 1957

Jim is the oldest child of a US Marine Corps drill instructor and a nurse. He was named for an uncle who died at Iwo Jima. He attended Catholic grammar and high school before graduating from Columbia University, Georgetown Law, and Harvard's Graduate School of Education. He also attended the London School of Economics. After working as an assistant prosecutor, Jim entered politics in 1990. He had all the skills, an easy smile, a great laugh, and a firm handshake. Plus, he was smart and telegenic. He was immediately successful and rose rapidly. He served as state representative, state senator, and mayor

243

of Woodbridge. In 2001, at age forty-four, he was elected governor of New Jersey in a landslide. At the time, Jim had two daughters, one of whom he was raising with his second wife. In August 2004, he announced that he was gay, had had an affair with a man on his staff, and would resign from office. His wife and parents stood by him.

The announcement made Jim the only openly gay governor in the United States and ended a remarkable political career, one that some thought would lead to a presidential bid. It also produced a divorce, tabloid headlines, lawsuits, and, most significantly, a long period of reflection that caused Jim to redirect his life. He attended theological seminary and earned a Master of Divinity degree with the intention of becoming an Episcopal minister. In addition, he began working in Harlem with former prisoners.

Today, he continues that work, counseling female inmates at the Hudson County Correctional Facility and former convicts at Integrity House in Newark, New Jersey. He is immensely popular with these groups and in the very rough neighborhood where he works. In a three-block walk to a coffee shop, at least a dozen street folks and merchants greet Jim loudly and warmly. At lunch, three or four women residents swing by our table to hug him, thank him, or bless him. He knows their stories and gives each one personal encouragement.

Jim is happily married. He and his husband, Mark O'Donnell, share, with his former wife, the child-rearing responsibilities for Jim's youngest daughter. His older daughter lives in Canada and is about to graduate from college.

In 2006 Jim coauthored a New York Times best-selling memoir, *The Confession*. It described his intense ambition, his ethical challenges, his political successes, and the internal conflict he lived with for forty years as a gay trying to appear to the world as a heterosexual.

**In the spring of 2013, HBO aired a documentary, *Fall to Grace*, that traces Jim's path from resignation to his current work at the Hudson County Reintegration Program, counseling women prisoners and helping them with housing, jobs, and other services. The Hudson County Reintegration Program has cut recidivism in half and has been recognized as one of the top reentry programs in the country.**

About three weeks after my resignation, I realized the phone had stopped ringing. It was a draconian silence. It was an awkward, fear-inducing silence. The fear stemmed from the reality that life, as I knew it, was over. I was irrelevant to the political process.

The political elites ignored me. I didn't immediately understand the potential good in the situation. For a while I relied on the same strategies, strategies I should have abandoned. I just tried to put the same ladder up against a different wall. I joined a law firm and soon was as busy and intense as before.

Then, a friend pointed out that I hadn't grappled with the enormity of what had happened, and that I needed to take a break to reassess aspects of my life—the things to keep, the things to discard, and the things to reassemble. So, I went to a rehabilitation facility, The Meadows, in Wickenburg, Arizona. I planned to stay a week and get everything figured out. Check in and check out, cured in a week. It was the ultimate in hubris. My counselor told me that I had no idea how much time it was going to take. I ended up staying thirty days. It was an impactful time. I had to grapple with my sexual orientation and the compromises I had made in my life and my political career, and to reexamine what I wanted to do with the rest of my life.

I recognized that I had to deal honestly with my sexual orientation, but I also came to recognize that I was driven and ambitious, with a need, like many politicians or actors, to feel liked, admired, and be knighted. It was hard to separate these influences, but some of the need for acceptance was to legitimize who and what I was. I could develop a different value system, but the drive, the ambition that's there, that's who I am.

In the beginning, I wanted a low-key, anonymous life. The aftermath of my resignation and the divorce were so acrimonious and painful. The public sphere is replete with thrust and parry, accusation and recrimination, rise and fall, and fall and rise. I just wanted to be in a different place.

Likewise, I tried to turn the drive off because that's what I thought was asked of me. But then a Benedictine priest told me that I should use the gifts and skills I have for a bigger purpose than just me. From AA I learned that I'm here to do the will of God and that I must use the skills I have, including the drive, for a purpose outside myself. Even now I grapple with this, but I do understand being ambitious for others is permissible, provided you approach it with humility. Still, there is danger when ego and self are being derivatively benefited from service to others. When that occurs, I have to quash it, or at least control it. Now, I'm less anxious. In my former life I had been tightly wound and tried to control everything, even things beyond my control.

My values were never material, but all about power and the acquisition of power for good, particularly when I was mayor. The job was rooted in the community, births, deaths, and illnesses. In the legislature, it was about deal making over individual pieces of legislation. As governor, it was about sustaining influence and promoting an agenda. I became separated from the people I was meant to serve and their grounding influence.

When I stepped down, it gave me an opportunity to consider the question: "If you could do anything with your life, what would it be?" I realized this was a blessing. Seminary was a significant retreat from the world in the best sense. It took me out of the day-to-day business and noise of life. It gave me time to study scripture and to work with ex-offenders and in hospices. I've always enjoyed building intellectual castles in the sky, but the human contact with populations in need affected me the most.

Yet, the transition to service was not without difficulties. Even as I was trying to live by AA's steps, I experienced the stages of grief, finally coming to accept that my political life had died. I remember attending the funeral of a close friend and crying as much for my political career as for my friend. During this period I had a vivid, recurring dream of approaching a casket and viewing a deformed body, my own sense of self as deformed by my engagement in the political process.

My parents stood with me through the resignation. That had to be hard for them, yet they did. Their example of resilience helped me in the transition. I became realigned with their values of community and service. It was as though my political life had been an aberration. My parents and grandparents had always felt blessed to be in this country. There was always the view that life has been exceptionally good and that service to others was a way to move beyond self.

Now, I'm working with folks, trying to get them back on their feet. I know government; I know the housing and addictions programs; I know the unions, their representatives, and their requirements. Being able to put these disparate elements together has made me better able to help. As governor the accomplishments were statewide and benefited a large population. Now, I am operating on a more individual level, helping one person at a time.

Everyone has a right to redemption. I believe that. I accept that humans are flawed. We make right decisions and wrong decisions. Moral development is incremental and uneven for individuals. That's my understanding of original sin. It's far more gray on a daily basis than a stain that we can't get beyond. Practically, neither I nor any of the inmates at Hudson County have the ability to always make the right decision. We struggle every day to do that. Some people may get beyond the struggle, but not me. I'm still on the ground floor, struggling. We are all flawed by virtue of our existence. We're imperfect, but we're capable of responding to our better angels, to move beyond our baser instincts. To move from thinking about ourselves, to thinking about the consequences of our actions, to thinking about the greatest good for the greatest number, to doing the next right thing, regardless of the consequences.

We can do this by constructing a new life narrative. It's powerful. We are, to some extent, who we tell ourselves we are. One exercise that we use is to have the inmates write their obituary as it would be now, and then write another, the one they'd want. They have to understand that what has happened in their lives to date doesn't determine their future lives. It provides context for the present, and their lives will continue on that trajectory unless they make an effort to change. If they don't, it will be propelled in the direction it was in the past. They have to imagine a different life and bend the arc.

Longer term, I'd like to address the problem of incarceration in this country. It's an utterly broken system with a massive failure rate; two-thirds of felons commit another felony within three years of release. It's terribly expensive; $74 billion every year on courts, parole, and probation. It's misguided; 70 percent of the population is clinically addicted, yet only 11 percent receive treatment. In prison nobody works; they lift weights and fight. In the Hudson County program, everyone works. There's a dignity to work. I want to do more with the Hudson County program. We've cut the recidivism rate to 22 percent. Governor Christie has put me on a statewide opiate abuse task force, and I've begun discussions with a major university about looking at the policy issues.

My need for admiration and public approval was to some degree related to my own inability to accept my sexual orientation. I found some solace in political acceptance. On the other hand, I have received some brutal comments about my current efforts. As to such disdain and negativity, I keep in mind the old AA adage, "What you think of me is none of my business." Also helpful is the poem "Love Them Anyways" by Mother Teresa. People are unreasonable, illogical, and self-centered. Love them anyways. In the final analysis, it is between you and God. It was never about them anyways. I am who I am. The flaws that I have are the flaws that I have. As long as I'm trying to do the next right thing, it's all good. Daily, I see guys in group therapy who can't make progress because they're afraid of what others may think. It doesn't matter what others think.

I've been doing this for three years, and the most gratifying experiences are seeing women reunited with their families. For parents, prison is a very difficult time. Often, the children are being raised by someone else. The children move on and pass the parents both emotionally and psychologically.

Another impactful moment occurred at Thanksgiving, when one of the women stated that she was thankful she had AIDS because until the diagnosis she had taken life completely for granted, and since the diagnosis she cherishes every day. That statement changed the perspective of all who heard it. These experiences have given me a sense of self-acceptance, an inner peace, and a comfort with the idea of death. That could never have occurred in the political realm. I was climbing the ladder and you don't get off until the top rung.

A while back the Episcopal Diocese deferred my ordination. It legitimately wanted to be sure that I was not just "escaping to the priesthood." It's probably just as well. I feel that I've found what I should be doing, working with these women and on issues surrounding incarceration. I get along very well with the women. I think ordination would confer a status and a sense of separation.

Another issue that's important to me is the discrimination people in the lesbian, gay, bisexual, and transgender communities face. When I am traveling and speaking to different organizations and colleges, I'm amazed at how much things have changed, and how little. For many young people, being gay is the same as left-handedness. They do not ask about my coming out. They ask about policy matters, e.g., the Defense of Marriage Act, the Supreme Court, education, and social services. For me, being gay was not about public policy; it was deeply personal.

Yet, discrimination and homophobia exist, even in many ostensibly cosmopolitan places. A brother of one of the Integrity House participants was recently brutally beaten on the Upper East Side of Manhattan. On my book tour, I witnessed people in San Francisco and Atlanta who, despite their pain, stayed in the closet because they feared discrimination. I don't face it on a daily basis. In fact, the women I work with act like it's a blessing. They feel safe and will good-naturedly joke about it. One of them told me, "Jim, I know you're not gay. You like black women with big butts." I told her, "I do, but not in that sense." Occasionally, an ex-offender will say derisively, "Oh, he is a faggot. Oh, he's gay." But, I think my being there says something to them.

My idea of happiness has changed dramatically. It used to be a crowded room, a lectern, an election victory. Today, it's being with my daughter after communion, or reading the paper with my partner on a Saturday morning, or watching the progress of women who have been so violated in life recognizing their inherent dignity, goodness, and potential. It's trying to achieve transcendence through activities focused on love and faith. For me, the challenge is to continue my spiritual development, not get distracted by the world, and stay aligned with what I know is critical to my spirituality.

# X. ATTITUDE

## *"A Pathological Optimist"*

# DR. JOSEPH E. MURRAY
### Born 1919 – Retired 1986 – Died 2012

Dr. Joseph Murray won the 1995 Nobel Prize in Physiology or Medicine in recognition of his pioneering work in the field of organ and cell transplantation in the treatment of human disease. This was the culmination of an over forty-five-year career that included surpassing achievement as a surgeon in two distinct specialties: organ transplantation and plastic and reconstructive surgery.

He was the youngest child of a lawyer/judge and a schoolteacher. After graduation from Holy Cross and Harvard Medical School, he served in a World War II plastic and reconstructive surgical unit treating severely wounded and burned servicemen. There, he met many courageous patients who underwent long, multiple surgical procedures (sometimes without the aid of anesthesia) to re-create their lives.

After the military, Dr. Murray completed his surgical residency in Boston and New York hospitals, began work in plastic reconstructive and general surgery on the staff of the Peter Bent Brigham Hospital, and worked with the dental service unit at the Children's Hospital.

In the early 1950s, Dr. Murray became involved in the renal transplantation research taking place at the Peter Bent Brigham's Surgical Research Laboratory. To some, the idea of organ transplantation was a far-fetched dream, and those pursuing it were a "bunch of fools." This was because no one could know all the obstacles or whether any of them could be overcome. Yet, Dr. Murray joined the research group and pursued the uncertain effort for almost eleven years. He and other members of the team persisted because without successful transplantation, patients were certain to die.

In the early 1960s, after success was achieved, Dr. Murray redirected his career and returned to plastic and reconstructive surgery. In this field, he repaired the physical appearance and healed the spirit of many.

Dr. Murray's memoir, *Surgery of the Soul: Reflections on a Curious Career*, recounts the course of his career and his many achievements, which individually would be remarkable, but are especially so in the context of one man's life.

I've been called a pathological optimist, even in my youth. At family dinners and discussions, my sister would say, "Joey, I can't stand you. You're always smiling." And I'd say, "Why not?" I just enjoy being alive, and the pleasure of being an optimist.

As early as I can remember, I'd tell people that I wanted to be a surgeon. I don't know why; I had no real understanding of what they did. I read books and they probably contributed to my desire. I was very influenced by our family doctor and the effect his visits had on our entire family, particularly my parents. The family unit was every-thing, and I could see the wonderful results that his presence and skill brought to a normal family.

Before I came to practice in Boston, I had had a good surgical expe-rience in plastics and reconstructive surgery at Valley Forge Hospital treating wounded and burned soldiers. I knew what was possible. Yet, when I got home to start a practice, I saw that the so-called "Boston greats" didn't know a lot. I was unhappy. I'd say, "These guys think they know everything, but they don't know a lot." My mentor told me, "Joe, keep your mouth shut. Learn to listen. Everything will come out all right." That was one of the greatest lessons in my life—learn to listen.

In 1952, when I began working at the Peter Bent Brigham in the kidney transplant research program and the Surgical Research Laboratory, my real interest was in the problem of transferring skin from one person to another. Studying the biology of kidney trans-plants presented a more easily detectable and observable event. Yet, organ transplantation was considered a fringe project. We had no idea whether it could be done. It was an exploration into the unknown. Accomplishing one step didn't mean that we were any closer to our ultimate goal because we never knew whether the next obstacle could be overcome. It was eleven years from the start until we successful-ly accomplished the transplant of a kidney from a cadaver. The key was the development of immunosuppressive drugs that prevented the body from rejecting the transplant.

During that period, of course, there were frustrations and disappointments.

People come to me all the time asking advice on this and that, in-cluding how do you deal with frustration. I say, "Hell, I don't know." I think I responded to those disappointments because I was so curious, and that fed my optimism. We're curious animals. A good friend and former colleague used to say that you need curiosity, and persistence, but don't confuse persistence with obstinance. Persistence is driven by picking a problem you're interested in. Pick a subject you like, your heart is in it, and you're going to follow through, not for any purpose other than it is really what you want within yourself. It's the inner drive that keeps you going.

Of course, I've had a lot of support from my wife. We've been married for sixty-seven years. When I was starting out, we had four kids early in life. I was frustrated, and sometimes as we sat at the table after dinner I'd question whether I should quit focusing on the research and concentrate on a local hospital. My wife would say, "Oh, Joe, you'll be long at the Peter Bent Brigham Hospital and at the [Harvard] Medical School." Picking your mate is a wonderful thing. Of course, there are ups and downs. But, we have always had a unity of thinking, a unity of a marriage.

In the 1960s, when I was in my early forties, we had success transplanting a kidney from a cadaver. At this time, I decided to redirect my career to reconstructive surgery. At some level this was starting a new career, although not completely so because the skills were similar. But, nevertheless, it was a big change in the direction of my career, sort of a "retiring" from transplantation and beginning anew, in reconstructive surgery. I refer to it as returning to my true surgical identity. In this regard I was strongly influenced by Dr. Sidney Farber, founder of the Jimmy Fund and the Dana Farber Cancer Center. Of course, there were challenges and frustrations and uncertainty with this redirection. What sustained me through those challenges was that I was doing something that was within my heart. I was taking care of fellow human beings. It sounds lofty, but it's true. The patient is the center of any physician's life.

I am very happy that I turned my efforts to reconstructive surgery. You must understand the suffering that those with facial or body deformities live with daily. They are isolated, rejected by peers and sometimes by their own mothers, and experience loss of self-esteem. Surgery that addresses, alleviates, or resolves these deformities promotes self-respect and acceptance, and gives these patients lives with dignity. That's what my book, *Surgery of the Soul*, refers to. When I talked about optimism earlier, I think it's true that I was born with a good measure of it, but I believe that my exposure to the courage with which these patients faced their problems and the lives they led has greatly enhanced my optimism. I was helping them, but they were inspiring me.

When I was sixty-seven, I was nearing retirement and contemplating scaling back, but I was extremely busy trying to smooth the transition at the hospital to a new chief of plastic surgery, and I was lecturing all around the country and abroad. One morning, I was getting ready to travel to a lecture and experienced a dull ache and weakness in my left leg and left arm, and it got progressively worse. The left side of my face started to tingle and my fingers were getting numb. My wife drove me straight to the Brigham. By late afternoon I was totally paralyzed on my left side.

While I was in the hospital bed, I assessed my situation. I had no feelings of anger or self-pity. The children were raised; the house was paid; I had had a forty-two-year career in surgery. I didn't know what I would be able to do. I resolved to use whatever faculties remained to the best of my ability, and to live with my wife and family as my first priority, and my profession second. I had great doctors and very good friends advising and working with me in the rehabilitation period. It was a struggle.

A colleague insisted that it be a learning experience, echoing the motto of an Indian leper I had treated years before: "Difficulties are opportunities." He gave me that sign with that motto on it years ago. It's right up there [*points*]. It inspired me then, and it still does. I don't know why I did not feel anger or self-pity. I had been taught to avoid pride, anger, and envy as deadly sins.

I suppose rebalancing my priorities would have been a natural occurrence even without the stroke. People often do so at that stage of life. I don't know why we don't do it earlier. That's really asking: Why don't we achieve wisdom earlier in life?

I'm not going to live forever, but I'm at peace, although I keep finding stuff that I want to do and am a bit anxious to get it done. Peace is what we all want. Peace comes from within. No one is ever satisfied completely. It's human nature to be dissatisfied. Mother Teresa set out how to achieve peace in her poem "The Simple Path": faith leads to love, love to service, and service to peace.

I am the greatest fan of Emily Dickinson. Her poetry is very meaningful to me, and the words on her gravestone, "Called Back," suggest the level of peace we all seek.

About four years after the stroke, I was awarded the Nobel Prize in Physiology or Medicine. It was only the fourth time a clinical surgeon involved in treating patients was awarded the prize. It is usually given for basic scientific research and many winners have not even had degrees in medicine. I was elated when I won. I had been nominated in years past, but I thought prizes awarded in earlier years represented the committee's acknowledgment of the field.

We donated the prize money to the Harvard Medical School, the Brigham and Women's Hospital, and the Children's Hospital, each of which was essential to success in the field. The prize did change my life, in that it increased my visibility and my sense of responsibility to practicing physicians. It's a responsibility I feel even today. I suppose you never feel that you've discharged all your responsibilities.

But even with our day-to-day responsibilities, it is important to appreciate the richness of our lives as we are living them. In my favorite play, *Our Town*, Thornton Wilder delivers that message very clearly. For some reason I understood that message right from the time I saw the play in college, not just at an intellectual level, but actually tried to incorporate that message into my daily life. The most important word in the English language is: *is*. What is, not what was. Not what will be. What is. That's what's important. We're here now talking. It will probably never happen again.

Sometimes I think childhood was the best stage of life, but then I realize being ninety is awfully good, too. I think being alive is the best, I really do.

I can't believe the good fortune I've had. We've been in this house for fifty years, and I've always loved it. I sit here in my office and look outside and see the kids playing. I look around in this space and see that picture of my wife before we married, when she was a model and a music student. I look at those lists of my children, grandchildren, and great-grandchildren, and individualize each of them. Of course, we don't know how they are going to end up, but I'm not anxious about them.

I would love to get my chain saw, go out back and cut up some trees and stack the wood, but I can't, and I accept that because there's no alternative. [*Laughs.*] It's almost scary how fortunate we've been, with people caring for us and visiting. But still, I can't get the chain saw and cut the wood. So what.

# "I Decided to Be Happy"

## ANDREW MONACO
### Born 1936

**Andrew Monaco was born in a third-floor walk-up and lived there with his parents, two brothers, and three sisters. His father worked at a rubber factory and died when Andrew was four. He has only a vague memory of his father. Andrew owns his own barbershop and works five days a week. He has been married fifty-one years and has five children and ten grandchildren. Andrew has many interests: woodworking, gardening, opera, reading, traveling, and Italy. During lulls in his workday, he will use the time to read about these topics. Until a few years ago, Andrew would even do a little wood carving in his barbershop.**

M y mother and my older sisters raised us. My three older sisters worked as stitchers in clothing factories. During the war, they made military coats and supported us. We moved around some. I never finished high school. I went to work after my first year of high school. I worked in a factory as a floor boy/laborer. I was sixteen. I did that for about four years, and then I worked for Raytheon in its power tube division. I worked as a welder and as a utility man in the machine shop.

By the time I worked at Raytheon, I had a couple of kids. And at Raytheon, every year or two you'd get laid off. So I said something has to be done here. I decided to go to school to either become a chef or a barber. In those days a chef was not glamorous. So I decided to be a barber. So I quit my job, went to work for a printing company nights, and went to school days.

I suppose it took a little nerve just to quit Raytheon with a wife and three kids to support, but I had to do something. I had to do something. I wasn't going anywhere. Although, if I had stayed, I'd probably be retired by now with a pension.

Barber school was six months. When I got through, a guy who had a couple of barbershops called the school and said, "Hey, listen, I need a barber." I was the guy. I started in August 1964 and have been in the same town for forty-eight lovely years.

My wife was an extremely good mother, but the years raising children were kind of tough. It was work. Sometimes I worked three jobs, barbering and cleaning offices. I can't remember the year I stopped doing three jobs, but I remember how it occurred. I'm a praying person, and my family is a praying family. I was cleaning offices late one night and I said, "I'm tired of doing this, God. I'm not going to do this. When I finish this job I'm not going to come back doing this." And I never did. From that moment on my barber business began to flourish. My business started growing and people started getting haircuts more often. I give credit to my faith. The decision to stop cleaning offices, it was more a matter of faith than courage.

Eventually I bought the barber business in the early '70s. In the '80s, my daughter joined me and we opened a beauty shop. I went to school to get more depth in hairstyling. We worked together for twelve years, and then when I was about sixty-one, she had children and wanted to leave the business. So I sold the business and I returned to barbering.

The word retirement never entered my mind at that time, and even now, only occasionally. I like the work. I have interests in woodworking, opera, food, travel, and the work permits me to satisfy these interests. The interests all began to develop when my kids started getting married.

I started to listen to opera more, but only started going to see productions in my seventies. I haven't seen opera on any of my visits to

Italy. I have a schedule for La Scala, but probably will never go. I see simulcasts regularly. They're terrific, wonderful.

I went to the local trade school nights for about six years to learn woodworking. I don't know where the idea came from. It just came to my mind one day. I took lessons from one of my customers and then followed up with the courses. I've always liked artisans, people who make things and can put a thing together; carve something, put a building together. I had a natural inclination towards that sort of thing. I like doing it. I used to do some wood carving right there in my shop, but not now. I'm going to work on a clock when I go home tonight.

I sometimes think about retirement now, but I have the desire to work. My oldest brother worked until he was eighty. What am I going to do if I stay home? I have a lot of control over my schedule. I like the conversations with the customers, and if I have downtime, I can sit and read a book, like *A Thousand Days in Venice*. I find reading about the experiences of people doing different things fascinating.

I go to breakfast every morning at 6:00 a.m. with a bunch of people I've known for forty-five years. Sometimes during the middle of the morning I go to coffee with some guys from my old neighborhood. I got a lot of customers coming and going and people stopping by to say hello, or tell a joke; it's a clubhouse. I try to make it relaxing. I sincerely like all my customers. I think of them as friends. Some are incredibly considerate. One who had done well when his company went public gave me a convertible. I love driving it. So, I got my friends. I got my opera. I got my books. It's very fulfilling, it really is.

I get interested in people's lives, careers, or what they do. It's interesting. So I'm always getting stories from my customers and the stories are all at different stages. What's marvelous about this is that I remember something about the last conversation with every one of them so I know where it left off. You remember, if you like people. Some of my relationships with customers go back over forty years.

Health would be the reason I would retire. If I couldn't handle the job. But I'd have to be pretty sick or pretty feeble to do it, and I'm not that way yet. My intention is to do this as long as I can. As long as the income is what it should be, I'll stay there. I expect to work for another three, four years. I hope I can drive my car when I'm eighty, with the top down on a nice summer day with my beautiful wife, and drive anywhere I want to go.

Thinking about retirement doesn't make me nervous, but I do wonder how I would replace all the contacts I've had. The business has slowed, and I welcome that because of the fatigue. When I recently came back from a trip to Italy, there was a big backlog. I had been gone for three weeks. Guys wanted to get their haircut. Getting caught up was tiring. It was a lot of work.

I have no big plans for when I stop. The biggest challenge for me would be to stay busy. But it all depends on my health. I'm very healthy. I don't take any medication. I feel healthy. I spent all day yesterday and this morning getting my yard ready for winter. I have very good genes; my mother lived to 103. She was good right up to the end. I saw her just before she died. I sat with her and she told me these things that I should know about life and what I should do. She told me that I should not forget the family and that I should stay true to my beliefs. She emphasized always stay close to the family. And then she blessed me. That was it. It was wonderful.

I have always had a strong faith and grew up in a churchgoing family. There have been times when I have not been as faithful to my religion as I should have been, but down deep in my heart I have a love for God and know the way I should live. Things become more clear with more time.

My brother, a couple of years behind me, and I take trips to Italy once a year for three to four weeks. Sometimes, we stay with cousins on their farm. Sometimes, we get a car and drive. I love Italy. I love Rome. Sometimes, I'll go to the Pantheon and study it; it's so calm and restful in there.

My wife and I have gone on cruises to Bermuda and Canada. When we got to Bermuda, I didn't even get off the boat. For me it's all about the activities on the boat—nice breakfast, lounge around, read, maybe go to a lecture, take a steam bath. My wife had a bout with cancer and she gets fatigued; she has trouble with her knees. But she never complains. In fact, I'm looking at travel to the beaches of Normandy next year. An organized trip, but you get to learn more history.

My ideal retirement? I wouldn't mind going to an opera in New York one time, but I don't see that coming true because I wouldn't want to go alone. If possible, I'd like to see *The Magic Flute* by Mozart. Papageno, the bird catcher, is so comical.

There's a goal maybe no one knows except me. I would like to go to Italy and work on a farm for a month in September, when they gather the grapes. At my cousin's farm we did something like that. We'd cut the grapes and have a good time. At the end of the day we'd have a big meal. The camaraderie, the physical labor, the joking, the hard work. I don't know if I'll ever do that, but I'd like to. It sounds like fun. There are places you can go to do that.

I'm a happy guy. I decided to be happy about the time my children were growing up and leaving, and I started working with my hands and accomplishing things. It took a lot of years for me to become that way. The first time I felt secure in myself, I was in my late thirties, early forties. I always knew I was loved, but somehow it became real to me and I felt very secure. As time went on, and I did more things and became more accomplished, those things bring you to the point, "I'm going to be happy." It comes from becoming older. When you succeed, you accomplish something when you got a goal and you succeed at it. There's a feeling of accomplishment. But other parts of it are to be content with what you have and appreciate what people do for you. Appreciate people more. Say thank you.

I have a few regrets. I didn't always make good decisions, but I ended up pretty good, I think. I don't know how that happened, but I have to give credit to my praying mother; that's all I can say. My biggest regret is I quit school, but I'll get over it. Another relates to my older brother. He was at the Battle of Anzio in World War II. I regret he never came to Italy with us. If we had to push him in a wheelchair, we would have. I also regret I never went to Italy with my mother. My mother went with my aunt. They were so funny together.

My mother would say to my aunt, "I have nothing to leave you. When I go, Andrew is yours." So now, I say, "Auntie, am I in the will?" She says, "Yeah, you're in the will."

# *"Two Thousand Daffodils"*

## GAYLE SWEDMARK HUGHES
### Born 1940 – Retired 2010

Gayle Swedmark Hughes is a wife, mother, grandmother, artist, musician, published author, cook, volunteer, sports fan, and cancer survivor who works to keep old friendships and make new ones. Every summer she and her husband spend a week in her hometown, visiting familiar places and catching up with friends and the community. She attended Florida State University and is an avid fan of the school's athletic programs. She graduated from the University of Iowa Law School at the time when few women attended. On graduation, she returned to Florida, clerked for a state appeals court, and then entered a trial practice. Before she was "set free by retirement," Gayle had a distinguished career as

**a trial lawyer in North Florida, the highlights of which are contained in a 2011 memoir, *Two Thousand Daffodils*.**

T he only fear I had as I approached retirement was that, because I am a type A and a strong personality, I might miss being number-one chair in a trial. I was used to being in charge and running the show. And I thought I might miss that. Friends said I'd miss it, because at trial I'd go into full-bore steamroller mode. They said, "You'll miss it so much." I didn't miss it one day, not one hour.

I weaned myself. I got cancer, so I was out of work for a time. I'm over that now. But during that period, my firm told me I could have my office as long as I'm alive, and I could work when I wanted. At first, I'd work five days a month, and then sometimes I'd work six or seven days in a row on a trial. But I was never lead counsel because I didn't want to be on call. I had calendar freedom.

My partners were sweet. They said, "Do what you want." That made it easier. That went on for about a year. Then one day I thought, *Heck, I don't want to get dressed. I'm out at the farm. I got my shoes off. I got my dog. I don't want to get dressed and go down there.* It was nice to have approbation and recognition, but the trade-off was the stress. Is it really worth waking up with sweaty palms, thinking you have forgotten some detail? It wasn't worth it. I had other interests. I realized that I hadn't been in the office for two weeks and what I really missed was talking Florida State football with the guys, the camaraderie.

Key: Lawyer was not what I was, it's what I did for a living…it wasn't all I was. I evaluated how much money I needed and reassessed my values. What's important to me? You're voting with your money, and unless you're Rockefeller, you have finite resources. Now I have the luxury of learning new things. What a joy!

I painted in college and started again when I was sixty, but I didn't have time because I was working. So now I'm getting better, so much better. One of my watercolors was accepted in a juried show, the

Gasden annual show. The jurors are from the Smithsonian. It is huge recognition, and I submitted my painting on a whim. It was pretty cool to be accepted and that gave me encouragement.

I started piano lessons when I was six and continued through high school. I was a partial music major at one point. So I've always been in composition. I have a serious music background and now I just write. I spent one summer writing something that was in my head, and then I realized it was already written. But it's very enjoyable. My husband gave me a baby grand piano for my sixty-fifth birthday. So I'm very fortunate that I have that to work on.

The only schedule I have is for art classes twice a week, and I have a writing group, but that's mostly a social thing and it keeps me going, making progress. I do like to cook and now I have more time to do that—bread, lemon pudding cake, whatever. It's a way that I show my love.

Some people are positive and some are negative, and you take that personality into retirement. You know there are some people for whom the water's never quite wet enough. For them, retirement would be bad because things are just bad, just dreary and bad. They have a Hobbesian approach to life. If you're a person who is generally upbeat and positive, retirement will be fine.

The problem for some retirees is they're so caught up in their employment identity. It can be scary. Marriage was a transition. It may not have been scary, but it sure as heck was going to be different, and you felt that as you approached your wedding. I think retirement is like that—different and a little bit scary.

But as far as your self-esteem and emotional well-being, if you like yourself, and you've not completely identified with your profession or your physical appearance, you're going to be fine.

As much as I loved hanging out with the lawyers, I have no new lawyer friends. I have old friends forever. I'm meeting people down the road who are fascinating, whom I would never have known if I stayed on the treadmill of work. Now, through the art classes, the music, writing group, it's a real eclectic mix. I never had enough time for women companions and I'm enjoying the companionship of females. I never had that luxury previously. I'm enjoying learning what other women think.

I don't have a schedule or any new goals other than I want to be better. I'm writing a novel; I'm enjoying my husband and life. A side benefit of writing *Two Thousand Daffodils*, my memoir and family history, is that my son learned a lot about his momma and his great-great-grandpa. He's read the book three times. It took me a year to write. I was just piddlin' with it, but when I got serious, I finished it in a month.

I always volunteered a little bit. Always had the interest, but not the time. Now, I go to three different nursing homes and read the sports page to elderly men. If I find them listless, then I get them going by telling them, "The University of Florida Gators stink!" Then they get going and we have a good time. Sometimes we play cards. And if they're dying and they want me to hold their hand and pray, I'll do that, but I don't force that on them.

I do stuff with my church. I do the flowers and all the little sissy things I couldn't do when I was working sixty hours. I find it liberating. That's the word.

Except for learning to fly and falling in love, retirement is the best. Although your eyes and knees aren't as good. Everybody says health is a factor, but I found that health has very little to do with how happy people are. It doesn't seem to be the only factor. Surprisingly, people can be happy even when they're not healthy.

A happy marriage is a huge factor in being happy in retirement. If you're going to be spending a lot of time with someone, let's hope you enjoy each other. If you don't, then you need to figure something out, maybe live in different nursing homes.

I plan to take care of other people, be as healthy as I can, and write my book and my music; enjoy life. This is a gorgeous fall day, I'm going to get outside and enjoy it. I don't want a schedule, and I don't want to meet the same people for lunch every Thursday. I just stay away from that. One of the huge warnings, a real caveat: be careful not to over-schedule. You think you'll have so much time, but if you're not careful, people'll eat it up. So don't plan to play cards with somebody every Friday, or have lunch with the same person ever Sunday; pretty soon, it takes up all your time.

I'm religious, but I'm not doctrinaire. I go to church and am a regular participant in the activities of the Presbyterian Church. It's a vehicle to do things; feed the needy, build houses for people who don't have houses. We have an event called Manna on Meridian. We, along with other churches and organizations, collect food and distribute it to families caught in the cracks. I'm so sick of people referring to organized religion as if it's organized crime. Organized means that you have a way to get things done. Organized in that people have a way to give because they need to give. People love to give, but they need a way to give.

I'm not scared of dying. Once you get that settled, it's pretty sweet. I got that settled when I had colon resection. I had a near-death experience. And I realized that I might die. I struggled with it. I almost died and I realized I was OK with it, and after that I was never really truly afraid of it. If you get over that fear, you're a lot freer.

I've traveled and enjoyed it, but I'm satisfied with a smaller universe right now. I don't have the itch that I used to have. We go to the beach and to the mountains every year.

Football season in the South is like the holy days. We have a lot of activities in Tallahassee tied up with sports. I am a huge, huge sports fan. I watch all kinds of sports on TV. I'm a rabid Florida State Seminoles fan. When I was in college, four thousand fans showed up at the airport to greet the team just because they had scored against—not beat, just scored against—the number-one team in the nation.

I don't have an exercise program; hate it. I don't need a knee replacement or have any heart problems. I'm fine physically, but I'd love to have a fifty-year-old's body and know what I know now. That would be dynamite.

If there is a strong sense of self, a love of other people, a faith, talents to be explored, retirement is magic. Some fun. Some art. Some good works for others. Lots of good family life and love. Friends. Work. Balance. I am positive that you'll agree.

# XI. THE LONG VIEW

# "Something Really Exciting Right Around the Corner"

## DON HOUSE
### Born 1947

Don was born in the "little bitty town" of Angleton, Texas, between Houston and the Gulf. His dad was a Methodist minister and his mom was a homemaker. His family moved around Texas with his dad's assignments and finally settled in College Station.

He went to Texas A&M and got his PhD there. Later, he taught at Auburn and A&M, worked as an in-house economist, and finally joined an economic consulting group. Don is also a rancher, blacksmith, entrepreneur, and quite active in his church.

He is married, and has a large extended family in and around College Station. After Don discusses his views on the years ahead, he visits his ninety-year-old parents, Morris and Mary, to get their perspectives.

A s I approach sixty-six, I've thought a lot about what the coming years might mean. It's an important topic and a little daunting. It's not that I don't have my interests. I do. I have my toys and hobbies: a small cattle ranch, blacksmithing, and a small-town drugstore we restored some years back.

I've been in the cattle business since 1986, always losing money, but having fun. I had no connection to it as a kid. I grew up in towns and never owned a horse or spent much time on a farm or a ranch. But relatives did, and it always appealed to me. I wanted to see what it was like and expose my kids to it. So I did. They've helped me work the cattle.

Plus, it's fun for me. It's a place to play. It's like my psychiatrist. When I'm stressed, I go up there and all the stress goes away, immediately. There's a house and we had planned on spending some nights there, but it's hard to keep the mice out, and so it's hard to get my wife up there. I still go up about twice a week to put hay out.

There's a barn that some Amish friends helped me build, an old-style barn that could have been there for one hundred years. It's a fun place. A few times a year, we have gatherings, fund-raisers, dances, and stuff like that for church groups and college kids. I built it to capture some of the old technology and show people how things were done. I've always had an interest in old ways. I enjoy understanding the past.

That's how I got involved in blacksmithing. I was visiting Washington-on-the-Brazos, where the Texas Declaration of Independence was signed in 1836. The site had a working blacksmith shop. I was fascinated. That was the spark thirty years ago. Using pieces from an old shop I built a replica, a working museum from the 1860s—the hammers, the sledges. I have a mechanical trip hammer when I want to move some steel. I've made fireplace tools, candlesticks, and ornamental stuff, like in Williamsburg.

Preserving the old ways is a real interest for me. Recently, we came across an old drugstore in Leona, Texas, where my dad grew up. He and his brothers and sisters used to go there on a wagon on Saturdays. It was about to fall down. We bought and restored it to what it was like in the 1920s. The old soda fountain serves ice cream sodas and phosphates. Old marble counter and gooseneck dispensers. It's a lot of fun.

I used to hunt as a kid, but I've found it less and less interesting. I remember hunting white-tailed deer and freezing to death. As I've gotten older, I don't want to be cold! I don't want to sit in a blind, freezing, waiting for a deer to come by. My parents were avid hunters and were on a deer lease with other families. That's how my mother found her way into a hunting blind. Mother would always go hunting with Dad, as recently as two years ago.

So, I do have my hobbies, but the thought of pursuing them for the next forty days...after two, I'd be saying, "Enough of this, I want a break from retirement." So, I'm afraid of absolute full-time retirement. I want to continue to do meaningful things, but I want to transition to something more meaningful than making a payroll, something where I can make an impact on my church with my skills as an economist. If I can do that, it's a win-win.

That seems possible. About forty years ago my involvement in the United Methodist Church began to evolve. I've been a delegate to the General Conference and an advisor to the World Church Finance and Economics Committees. This exposed me to a wealth of information and very rich, detailed statistical records. It really provides the basis for understanding what causes churches to grow or decline. Sure, a fantastic pastor can make a difference, but how many of them are there? My focus is on the average church. This aspect of my work has become increasingly serious and fruitful. I'm excited to use my analytical and research skills on something that matters to me. When I'm working on this, I can't wait to get to work. It's a nice thing that's happened.

I do have anxieties and questions about what's ahead. I don't know when I'll stop working. I am a little bit driven. If this transition is successful, then I'm going to continue doing it for as long as I'm capable—maybe not full time, but I can see myself continuing to work. Maybe at some point far down the road we close the consulting firm. My wife, of course, has dreams of vacationing here and there, which I will want to do, but not quite yet. The concept scares me. Taking three days off is no big deal, but taking three months off is a big deal.

I'm figuring, given the genes I have, maybe I have twenty years of good health and ten years of difficult times with fading health. Still a happy guy, still like living, but I can't do the things I'd like to do. Twenty, where I can work in the blacksmith shop and travel anywhere, and ten, where I won't be able to move about. My dad now spends a lot of time watching sports, but has trouble getting out. So I think I'll have ten years where I better find something I want to do when I can't physically get around. I'm thinking I'll read and write, a lot of writing perhaps. So I'm thinking I got thirty years, at least that's how I'm looking at it. If it's cut short, it's cut short, but I'm going to plan for thirty.

Travel would probably take us back to where we've been. My wife loves the British Isles and London, Ireland, Scotland, Rome, and Southern Italy. We go to Colonial Williamsburg for a few days and enjoy it around Christmas. I have trips to Chicago and my wife likes to go with me, just going back to favorite places and seeing a few more.

As to finances, I'm not skilled at budgeting. I keep thinking I'd like to be able to live comfortably off interest income. That's where I want to be. The idea of having an estate that you're spending down each year, so that when you go on to Glory you have a modest amount left, I don't know how to do that. Budgeting time is even harder because you don't know how much you have.

I'm a happy guy...I'm optimistic. I always think there's something really exciting around the corner. Let's see if we can make it happen.

I don't expect retirement will affect my self-esteem if I'm doing things that are purposeful. That's why I'm focusing on the new work, because it's purposeful. I'd like to spend more time studying the Bible and visiting with people. I'd really enjoy more leisure time to seek some answers. I'll have more time to read and write, and that will be more fulfilling. I'd like to write a book or two, one on what I'm doing, and one on the relationship between free markets and the growth of religion. I'd also like to dispel some of the misimpressions about businessmen as greedy, always taking advantage of everyone. That's interesting storytelling, but that's not life, and religious leaders and common folks need to understand that.

I'd like to visit with people, volunteering and having fellowship with people. I like to know people; they're fascinating and there's tremendous good in people. Everybody seems to have a shell, but once you get past the shell, boy, they're awfully good people out there and I'd like to get to know more of them. I'd like to learn some perspectives, what more people think, particularly from theologians who are a lot smarter than I am. You're on a journey.

# *"Not Waiting for the Bus"*

## MARY AND MORRIS HOUSE
Born 1921 (Mary), 1918 (Morris) – Retired 1988 –
Died 2014 (Morris)

*Don with Mary and Morris who recently celebrated
their 75th wedding anniversary.*

When Don House agreed to be interviewed for this project, I pressed him to see if his mother would participate. I was eager to talk with her because years ago Don had told me that his mother was still deer hunting in her mid-eighties. I thought a woman with that much gumption and life experience was somebody with whom I needed to talk.

Shortly after Don's mother agreed to be interviewed, his dad, Morris, also agreed to talk. After our interview, Don drove to his parents' house to continue the conversation.

MARY: I was born in 1921 in Sinton, Texas, the youngest of eight, five sisters and two brothers. My parents were sharecroppers and we moved around, wherever they needed sharecroppers. I went to school in Marble Falls, Texas, in a one-room schoolhouse. My oldest sister was my schoolteacher. Then, we moved to San Marcos, where I graduated high school. I went to college in Huntsville to study music and be in the band. In 1939, I married Morris after one year in college. For that one year I studied all the instruments so I could teach music. My favorite was the clarinet. Morris was in school studying to be a Methodist preacher. So I quit school and married him. We've been married seventy-two years.

AUTHOR: So how did that work out?

MARY: Well, I've been married seventy-two years.

AUTHOR: You haven't answered the question.

MARY: You think that I would have stayed seventy-two years if it didn't work?

We moved to Queen City, down on the Texas border, with his ministry. I got a job with a munitions plant in Texarkana and he preached and taught school. Then the church moved his assignment to another location and I retired, quit, or they kicked me out. It was the one and only job that I ever got paid for. So I retired from that.

I stayed home and raised the two boys. [*Nods at Don.*] I did good on that one. Took a lot of my time. My other son is two years older than Don, and a practicing lawyer in East Texas. He can get you out of jail if you get in trouble.

I worked at the church in civic organizations, and at Texas A&M in the Wesley Foundation, and in the Food Bank where we served hungry people. All of it was volunteer. I've been busy working my whole life, but I haven't got any money for it.

When my husband's retirement was approaching, I thought he'd still work a lot because there'd be a place that needed a preacher or he would hold funerals for people that we had known and teach Sunday school. He'd stay busy volunteering. No anxieties about it because we were real close to a lot of ministers that we had known for years. So they were retiring and they found things to do, and I knew I could stay busy going to church meetings and enjoying retirement.

Now we meet the whole group about every month. There will be about thirty-five of them and they'd come here and visit, and the next time we'd go to somebody else's house. So we kept up. So I had to cook and serve lunch a lot. And we continue to do that. Plus, I joined different women's clubs, enjoyed my family and taking care of grandkids.

All of my sisters are older than I am. So a lot of the things I do are to help them. Go and stay a week if one of them is sick. When you got that much family, there's always somebody who needs visiting, or you go to them for enjoyment or take trips together.

I have a sister, 103, in a nursing home nearby. I went to see her yesterday and she was up doing exercises. Most of my sisters were schoolteachers. She taught school until she got too old. Now she paints, does that sort of thing. She has a big family.

I do a little bit of gardening. I help pick the beans after Morris plants them, and if I can, I keep the deer from eating them in my backyard. I joined a sewing club and a quilting club, but stopped because I can't see to thread the needle; I'm too old. I'm going to get Don started on helping me with that pretty soon.

My health is good. I had pneumonia when I was in the third grade and that messed me up pretty bad, and they're still fussing at me for having had it. And I had smallpox. We were quarantined in elementary school. They'd leave the mail at a tree close to our house, but they wouldn't bring it to the house because they didn't want to get close to anybody who had smallpox. Doing very well now, get around good. I still drive and so does Morris. I passed my driver's license about a month ago. I was real glad. Morris just had a new pacemaker put in. He wore out the first one.

I do like deer hunting. I began when my children were born, about sixty-seven years ago. We'd get a deer lease out from New Brazos and they'd be four or five couples. We'd get a cabin where we'd spend the night. We'd have a lot of fun; the boys would be playing dominoes and we'd go shopping, and get back in time to go to the deer lease at six o'clock; lots of good fellowship.

I had little experience with guns before that. Except when we were kids, maybe we'd try to kill a possum that was in our yard. Usually it was my older brother or sisters who would use the gun. I learned to use the gun by going to classes. My first gun was a Remington .30-06. I keep it hidden because Don will steal it if I don't hide it from him; it's an antique.

I hunted about sixty years. We tried to go every year just to be with the friends. We'd go three or four days at a time. One time I shot an eight-pointer and the rack was really wide. The points were really far apart. And Morris shot one with more points—ten, I think—but they were close together. So I put his ten-pointer inside my eight-pointer. I keep them in my garage so he won't forget. Over the years I've killed at least one deer every year. We drag them in and take them to a company that will skin and dress them. We eat the meat—venison sausage, venison steaks, and chili. We eat a lot of venison.

Since the drought, the deer come into our yard. They're hunting water. It's getting real bad around here. Trees are dying and the deer out in the pasture don't have anything to eat or drink. Two years ago we planted some beans in a garden and they were about twelve inches high, covered with leaves. A deer came in and ate every leaf off two rows of beans.

In one of my hunts with Don, I hit a deer but it ran off. We followed it and got it. In the brush you can't tell how far it is because you have to go around through the trails. You walk a good while. Not a mile, I don't imagine, because you can't see through the timbers. I retired from hunting because I have trouble with my eyes, wet macular degeneration. My last hunt was four years ago. The macular degeneration started twenty years ago, but I keep driving, I keep reading, I keep sewing.

AUTHOR: Should I be concerned that retirement will affect what I do, my self-esteem, my optimism?

MARY: No! Look forward to it! Because you can travel, you can go with a group to Canada, and have fun seeing the world, and come back and do whatever you want to do. We keep doing.

AUTHOR: Has it impacted your sense of optimism?

MARY: Well, I think we're doing OK.

AUTHOR: More excited in the beginning or now?

MARY: Well, I miss being able to do the things I did, but then I enjoy doing stuff in the house, too, cooking lunch for Don.

AUTHOR: Where have you gone?

MARY: Europe and the Holy Land. We used to visit my sister, who'd host visits by students from A&M down in Ole Mexico for a couple of weeks at a time.

Well, I've had a good life. I enjoy just about everything I do. And I've got a good family and a big family. My family is growing. My children were having so many babies that my brother-in-law said, "They're catching them faster than you can string them." I have twelve great-grandchildren, five grandchildren. See, there's so many we can't even count them, and we see them at least once a month. Usually over Don's house because I don't want them messing up my house. All those toys out, dominoes and balloons and crackers and stuff...When my whole family gets together there'll be twenty-seven. We had twenty-seven for Thanksgiving.

The biggest challenge is taking care of my health so I can have fun with my family.

AUTHOR: Is that your biggest worry?

MARY: I don't have anything to worry about.

AUTHOR: How is that possible?

MARY: Look on the bright side and say your prayers. You walk through the valley of the shadow of death. But you go through the valley of the shadow of death, then you go up to heaven on the other side.

Things like that are very important to me. When my father died, I was reminded again of that scripture that we go through the valley of the shadow of death. He's not still in there. He's up in heaven now.

That's comforting to me. My father was a Sunday school superintendent when I was a little itty-bitty girl. Age has made me more conscious that I better be good or I won't go to heaven.

AUTHOR: What have you done to be good?

MARY: I volunteer. I go to a retirement home about once a month
and serve coffee—Coffee Klatch—to those in poor health. We entertain them. Let them come out and sing and play games. I go up there
three different times. Then there's my Sunday school class. I'm chairman of the Bereaved. When someone dies in our church, we serve a
meal to the family at the church if they'd like it, and I'm chairman of
getting the meals together. One time we fed lunch to 123 people.

At this stage I miss friends who pass away. I hate to see them die.
One of my dearest friends recently passed, and I'm sorry about that
and I miss him and worry about his wife, who is now in the house
alone. I worry about things like that. I know God will take care of you
in heaven and we'll see each other in heaven.

MORRIS: I want to straighten out that deer story first. She stretches
the truth about that. Back when I retired and closed the church office
and came home, it felt like the world had dropped out from under me.
I just wondered what I was going to do. I had been active for years and
years. I had been preaching every Sunday and prepared two sermons
every week. Then I'd go home and think about things I needed to do.
Not enough hours in the day.

But seventy is a strict retirement age. There's no choice. I spent
the next fifteen years preaching about half the time, marrying people,
holding funerals, and visiting sick in the hospitals. So, I had a little
adjustment to make, and I made it, and we've had a happy retirement.

We started traveling and working in the yard and group garden.
We got three retirees out here that we're friends with, so we got a real
good fellowship. We enjoy each other and it's been good for us. In retirement I haven't had any challenges other than trying to do something worthwhile. I didn't want to just sit in the chair and do nothing.
I told myself the Lord called me into the ministry, but he didn't give

me a retirement date. To feel worthwhile and purposeful I read a lot and visit the hospital. I do a little of what I did when I was active, a little less demanding and I choose what I want to do.

I grew up in Leon County about forty miles from College Station. I had three sisters and two brothers. My dad became an invalid when he was in his fifties with arthritis; he couldn't do anything. We struggled during the Depression.

I did not plan to become a minister. They didn't pay the preacher enough to really live on. So I looked on the ministry as a declared poverty in most instances. My mother thought I would be her preacher boy, but my brother went into the ministry before I did. I went to college. I had decided to be a lawyer, but I got there late. We had to get through with the crop before I could enter school. When I got there, all the classes I wanted to take were full.

So I took the Bible and I had a really great teacher. I resolved the questions I had about scripture. It wasn't clear that I'd become a minister. I wanted the Lord to knock me down and tell me that I had to do it. Even though the Lord didn't do that, I kept feeling that I wanted to and needed to. So in 1937 I started in my ministry.

My current goal is to do what I've been doing. Preach when I get a chance, teach Sunday school, hold funerals.

MARY: Let me interrupt a minute. I wanted to tell you that when he served a church for a good while and we loved all the people there, then they'd tell us we're moving. I'd cry all the way from packing and moving to another place because I was leaving my dear friends. Then I got to the new place and made new friends and loved that. That's what happened every time I moved to a new house.

MORRIS: I found meaning in serving and helping people. I felt that's what I was called to do. I've had good relationships with congregations. Now, I'm committed to hold a number of funerals for old friends. I keep telling them that they better hurry and die because I'm not going to be around much longer. One neighbor wrote me that, "I want you to do my funeral, but my wife has not scheduled it yet." I wrote back and told him that we could have the memorial service anytime, and when he died she could just take him out to the cemetery.

Most of the services now are of people who I knew and loved, and they know me and love me. So, it gets to be very personal and meaningful. Last week there was a man, ninety-six, whom I've known since 1959.

I don't worry about what's going to happen to me. I am ninety-four and have had some health problems. I don't have many years left, but it doesn't bother me. I'm not afraid to die, but I'm not waiting for the bus to come and pick me up. I enjoy living and I hope I can live a long time yet and be active. When I get to be inactive and can't do anything, I hope the Lord will take me home.

DON: When people like us are approaching retirement, what should our vision be? What should we be thinking? How should we spend the rest of our lives? It's a question we all have to ponder.

MORRIS: Well, Don has so many different hobbies, I don't know what he'll plan to do when he retires. I really didn't retire, just kept doing the same thing only on a lesser scale. Teach Sunday school, hold funerals, visit sick people, but that's been my life all along. So I keep doing as much of that as I can. I just don't get paid for it.

I don't know that Don can keep doing what he's been doing. So you need to have some interests to challenge you and keep your mind sharp. That's so important. Find things that you enjoy doing that are worthwhile. I don't believe in having a big time, or doing things for my personal satisfaction. Most of my life has been spent trying to help other people. That's been the joy of it, to see that you've done something worthwhile and helpful. For example, I picked out Don's wife for him. That's an Old Testament deal, and I did a good job. That's what made him what he is.

# *"I Just Do What I Can"*

# BROTHER BEDE J. BENN, CFX
## Born 1920 – Retired 2000

*Brother Bede (c.) on the Rosebud Sioux Reservation.*

**Brother Bede was raised during the Great Depression in a hardscrabble town outside Boston. One of six children, his mother was sickly. He lost one of his brothers at a very early age. His oldest sister became like a second mother to the family. In his sophomore year of high school, in a particularly vivid and memorable moment, he was struck with a clear message about how he should spend his life. He would ultimately join the Roman Catholic Congregation of St. Francis Xavier, a religious order dedicated to education, where he would serve as a religious brother, taking vows of poverty, celibacy, and obedience, and dedicating his life to serving the community as a teacher. When he joined, as is the custom, he selected a new name: in his case, Bede.**

He taught math, science, chemistry, and physics in Xaverian Brothers high schools in the Northeast—Utica, New York; Worcester, Malden, and Westwood, Massachusetts—for over twenty-five years. He was well-known by his students as someone who would spring surprise quizzes, always with the introductory phrase, "Half sheet of paper for a quiz."

Then, at age fifty, he and three other brothers went to the Rosebud Sioux Reservation near the Black Hills of South Dakota to teach. He spent the next twenty-nine years there, teaching math and science classes, religious doctrine classes, and a GED program, as well as teaching math at Sinte Gleska College and serving as an archivist and tour director in a mission museum. In his sixties and seventies, he retired and unretired at least four times, each time taking on a new challenge.

At eighty, he returned to Boston to be near an aging brother and sister. He now lives in a community of retired brothers at a home run by his Order, set on the campus of an affiliated high school with a population of one thousand students. Because of the home's proximity to the high school, there is vitality all about, something always going on, including many athletic activities.

W ho am I? A guy without too much talent, I think. Never the smartest kid in class, never the greatest athlete. My gift is my personality—I get along with people. And in my life I've been rewarded for that. Because of it, I found something that I loved to do and that I could do well. The kids I taught respected me. We got along. I helped them.

Back in 1968, I was planning to go off to teach in Africa. At that point, I was almost fifty and I'd been teaching in schools around the Northeast for twenty-five years. I enjoyed it, but I'd always wanted to work with the poor. The mission in Africa seemed like the perfect opportunity. I'd been getting ready for it, making lesson plans, everything. At the last minute, the head of the school where I was working said to me, "You can't go, we need you here." He told me the school wouldn't be able to replace me. Looking back, he might've been feeding me a line. Anyway, I stayed.

At first, I was disappointed. Then, after a bit, I told myself, maybe this is just how it's supposed to be. Maybe God has other plans. And don't you know it, one year later, I got the opportunity to go work at the reservation. That—I'm sure of it—that was what God wanted me to do all along. I enjoyed that work so much, all twenty-nine years that I spent out there.

The first time I saw the reservation—I still remember riding across those plains and spotting it off in the distance—right away, I knew I was home. Still, it was an adjustment, both for me and for the locals. When I first arrived, I'd never seen a Native American before. And some of the kids I taught were in the same position. They were very respectful, almost to the point of shyness. Sometimes, they'd run away at the sight of strangers. Gradually, everyone came to accept me, but it took a long time.

Many of the people on the reservation were Catholics. But many of them had a different way of praying. Well, different from the way I pray. They connected their faith to their heritage. They'd conduct sun dance ceremonies, sweat lodge ceremonies, powwows. I liked learning about all of that. I still remember watching the powwows, how everyone kept so silent. It was a spiritual experience.

Conditions on the reservation were difficult, to put it mildly. The poverty was staggering. Every year, the schools out East where I'd worked would send money. I'd write checks to the local food store and give the checks to the kids. Of course, almost everyone used the money for food. Every so often, someone would sell a check and use the cash to buy liquor. Alcoholism was a major problem. Much worse than what you'd find in any big city. It was at the root of so many problems. It ruined families. People lost their lives to it. The other basic problem, which contributed to the alcoholism, was that there were no jobs. I think there was about 80 percent unemployment. The isolation made it worse. There was no industry. Basically, if you wanted to work, you had to leave.

And the closest large city was two hundred miles away. Another big problem was health care. There was one hospital, and any serious illness meant a long trip. Infant mortality was high—three times the national average. And the life expectancy was far too low.

So, of course, with conditions like that, educating kids was difficult. When we first arrived, the kids wouldn't pay attention in class. They'd put their heads on their desks and ignore us. We put a stop to that, but keeping their interest was difficult. With all that was going on in their lives, you couldn't blame them for not paying attention.

Around the time I first moved out there, a group from the tribe founded a local college. Eventually, it grew. More students began attending and it helped to broaden everyone's outlook. Even for the young kids. A lot of the graduates made a point of helping the community. Slowly, conditions improved a little. It was wonderful to watch that happen—especially to be there for almost thirty years and to see progress. By the time I left, many more students were interested in getting an education.

I found contentment on the reservation. I met a lot of fine people. Devoted, hardworking people. I found peace out there. I thank God for that experience. And yes, I'll admit it—I had a hard time leaving. I think, during the last fifteen years I was there, when I was in my sixties and seventies, I think that I retired and unretired about four times. Every time I got ready to quit, I saw something else that needed to be done. I knew no one was doing it and that I could help, and so I did.

I think—no matter what I did back then or what I'm trying to do now—I think that my basic job has always been to help people. To try to think outside of myself, beyond my own concerns, and to act accordingly, even if it's just in the small things. Even if it's just in my attitude, or how I treat people and how I look at the world. I just do what I can.

During those last years on the reservation, I think that staying so busy was also my way of putting off retirement. Back then, I had no idea what retirement meant and I didn't want to find out. As it got closer and closer, I thought...well, frankly, I thought that it would just be a time for me to prepare myself for death. And so I thought I'd keep working as long as I could and that I'd live on the reservation until I died. As I said, I was happy out there. I was helping people. I felt accepted. Life was pleasant. Eventually, I realized I had other obligations—that my family needed me back here. Two of my siblings had become ill, and so I moved back here to be with them.

After I came back, I tried to stay busy with other things. I helped in the library and tutored. In those first few years, my health was great. It's funny—when I was young I wasn't very athletic. But all my life I've managed to stay active. And so I made it into my eighties with no real health problems. Actually, without even any real aches or pains. Then, after about five years—when I turned eighty-five or so—I realized I couldn't keep tutoring and helping out at the school. I got to the point where it became a problem to spend long periods of time standing up. Physical decline isn't sudden. It's progressive. Still, I'm lucky. Even now, I don't need eyeglasses. I use a walker, but I can still get around pretty good.

I'm grateful I don't have a lot of the issues and insecurities of some my age. My life is well organized. That helps. Structure is important. A schedule allows you to focus. At the same time, I'm not too rigid. Every morning, I pray and go to Mass. I usually take two short naps a day—one in the morning, one in the afternoon. Also, I meditate twice a day—twenty minutes every morning, a little longer every afternoon. I've been able to do that more regularly since I retired. It's become very important. Exercise, too. I do that every day. And, five days a week, I spend time with another of the brothers here at the home. He's become a little withdrawn, so the company is good for him.

My older brother is ninety-three. He lives in Florida. We keep in touch regularly. I have nineteen nieces in the area. About once a month, a few of them take me out to lunch. We get along wonderfully. It's my fault I don't see them more often. I could call them up more, but I don't want to impose. Of course, I still correspond with the people on the reservation. I made lots of friends out there. It's nice to keep in touch.

So yes, I like being retired. The easy life! No, only kidding. Actually, sometimes I forget that I'm retired because I'm always doing something. Except, you know, when I'm getting my beauty rest. But yes, almost always, I feel like I want to be doing something. Inevitably, I run out of time. It goes by fast. I know people who say that old age is boring. That everyone just sits around all day doing nothing. Well, not me.

I don't really think too much about the hardships. A while back, I read something: that life breaks all of us, that we all have hardships to bear, but that's a blessing. Because it teaches us that we need each other and God. And it shows us how to give to each other. I can't remember the exact quote, but it's something like that.

These days, I don't really get optimistic or pessimistic. It's not how I look at life. At my age, I know that one of these days I'm going to die. I accept that. I hope I'll be ready. I pray that I'll be ready. I think we're all chosen to live the lives we live. And death is a part of that. So I know that when the time comes that it'll be God that calls me.

Did I ever tell you about how I came to be a brother? It's the most memorable moment of my life. I was sixteen, in tenth grade, living with my family in a three-decker in Somerville. For a while, I'd been feeling anxious, not knowing what I was doing with my life. Anyway, one day—a very ordinary day—I left for school. I was walking up Lowell Street when it happened. It was sudden and clear. Somehow, all at once, right there on the sidewalk, I just knew that I should become a brother. It was that simple and that profound. I couldn't deny it and didn't think to. Even though I had never met a brother of any kind, I went down and joined the only order of brothers that I knew. And it happened that they were teachers. If they had been a nursing order,

I would have become a nurse, even though I can't stand the sight of blood. So that was lucky.

That one moment on Lowell Street was the most important moment of my life. It allowed for everything else. I still thank God for it. So yes, I know that I was blessed. I was happy doing what I did. I helped a lot of people, made a lot of friends. Always kept learning, always stayed busy. Laughed a lot. Did my best to be kind and to enjoy life. What else is there?

# "Ninety-Seven Years of Luck"

## AL PORKOLAB
### Born 1914 – Retired 1983 – Died 2014

*Al in World War II, and celebrating a birthday with his late wife, Jean.*

Al, ninety-seven, lives in an immaculate single-story brick home on the well-kept grounds of the Otterbein retirement community. Situated on 1,200 acres north of Cincinnati, ringed by cornfields and low green hills, Otterbein was founded by the United Methodist Church in 1912. Today, the site might be mistaken for a small college. In addition to its medical facilities, it features a large activities center, dining hall, general store, bank, chapel, post office, and several miles of paved walking paths. Many of its residents, though elderly, exhibit something of the collegiate spirit. Rolling by on golf carts, laughing together over lunch, gathering in the parking lot for day trips, they are active, energetic, and social—none, it seems, more so than Al.

The son of Hungarian immigrants, Al grew up during the Great Depression on a small farm in Ohio. Unable to afford college, he spent much of his early life working in steel mills before enlisting in the army at the start of World War II. He joined at the rank of buck private and, four years and eight ranks later, returned home a master sergeant. During the war, he served as chief clerk of the Allied medical division in the UK, and was later shipped to Le Havre in the wake of the D-Day invasion. While en route from England, he survived a German attack in which several Allied boats were lost.

Landing in Normandy, against great odds, he established and administered a massive medical supply depot near the front line. Al's service earned him a Certificate of Merit and a Bronze Star. After the war, he returned home where, after spending an unhappy year working in a steel mill, he opened a small insurance agency. For decades, as his business flourished, Al pursued an extraordinarily active role in community affairs and public life, working with numerous charitable and civic organizations, and holding various positions in state and federal government. According to his son, "There wasn't any local civic or charitable activity that he wasn't involved in."

Now widowed after seventy-three years of marriage, Al lives alone, though he is close with his son and grandchildren and is popular with fellow Otterbein residents. Nearing one hundred, he remains an impressive figure: physically fit, dapper, with a warm, self-assured bearing. His apartment is similarly impeccable, as if prepared by Al for the surprise appearance and inspection of some long-departed drill instructor.

W hen my wife, Jean, was four years old, her family moved from central Pennsylvania to Lorain, Ohio, which is where I'm from. Her father built a house there, a duplex. After Jean and I married, that's where we lived, the two of us in one half, and her family in the other. It worked out well. When I went off to the war, Jean stayed in that house and got a job in Lorain. But, when I was stationed in New York, getting ready to deploy to Europe, her boss told her that she couldn't come see me off. So she quit. How about that? She just quit, came out to see me, and then went right back to Ohio and got herself a bigger, better job.

There's nothing worse than going to work and watching the clock. I did that when I first came back from the service. I was working in the steel mills, which I'd also done before the war. It was a steady job and a salary, but I was just a clock-watcher. That lasted for about a year, and it was the most god-awful time of my life. I had this horrible feeling that the work I was doing didn't matter. It felt senseless. And Jean could see that. She saw I couldn't put up with it. One day, she said: "Honey, I don't like that you don't feel rewarded by your work." And that was that. I quit and started my own little insurance agency. And from that point on, I'm telling you, forget about watching the clock. When you work for yourself, the time just goes.

When I finally did retire, I kind of did it twice. The first time, I was about sixty-five or sixty-six. I'd been working two jobs: I had my insurance business and I was also an assistant to a member of Congress. Jean was working as the office manager for our business and was really the backbone of the operation. It was a hectic life: the two jobs; managing political campaigns; traveling back and forth to DC and across the district here in Ohio. So when the congressman I was working with retired, I thought that'd be my time, too. And I felt fine about that. Just fine.

But before I could settle, I got a call from some friends down in Columbus. They knew about my insurance background and they wanted me for a position with the State. I talked to Jean about it. She was very gracious, and so I decided to accept it. That job was about five years. I became head of the State's Administrative Services Department and served as part of the governor's staff. And so when the governor was voted out, that was my second retirement. Around that same time, Jean decided to retire as well.

We were living in Columbus, but we went through a disruptive, abortive attempt at retiring to Florida. We were always looking for a place down there, thinking we'd find our ideal home. Eventually, we bought a place in Naples, which was a horrible mistake. We started leasing it and the tenant trashed it. Trashed the whole place. We sued and got enough to restore the property. Then we sold it. That was the end of Florida for us. It was a bad, bad move. Actually, from the start, Jean hadn't been too keen on the idea. For one, Florida was too far away from our grandkids.

A couple of years after we retired, we moved from Columbus to a new home in Landen, Ohio. That's where we finally found our retirement, where we finally settled. That was our ideal place. We lived there for about eighteen years. And those were the best years. Better than any other stage of life. Nothing compares to that time. We were finally retired. The pressure was finally off. It was a big, big relief.

I think that's a key to retirement, finally doing what you want. When we bought the new place, I knew that I had to have a basement space for a workshop, because I wanted to be a wood turner. I hadn't really done it before, but I'd loved woodworking when I was in high school. So it was an old love, I suppose. I got myself a workshop with everything: lathes, saws, the works. It became my favorite hobby. I didn't waste any time playing golf. I'd go down after breakfast and start working. Eventually, I'd hear Jean holler: "Hon, time for lunch." I'd have lunch and then I'd go back down again. The next thing I knew it was suppertime. In that workshop, the rest of the world was absolutely foreign. You have to be so intensely concentrated when you're doing that type of work. It's amazing to pass the time like that, totally focused on a single task.

After my two eye operations, I decided I'd better give up the wood turning. It was too dangerous. My eyesight was restored, but it has to be perfect when you're doing that type of work. So I had a good twelve years with it, and I've still got many of the pieces I made.

In 2004, everything changed. Jean became ill. We discovered she had a brain tumor. That changed everything. Everything. All the happiness, all the good times and the good feelings, all of that disappeared.

We sold our house and moved here, to Otterbein. Caring for Jean was my number-one job. Of course, I coordinated all of her health care. We were lucky that, by the time she got sick, we'd managed to put away a few dollars. It's very expensive when you get sick—really very expensive. Also, I tried to make sure that she had the amenities she was used to. I'd bring in the people from the beauty shop to do her hair. They'd do it in her room because she couldn't get out anymore.

Mostly, I just spent time with her. I didn't like the wheelchair they gave her, so I bought her a nice new one. I used to walk with her through the wings of the campus center. When the weather was nice, I used to walk with her outdoors. Spending time with her. Feeding her. It was trying. It was the roughest time of my life.

She's been gone now for over three and a half years. At first, I handled the grief very badly. I took some classes, courses that the church gave about how to deal with grief. But I didn't feel right. This place offers so many activities, but I shunned them. I shunned practically everything. I didn't want any companionship. I'd go to supper and sit and eat alone. There was no purpose to anything. It all seemed empty. Everything. After living with Jean for seventy-three years...well, when she's gone, it's hard to make a change.

For about two years after she passed, I was pretty sad, really pretty sad. Eventually, those grief courses started to help. I started going to meetings and getting involved in different activities. I'd volunteer to do little things in the community, delivering mail, things like that. Little by little, the grief receded; the purpose of life seemed restored. By picking up activities, it became less of a burden. It was redeemed, somehow. Now, I've sort of grown with it and accepted it. And because I'm living in a retirement community, death is not uncommon. In a way, that brings you up. You say to yourself: Well, after all, that's what you're doing; you're waiting for the call. Most of us have realized that we're not here forever. You accept that. And that acceptance changes your perspective on living.

Now I do almost everything myself: all the cooking and the cleaning. You get organized. You get into a routine. You get caught up in it and it becomes a habit.

Last October, I had to renew my driver's license. I was apprehensive. I thought, *Oh God, at my age, am I going to make it?* But if there's one thing that I dread, it's being without wheels. And so I took the exam and passed it. And now I have my license for four years, until I'm one hundred.

Right now, I'm planning to take some of my assets and give them to my grandkids. I've already given some to my son. It's silly to wait. They should enjoy it. Why do I need it? My needs are minimal. There's nothing I want for myself.

Travel is out of the question. I think I'd find it burdensome. If I'm on my feet for a long time, I notice it. Jean and I traveled after we first retired. I remember we took a cruise in Alaska. That was amazing, seeing the whales and eagles.

My son lives in the area, and I'm very close to him and see him a lot. And, as I mentioned, I have two grandchildren. They both live out of state, but come in for the big holidays. And they call me, which is a blessing. I tell them, don't worry about the time, call whenever you'd like. And they do. I like hearing about their accomplishments. I take a lot of joy in my grandchildren. They're carrying on the name, and a good name is money in the bank.

I have some buddies here at Otterbein, but all my pals from the old days are gone. I remember, back when I was in the insurance business, I had certain friends who'd say, "Why the hell are you doing all that work?" And especially, they could never understand why I spent so much time working in the community—working and not getting paid for it. I'd tell them, look, I've got to give something back. This community's been good to me. I'm just trying to return something. Really, I resented those kinds of questions.

But they were right. I was a very busy guy. I was involved in everything. Here, have a look at this. [*He stands and walks to his living room, where two walls are covered with plaques, certificates, awards, photographs, and memorabilia. With pride, he explains the significance of them.*] That one's from the church, the VFW, the Red Cross, the Golden Gloves...that's from when I was president of the local YMCA. In the other room, I've got some of my woodworking. I'll show you those later. This is a letter from the Apollo 17 astronauts. They included a signed photo of Earth taken from the moon. There's my Bronze Star certification. And here's an award I got for being Otterbein's Philanthropist of the Year. I got it the year after Jean passed, because I bought an ice cream machine for the dining hall. They had one but it was always out of order. Jean loved ice cream, so I thought I'd buy a new machine in her memory. Also, that coincided with what would have been our seventy-fifth wedding anniversary. [*He returns to his seat, smiling slightly.*]

Looking at all that, I feel satisfied. I do. I feel satisfied that I made so many decisions that turned out to be the right decisions. I didn't make them lightly. I had a sense for right and wrong, and I always tried to do right. Even with the little things. Shortcuts, poor decisions—no matter how small—they'll always come back to haunt you.

Maybe, for me, maybe it was luck. Maybe it wasn't. I suppose ninety-seven years of luck is a long run of luck. Well, it's your life. You know what's right and wrong. You make choices. It's up to you.

I was certainly lucky when I found my wife. And that was a big part of everything. So yes, when I look back, I feel good about my life. And no, I don't think there's much about it that I'd change. Frankly, I think I'm ready to go.

# EPILOGUE

This book is rooted in a belief in the great power of stories. Throughout, I've tried to convey the experience of listening as another person reflects on his or her life and, as he or she does, turns the raw material of living into a richly meaningful story. If this project has a premise, it's that life itself is the greatest teacher, and that first-person accounts bear profound lessons, many of which cannot be expressed by any other means. Popular guidebooks on how to retire well, academic works of surpassing scholarship—none of these can capture the resonant wisdom contained in the story of a single life.

In assembling this book, I've come to believe that every life story contains many lessons. I've also come to believe that, in hearing or reading about another's life, every person will discover different lessons, each according to his needs. Like everything else, reading is affected by our individual limitations, preoccupations, and inherent subjectivity. What I've taken from the profiles in this book has not been the same as what my family and friends have taken. This fact prompted the book's epigraph, from Marcel Proust, who wrote, "Every reader finds himself. The writer's work is merely a kind of optical instrument that makes it possible for the reader to discern what, without this book, he would perhaps never have seen in himself." In this way, I hope that this book will serve readers as it has served me: as a kind of collection of optical instruments, with each profile offering a chance to see another person's view of life and, by doing so, also revealing a fuller, truer vision of one's own life.

Working on this book has changed me. As I wrote in the introduction, the project began as a way for me to confront my own anxieties about retiring and growing older. At the outset, the project did not dispel my anxieties but only deepened them. During the first weeks, I was full of prejudices. One of the early interviews that I conducted was in an elderly community in southern Ohio. Before my trip, I was offered the opportunity to spend a full day and night at the facility. I declined politely. The prospect made me uncomfortable. I expected the place to be depressing, filled with the frail, the lonely, and the purposeless. What if old age is contagious?

Of course, my prejudices were a product of fear, and my fear was a product of ignorance, of my habit of ignoring the realities of growing older. From the moment I stepped onto the grounds of that community, my prejudices began to dissolve. It was an impressive place, as vital and as sociable as a college campus. Its residents were changed by age, but not diminished by it. Indeed, their wisdom, their resilience, and their determination to live as fully as possible seemed to flow from their acute awareness of time's unrelenting march.

I cannot claim to have vanquished all my anxieties about old age, but I know that I am far closer today than I was when I began this project. I also know that my progress has been guided by the examples of the men and women I met while working on this book. They've taught me that aging is not merely a physical phenomenon, but also a psychological and spiritual one, the quality, shape, and direction of which is entirely my responsibility. They've saved me from the folly of spending my remaining years ticking off items on some artificial "bucket list." They've shown me that living in the present, however mundane or circumscribed, examining myself and my world, and pursuing a meaningful life can be endlessly challenging and rewarding.

In a sense, my experience over the two years of working on this book encapsulates a fundamental aspect of the aging process, or of any process that involves radical change. I passed through a challenging period of disorientation, during which many of my old habits, suppositions, and defenses were stripped away. The experience was valuable; indeed, it was necessary. When I began, I felt confused and constricted. Now, at the end of this project, I feel immeasurably freer, more purposeful, and more resolute. Again, I think that this is a fundamental process, and that it, or something like it, must accompany any major change.

As I write, I see that I'm advocating a life of introspection and philosophical contemplation, the very kind of life I avoided so scrupulously and for so many years. Perhaps my aversion to philosophy was another of my old prejudices, and was as misguided and as limiting as the rest. As I've worked on this project, I've learned that philosophy needn't be rarefied, or even academic. To the contrary, it can be simple and practical, and can offer vital instruction on how to live. In a sense, Western philosophy began as a way of confronting the very concerns that prompted this book. In 399 BC, Socrates concluded that all philosophy was simply a long instruction in how to die. Almost nineteen centuries later, the French Renaissance writer Michel de Montaigne returned to this theme. "All the wisdom and reasoning in the world," he wrote, "eventually come down to one conclusion, which is to teach us not to be afraid of dying." Montaigne argued that we must keep life's end always in mind, and that by doing so we might deprive death of its "strangeness," tame our anxieties, and be rewarded with a new sense of freedom and a richer, more joyous appreciation of life. In this way, the process of learning how to die is inextricably linked with the process of learning how to live. Indeed, on close inspection, the two, which at first sound so different, are identical.

We're all caught up in this process and will be until our last moment. By speaking so frankly and directly about their lives, the men and women profiled in this book have, I think, aided our learning. As Montaigne wrote, "anyone who teaches men how to die also teaches them how to live."

The men and women who appear on these pages don't offer neat lessons. Instead, they supply powerful examples. They have little time for self-pity. They appreciate that life is a gift and are grateful for its boundless variety, wonder, and potential. They are also keenly aware of its finitude. They are people of imagination and courage who have been bold enough to conceive of the lives they wished to lead and determined enough to pursue those visions, often in the face of adversity. Perhaps most importantly, they have continued to pursue life—ardently, creatively, joyfully—and to grow in wisdom and spirit, even as their physical capabilities decline and their time draws nearer to its end. They are alive, and are vivid testaments to the truth of Montaigne's admonition, that the richness of life does not flow from its length, but from its use:

> Life itself is neither a good nor an evil; it is the scene of good and evil, as you arrange it. And if you have lived a day, you have seen all; one day is like all days. There is no other light, there is no other night. This sun, this moon, these stars, this order, are the very same that your ancestors enjoyed and that will rejoice your great-grandchildren....Many a man has lived long, who has lived little. See to it as long as you are here. It lies in your will, not in the number of years, to make the best of life.

# ABOUT THE AUTHOR

B rendan M. Hare is a recent retiree. He lives outside Boston with his wife, near their three grown children.

Mr. Hare worked as a teacher, a college economics instructor, and for over forty years, as an attorney. He served as chief litigation counsel for a Fortune 50 company and later as the founder and managing partner of his own law firm. For over twenty years, he built and guided a sizeable national practice, with clients drawn from some of the largest corporations in America.

Few experiences in his career have been as rewarding as this book project. He spent two years traveling the country, meeting new people, and listening to them discuss their lives and thoughts about growing older.

Writing this book changed him profoundly. He hopes it will have a similar impact on readers.

Made in the USA
Middletown, DE
31 January 2015